Food Processing Industry in India

Unleashing the Potential of the Non-alcoholic Beverage Sector

About the Authors

Arpita Mukherjee is a Professor at Indian Council for Research on International Economic Relations (ICRIER), New Delhi. She has several years of experience in policy-oriented research working closely with the governments in India and the UK. She has conducted studies for various international organisations and Indian industry associations. Her research is a key contributor to India's negotiating strategies in the on-going Doha Round of WTO negotiations, in bilateral trade agreements and in domestic policy reforms. Dr Mukherjee has a PhD in Economics from the University of Portsmouth, UK. Her research interests include: services, WTO, bilateral/regional agreements; infrastructure, FDI, agriculture reforms, retail, migration and labour market programmes. She has over 80 publications including books, journals, working papers and government reports. Dr Mukherjee has presented her research at various international and national conferences.

Debolina Mukherjee is a Consultant at ICRIER. She has an MA in Economics with a specialisation in monetary economics and finance from the University of Calcutta, Kolkata. Her research interests include: retail and the food and agro-processing industry. At present she is working on a study of India's agro-processing sector with an emphasis on the non-alcoholic beverage manufacturing industry. She is also associated with a study on India's special economic zones (SEZs). Before joining ICRIER, she worked at Tata Consultancy Services, Bangalore, as a business analyst, where she was associated with an AC Nielsen-funded project that analysed the retail sector in the UK.

Deboshree Ghosh is a Research Assistant at ICRIER. Prior to this, she was with the Institute of Applied Manpower Research (IAMR)–Planning Commission for two years as a young professional. Her experience includes policy-oriented research on employment, skills and other areas of development economics such as sanitation. Her contributions comprise assistance in the *India Human Development Report 2011* and a report on factors impacting the growth of non-agricultural employment in selected states in India. She has co-authored a report on employment in the food processing sector and co-authored a paper on financing skills in India. Apart from research, she has taught macroeconomics to international students at IAMR. She has a BA degree in Economics from Delhi University and an MSc in Economics from the University of Warwick, UK.

Divya Satija is a Trade Analyst in the delegation of the European Union to India. Previously, she was a Research Associate at ICRIER. She has also worked on other bilateral trade issues such as the India-EU Broad-based Trade and Investment Agreement, and on sectors such as retail and consumer behaviour, non-alcoholic beverages and IT/IT-enabled services in India. Her broad areas of interest are consumer behaviour analysis, sectoral research, international trade and investments and microfinance. She has several publications as book chapters, journal articles and working papers. She has a BA in Economics from Delhi University and an MA degree in Economics from Jamia Millia Islamia, Delhi.

Food Processing Industry in India

Unleashing the Potential of the Non-alcoholic Beverage Sector

Arpita Mukherjee
Debolina Mukherjee
Deboshree Ghosh
Divya Satija

INDIAN BEVERAGE ASSOCIATION

INDIAN COUNCIL FOR RESEARCH ON INTERNATIONAL ECONOMIC RELATIONS (ICRIER), NEW DELHI

ACADEMIC FOUNDATION
NEW DELHI

www.academicfoundation.com

First published in 2014
by

ACADEMIC FOUNDATION
4772-73 / 23 Bharat Ram Road, (23 Ansari Road),
Darya Ganj, New Delhi - 110 002 (India).
Phones : 23245001 / 02 / 03 / 04.
Fax : +91-11-23245005.
E-mail : books@academicfoundation.com
www.academicfoundation.com

in association with
Indian Beverage Association
and
Indian Council for Research on International Economic Relations (ICRIER),
New Delhi.

Disclaimer:
The findings/views/opinions expressed in this book are solely those of the authors and do not necessarily reflect the views of the publisher or the organisations they represent.

Cataloging in Publication Data--DK
Courtesy: D.K. Agencies (P) Ltd. <docinfo@dkagencies.com>

Food processing industry in India : unleashing the potential of the non-alcoholic beverage sector / Arpita Mukherjee ... [et al.].
p. cm.
Includes bibliographical references (p.).
ISBN 9789332701137

1. Food industry and trade--India. 2. Non-alcoholic beverage industry--India. I. Mukherjee, Arpita.

DDC 338.4766400954 23

Typeset by Italics India, New Delhi.

Printed and bound by The Book Mint, New Delhi.
www.thebookmint.in

Contents

Foreword

Indian Council for Research on International Economic Relations (ICRIER) is one of the few think tanks in India that works closely with industry, academia and government to create and share knowledge for more informed and evidence-based policy formulation. Since our inception in 1981, we have engaged on diverse and often complex matters relating to India's economic and strategic relations with the global economy. Our research largely focuses on contemporary challenges with a profound penchant for enabling better policy. In the past, our recommendations have been implemented by different departments of the Indian government.

India currently faces serious macroeconomic difficulties. Growth has slowed, foreign direct investment (FDI) inflows have shrunk, fiscal deficits have been high, food inflation is stubbornly high, agriculture continues to absorb more people than it should while manufacturing has stagnated. The core policy issue is how to generate 'inclusive growth.' To address this issue, this report, sponsored by the Indian Beverage Association (IBA), focuses on developing India's manufacturing and export capabilities in the food processing sector, using the case of the non-alcoholic beverage sector. The choice of food processing is based on its pervasive links across the entire value chain from farm-to-final consumers. It is a labour-intensive sector and plays a crucial role in 'inclusive growth.' India's abundant supply of raw materials needs to be exploited to its advantage. In the past, the government has implemented various policies and schemes to support the growth of the food processing sector.

The situation of non-alcoholic beverages within the food processing sector is unique. It covers both perishable and non-perishable products and operates in an intricate network. It is therefore an ideal sector to study in the context of the challenges of linking India into global production networks. As a key component of the food processing industry, the non-alcoholic beverage sector has potential to generate significant employment and attract private investment. Interestingly, even at a time when the Indian manufacturing sector is not doing well, the non-alcoholic beverage sector has registered double digit growth consistently and a number of domestic and foreign multinationals have invested in this sector.

In keeping with ICRIER's basis for its research, this report analyses secondary and primary data, including a nation-wide survey of different stakeholders to arrive at the policy recommendations. The central research questions focus on identifying constraints to improving competitiveness of the Indian manufacturing, augmenting FDI inflows, increasing exports and developing a strong research & development (R&D) hub within the country. The vision of achieving 25 per cent manufacturing gross domestic product (GDP) must encompass the food processing sector in general and the non-alcoholic beverage sector in particular. While the report focuses on manufacturing, it also addresses other segments of the supply chain through retail and consumer surveys. I am confident that if the measures suggested in this report are implemented, Indian food processing sector would benefit tremendously from the policy interventions. I would like to thank IBA for sponsoring this study and I hope this report ignites interest and policy discourse on this very important subject.

(Dr Rajat Kathuria)

Director & CE

Indian Council for Research on International Economic Relations (ICRIER)

Acknowledgements

We would like to thank Rajat Kathuria, Director and Chief Executive, Indian Council for Research on International Economic Relations (ICRIER), for his continuous support and encouragement for this project. This project was commissioned by the Indian Beverage Association (IBA). We are extremely grateful to the Secretary-General, IBA, and to the members of this Association, especially to Coca-Cola India Private Limited, PepsiCo India Holdings Private Limited, Red Bull India Private Limited, Dabur India Limited, Tetra Pak India Private Limited, Danone Narang Beverages Private Limited, Cadbury India Limited, FieldFresh Foods Private Limited and Reliance India Limited (PET) for providing us with relevant information and feedback. We are also grateful to a number of companies that are not members of IBA, such as Mother Dairy Fruit and Vegetable Private Limited, Hindustan Unilever Limited, Haldiram Group, AMUL (Anand Milk Union Limited) and Bisleri International Private Limited, who have provided valuable inputs. The draft report was presented during two consultations with stakeholders jointly organised by ICRIER and IBA during 2012-13. We are indebted to the participants for their valuable comments. A number of companies in the non-corporate manufacturing sector as well as corporate and non-corporate retailers provided inputs for this study.

We would like to take this opportunity to thank Dun & Bradstreet Tangram Advisory Services Private Limited, especially Dipankar De, Kaustubh Rishi and Saurabh Mittal, for successfully co-ordinating the survey and in-depth interviews. We are grateful to all survey participants for their contribution. We had the opportunity to work closely with several industry experts, which enhanced our knowledge of this sector. Thanks are due to industry associations such as The Federation of Indian Chamber of Commerce and Industry (FICCI), The Associated Chambers of Commerce and Industry of India (ASSOCHAM), PHD Chamber of Commerce and Industry, and Indian Dairy Association for their valuable inputs into the study. Shilpa Gupta and Bhaskar Reddy (of FICCI), Kiran Sharma (British High Commission), Asitava Sen (Rabo India Finance Limited) and Kumar Rajagopalan (Retailer's Association of India) deserve special mention. We are also grateful to Ajay Jhakar (Bharat Krishak Samaj), Sameer Barde (TESCO India) and Pritam Banerjee (DHL India) for improving our understanding of agri-value chains. A number of officials from different ministries/departments of the central and state governments enabled us to improve our understanding of the subject. Our colleagues, Tanu M. Goyal and Shweta Saini, gave us valuable inputs and feedback. We would also like to thank Prof Parthapratim Pal (India Institute of Management, Kolkata) for reviewing the final paper. Renu Gupta deserves special mention for not only copyediting the report but also for her valuable inputs on the content and design. Anu Mohandas, Anshul Bhojwani, Raj Kumar Shahi, Chayya Singh, Manmeet Ahuja and his team and Rajeev Kapil and his team have competently helped us with administrative activities. Sanu Kapila of Academic Foundation deserves special mention. Last but not least, we would like to thank our families for their constant support for the late night work and handling project-related stress.

Abbreviations

3PL	Third-Party Logistics
4PL	Fourth-Party Logistics
AAGR	Annual Average Growth Rate
AEZs	Agro Export Zones
Amul	Anand Milk Union Limited
ANGOC	Asian NGO Coalition
APEDA	Agricultural and Processed Products Export Development Authority
APMC	Agriculture Produce and Marketing Committee
ASEAN	The Association of Southeast Asian Nations
ASSOCHAM	The Associated Chambers of Commerce and Industry of India
B2B	Business-to-Business
B2C	Business-to-Consumers
BIS	Bureau of Indian Standards
BRICS	Association of Brazil, Russia, India, China and South Africa
BRIEF	Bureau of Research on Industry and Economic Fundamentals
C&F	Clearing and Forward
CAGR	Compound Annual Growth Rate
CBEC	Central Board of Excise and Customs
CENVAT	Central Value Added Tax
CIFTI	Confederation of Indian Food Trade and Industry (Food Wing)
CII	Confederation of Indian Industry
CSDs	Carbonated Soft Drinks
CSO	Central Statistical Office
CSR	Corporate Social Responsibility
DFCs	Dedicated Freight Corridors
DIPP	Department of Industrial Policy and Promotion
DMI	Directorate of Marketing and Inspection
DTAs	Domestic Tariff Areas
EIC	Export Inspection Council
EU	European Union
EXIM	Export Import
FAO	Food and Agricultural Organization
FCI	Food Corporation of India
FDA	US Food and Drugs Administration
FDI	Foreign Direct Investment
FERA	Foreign Exchange Regulation Act
FICCI	Federation of Indian Chambers of Commerce and Industry
FIPB	Foreign Investment Promotion Board
FMCG	Fast-moving Consumer Goods
FPOs	Farmer-Producer Organisations
FSMA	Food Safety Modernisation Act
FSSA	Food Safety and Standards Act
FSSAI	Food Safety and Standards Authority of India
FTAs	Foreign Trade Agreements
FYP	Five Year Plan
GAAR	General Anti-avoidance Rule
GCMMF	Gujarat Co-operative Milk Marketing Federation Ltd.
GDP	Gross Domestic Product
GoI	Government of India
GST	Goods and Services Tax
ha	hectare
HDF	High-density Fiberboard
HR	Human Resource
HS	Harmonised System
HUL	Hindustan Unilever
HYV	High Yielding Variety
IAMR	Institute of Applied Manpower Research
IBA	Indian Beverage Association
ICBA	International Council of Beverages Associations
IGIDR	Indira Gandhi Institute of Development Research
IIP	Index of Industrial Production

ILO	International Labour Organization
IMF	International Monetary Fund
IMRB International	Formerly Indian Market Research Bureau
INR	Indian National Rupees
ISBT	International Society of Beverage Technologists
IT	Information Technology
MAT	Minimum Alternate Tax
MoFPI	Ministry of Food Processing Industries
MosPI	Ministry of Statistics and Programme Implementation
MRP	Maximum Retail Price
MSMEs	Micro, Small and Medium Enterprises
MSP	Minimum Support Price
Mt	Million Tonnes
NABL	National Accreditation Board for Testing and Calibration Laboratories
NCAER	National Council of Applied Economic Research
NCR	National Capital Region
NGOs	Non-Governmental Organisation
NIC	National Industrial Classification
NREGA	National Rural Employment Guarantee Act
NSDC	National Skill Development Corporation
PET	Polyethylene terephthalate
PIB	Press Information Bureau
PwC	PricewaterhouseCoopers
R&D	Research & Development
RFID	Radio Frequency Identification
RTD	Ready-to-Drink
RTM	Route-to-Market
SAIC	State Administration for Industry and Commerce
SEC	Socioeconomic Classification
SEZs	Special Economic Zones
SFDA	State Food and Drug Administration
SIA	Secretariat for Industrial Assistance
SLIB	State Light Industry Bureau
SMEs	Small and Medium-scale Enterprises
SQA	Supplier Quality Assurance
SSP	State Support Price
TFP	Total Factor Productivity
TMCs	Terminal Market Complexes
UHDP	Ultra-High Density Plantation
UK	United Kingdom
UN	United Nations
UNCPC	United Nations Central Product Classification
UNCTAD	United Nations Conference on Trade and Development
UNDP	United Nations Development Programme
UP	Uttar Pradesh
USA	United States of America
VAT	Value Added Tax
WHO	World Health Organization
WTO	World Trade Organization

List of Tables, Figures, Boxes and Annexures

Tables

Figures

Boxes

Annexures

Executive Summary

India is a fast-growing and large emerging market. Although consumption patterns are changing, food and beverages still account for a substantial part of Indian consumption (over 30%) compared to other emerging markets (Brazil at 17% and China at 25%). Within the food and beverage category, in recent years, there has been a shift towards packaged food and beverages and branded products. India is also a large producer of fruits, vegetables and milk. The government is trying to develop the country as a food processing hub, which is likely to boost the Indian food processing sector in particular and the manufacturing sector in general.

Given this background, this report focuses on the non-alcoholic beverage sector and its growth potential in India. Non-alcoholic beverages comprise all beverages that are alcohol-free and include a wide range of sub-sectors, such as carbonated soft drinks (CSDs), fruits and vegetable juices, tea/coffee/milk-based beverages, sports drinks, energy drinks and bottled water. The sector has witnessed continuous double-digit growth in the post-liberalisation period with the entry of a number of foreign and domestic corporates in manufacturing, and the proliferation of products and brands. The sector has significant forward and backward linkages and connects the entire agriculture value chain—from farmers to consumers. This report examines the contribution of the sector to India's economy in terms of its contribution to the GDP (gross domestic product), manufacturing sector, employment, FDI (foreign direct investment) inflows, technology transfer, exports and development of the agriculture value chain. It analyses the barriers faced by the sector and suggests policy measures to enhance the global competitiveness of Indian industry, generate employment, facilitate exports and inflows of FDI, develop India as an agro-processing hub and link it to the global production network. The report is based on a primary survey and secondary data analysis.

The study shows that globally the non-alcoholic beverage sector is undergoing changes in terms of product variety, business models and markets. Companies are customising their products to meet customer and market requirements. While developed countries continue to be the large markets for non-alcoholic beverages, both production bases and consumption are shifting to developing countries such as China and India. Unlike China, India is a much smaller player in the global non-alcoholic beverage sector not only in terms of manufacturing, foreign investment inflows, research & development (R&D) base and exports, but also in terms of per capita consumption of non-alcoholic beverages. India, with its large consumer base and availability of raw material and cheap labour, thus has huge untapped potential to develop the non-alcoholic beverage sector.

When one examines the global regulations pertaining to this sector, there is a significant difference between developed and emerging markets. While all countries seem to follow some common global standards such as the Codex standards, they customise it to their own requirements. In developed countries, regulations related to food safety standards, consumer and environment protection are more rigid, but they are also more transparent and better implemented, which has enabled the non-alcoholic beverage sector to grow and reach its potential. In developing countries, the regulations are evolving and their implementation is an issue. Since India is in the process of implementing the Food Safety and Standards Act, 2006, and other regulations that are likely to impact the non-alcoholic beverage sector, the report recommends that the country can learn from global best practices.

The secondary and primary data on the Indian non-alcoholic beverage sector highlights that non-corporate manufacturers dominate (around 75%) in terms of numbers, but corporate manufacturers dominate in terms of value, volume of sales, investment, employment generation and percolation and use of technology. The non-alcoholic beverage sector accounts for over one per cent of India's GDP and its share in the GDP is rising. The performance of this sector is better than in other manufacturing sectors and it is projected to have high double-digit growth for the next 10 years. It has the potential to create four indirect employments for each direct employment. The study found that the corporate sector works closely with contract manufacturers and has enabled a number of small manufacturers to gain scale economies. Although data on the share of the sector in investment and FDI inflows is not available, company-level information shows that companies are investing substantially in technology and skills upgrading, and in R&D in product development, customisation of products to local tastes and process upgrading. Through their backward linkages, they have enabled farmers to become more productive and efficient and have streamlined the supply chain. The non-alcoholic beverage sector has strong forward linkages—even corporate manufacturers work closely with non-corporate retailers, providing them with the necessary technology, such as storage facilities and freezers. Around 50 per cent of corporate manufacturers have taken measures to conserve water and large companies have invested significantly in waste management and recycling technology.

The survey of retailers highlights that the Indian retail sector is undergoing rapid changes with the entry of corporate retailers and the development of new retail formats. The private labels of large corporate retailers may compete with corporate manufacturers, but large retailers offer opportunities to small manufacturers to become a part of their supply chain. Globally, corporate manufacturers work closely with corporate retailers and this model can be replicated in India. Both corporate manufacturers and corporate retailers focus on streamlining the supply chain and thereby help to reduce delays, leakages and wastage in the supply chain. In a competitive scenario, these benefits can be passed on to the farmers and manufacturers in terms of higher prices for their produce/products and to consumers in terms of lower prices that they pay. This report also found that in India both corporate and non-corporate retail will co-exist and grow in the food retail business. At the same time, the growing corporatisation of retail will give an impetus to brand and product proliferation, thereby enhancing consumer choice.

Although Indian consumers are changing and they have shown increasing preferences for product variety and are becoming more brand-conscious, they still have a strong preference for homemade beverages and traditional beverages such as coconut water. Thus, per capita consumption of non-alcoholic beverages in India is low. The Indian consumer market is large and unsaturated and with the rise in GDP and per capita income and the evolving retail structure, it is expected that the consumer demand patterns will change and the demand for packaged beverages will grow. This report found that both traditional and packaged beverages will co-exist in India and the prices of products play an important role in consumers' purchase decisions.

The report countered some of the popular beliefs. For instance, all survey participants pointed out that allowing FDI in multi-brand retail alone cannot bring down inflation or help to streamline the supply chain, as has been envisaged by the government. It will depend on whether a single Goods and Services Tax (GST) is implemented and how the food processing sector in general and the non-alcoholic beverage sector in particular is treated under the GST. The treatment of the sector has to be such that it faces uniform low tax, and other fiscal and regulatory barriers to the interstate movement of goods are addressed. Herein, India can learn from the experiences of countries such as the UK, Canada and Australia that have used low taxes to streamline the agro-supply chain. Similarly, it is often argued that bottled water is a luxury commodity and, therefore, it faces high and differential taxes across states. In a country like India where it is difficult to get clean drinking water, such measures are anti-poor. The report strongly recommends that bottled water should be taxed at par with juices to increase affordability, especially knowing that access to safe and hygienic potable water is limited in India and there should be uniform low taxes for all non-alcoholic beverages across different states for consumer health and safety reasons. Contrary to popular belief, the report found that the subsidies given to the industry for cold chains or setting up of manufacturing facilities do not meet industry requirements. In fact, the high cost of doing business and the high and multi-layered taxes erode the benefits of subsidies and, therefore, the country is not receiving the desired investment from the corporate sector in areas such as cold chains and food processing. In fact, instead of subsidies, if the government streamlines the tax process, enhances transparency in governance and provides the necessary infrastructure, investment will automatically flow.

The report emphasises that to protect consumer health and safety, the government should take strong measures against spurious and counterfeit products. Government and industry interactions in this regard will be mutually beneficial. A number of reforms have to be taken at the state level. For instance, there is an urgent need to have uniform classification for the non-alcoholic beverage sector by the State Pollution Control Boards and all states should classify non-alcoholic beverages under the 'orange' category along with other food processing industries as is done by some states (such as Himachal Pradesh and Orissa) and the central government. This will streamline the clearance process for setting up manufacturing facilities.

The report highlights that India's ability to develop as a manufacturing hub for non-alcoholic beverages is inhibited by poor infrastructure. This includes power shortages that lead to an increase in overall production costs due to the need to install captive power units; limited availability of land near consumption centres, which requires production units to be set up at remote areas, thereby increasing sourcing and transportation costs; the high cost of land acquisition and cumbersome procedures that make investments unviable; inadequate and poor quality of surface water, which is crucial for the non-alcoholic beverage sector; and poor road conditions, delays in interstate borders, capacity constraints of Indian Railways and inadequate cold storage and warehousing facilities, which result in significant wastage in the supply chain. The competitiveness of the non-alcoholic beverage sector is further impacted by the inconsistent supply and poor quality of agriculture raw materials, rising raw material prices due to inflation and restrictions on imports. High duties on intermediate products, such as packaging materials and multi-layered taxes that vary across states, have adversely impacted processed food manufacturing in India. A number of complex regulations affecting the entire supply chain have not allowed the sector to reach its full potential.

Thus, unlike other emerging markets such as China or Brazil, India is not a part of the global production network in the agro-processing sector. Given that India has the raw materials and an abundant supply of manpower, the country has the potential to develop as a non-alcoholic beverage manufacturing hub and an agro-product sourcing destination. This will only be possible through a package of reforms initiatives that are presented in Chapter 7. It is important to understand that because the Indian economy is liberalising and globalising and the country is actively engaged in trade agreements, unless we initiate reforms at a rapid pace, Indian companies will also relocate to other countries and use the FTA (free trade agreement) route to cater to the Indian market. Hence, India should continuously strive to be a competitive, efficient and attractive investment destination through appropriate policy initiatives.

1

Introduction

India is one of the largest and fastest-growing economies in the world. Globally, it is the 10th largest economy in terms of nominal GDP ($[1]1.8 trillion).[2] According to the International Monetary Fund (IMF), in 2010 India's GDP grew at 10.1 per cent compared to 10.4 per cent in the case of China, 9.5 per cent among developing countries in Asia and 7.4 per cent among emerging and developing economies. Although India's growth rate slowed substantially in 2011 to 7.7 per cent, it was still higher than the average growth rate of emerging economies (6.4%). It is projected to grow at 5.7 per cent in 2013, which is higher than the average projected growth rate for emerging and developing economies (5.3%).[3]

With the rise in GDP and economic growth, there has been an increase in per capita income and consumption. The number of people below the poverty line has also come down. Between 2001 and 2010, the size of the rich consumer class in India increased by 21.4 per cent, while the middle class grew by 12.9 per cent (Shukla, 2010). McKinsey Global Institute (2007) forecasts that if the Indian economy grows at the rate of 7.3 per cent, then by 2025, 583 million Indians would join the middle class, increasing from around 5 per cent of the population in 2005 to 41 per cent in 2025; they would also account for 59 per cent of the country's consumption. Although the growth rate has slowed in recent years, the Indian middle class still has significant growth potential and India's consumer spending will increase.[4] There have also been demographic changes in the country (Sinha and Kar, 2007). More women are entering the workforce and nuclear households are replacing the joint family system. India also has one of the youngest populations in the world, with 54 per cent of Indians below the age of 25.[5]

Rising incomes and demographic changes have altered consumption patterns in the country, particularly for food and beverages. With higher incomes, a younger population and more women in the workforce, there is an increasing trend towards eating out and buying packaged food and beverages. With the liberalisation of the media, there is greater exposure to products and lifestyles, and with the increase in overseas travel, there is greater awareness of global shopping patterns and international brands (Rao, 2000). There is an increased willingness to try new products and brands, which has led to the proliferation of brands and products in processed food and beverages.

These factors have led to a demand for packaged food and for beverages. In the beverage sector, consumers now show a distinct preference for branded products for beverages such as bottled water compared to non-branded products. At the same time, there is a shift in preference within food and beverage categories. Within beverages, consumers are shifting from CSDs to healthier options such as fruit juices and sports drinks.

When we compare Indian consumers' spending on food and beverages to that of other countries, an interesting difference emerges. Food and beverages constitute a substantial part of India's consumption basket. In India, at least 31 per cent of the total consumption basket goes towards food and beverages. In contrast, consumers in other countries spend a much lower proportion of their income in food and beverages—9 per cent in the USA, 17 per cent in Brazil and 25 per cent in China.[6]

Thus, this is one of the most important sectors in India. The sector is changing rapidly through product diversification and brand proliferation to keep pace with consumer preferences. The large consumer base in India has attracted a number of domestic and foreign companies to this sector. In addition, the Indian government wants to attract investment in the food processing sector, which would benefit the beverage sector.

This report examines the non-alcoholic beverage sector, which is a component of the food processing sector. The non-alcoholic beverage sector has been selected because it operates across the entire value chain of the food processing sector—from the farm to the consumer. The sector comprises both corporate and non-corporate[7] players that produce and sell a

1. Unless otherwise stated, $ will represent United States dollar throughout the report.
2. *http://data.worldbank.org/indicator/NY.GDP.MKTP.CD* (last accessed in June 2013).
3. IMF (2013).
4. Ernst & Young (2012).
5. National Commission on Population (2006).
6. The Boston Consulting Group (2012).
7. Corporate or modern players have a corporate management. These are large companies that are professionally managed with a transparent accounting system and centralised quality control and sourcing. Non-corporate players are generally small businesses owned by a single owner or a family located in a particular region. They may not have an organised management with standardised accounting systems. The sourcing and distribution are also usually done locally.

wide range of branded and non-branded products. Some components of the sector are labour-intensive, whereas other components are technology-intensive. Hence, it offers employment opportunities along the entire chain as well as investment opportunities. Despite its potential, the sector has not been developed fully; very few studies examine the potential of this sector and its contribution to the Indian economy. This report aims to fill the gap and make policy recommendations on how to develop an efficient non-alcoholic beverage sector in India.

Specifically, the report examines recent trends and developments in the non-alcoholic beverage sector and its contribution to the Indian economy. It examines barriers in the sector that hinder its development. It offers policy recommendations to enable the sector to grow and to increase employment and investment in the supply chain. This would enable India to develop into both a sourcing hub and a large market for non-alcoholic beverages.

The report is based on secondary information and a nationwide primary survey.

1.1 Overview of the Food Processing Sector in India

The food processing sector in India is the fifth-largest sector in terms of size. It contributes to 6 per cent of the total industrial investment and to 12-15 per cent of the total manufacturing GDP (FICCI & KPMG, 2007). Between 2004-05 and 2009-10, the food processing sector grew from $9.8 billion to $13.8 billion at a compound annual growth rate (CAGR) of 9.3 per cent.[8]

The food processing sector in India has been a major beneficiary of the economic reforms of 1991. The reforms encouraged privatisation, removed restrictions on FDI, reduced tariffs, ended the strict licensing and quota regime and streamlined the approval procedures. Today, 100 per cent FDI is allowed in this sector, and the government has extended various fiscal and other incentives to encourage investments in this sector.

The sector attracted a total of $2.6 billion as FDI between 2000 and 2011, which is 1.8 per cent of the total FDI received by India during this period. The sector is highly labour-intensive; in 2009, the sector employed almost 8.5 million people and is estimated to employ 17.8 million people in 2022 (National Skill Development Corporation, 2009). In addition, India has abundant natural resources; it is the second largest producer of fruits and vegetables in the world, producing 74.9 million tonnes (mt) of fruits and 146.5 mt of vegetables in 2012.[9]

Despite these advantages, the food processing sector faces several supply-side constraints and regulatory barriers. Only 7 per cent of the total Indian perishable produce is processed, which is extremely low compared to countries such as the USA (65%), Philippines (78%) and China (23%).[10] In fact, India is a net importer of processed food (Joshi, 2009). The Ministry of Food Processing Industries (MoFPI) in its 'Vision 2015' plan identified some of these constraints. One constraint is the lack of quality raw material. The second is wastage, which is caused by improper handling and lack of cold storage facilities, which are available for only 10 per cent of the produce; as a result, almost 30 per cent of farm produce after harvest is wasted.[11] Other problems include the high cost of production due to lack of adequate working capital, lack of technology for processing and packaging, low economies of scale among marginal and small manufacturers, numerous taxes, regulations and restrictions, and a fragmented supply chain.

As a sub-sector of the food processing industry, the non-alcoholic beverage sector shares its potential as well as its constraints.

1.2 The Non-alcoholic Beverage Sector: Definition and Classification

There is no universal definition of the non-alcoholic beverage sector. The sector broadly includes all beverages that are alcohol-free and popularly known as softdrinks. Such beverages are drunk to quench thirst, for refreshment or for functional benefits, such as alertness, enhanced hydration or health benefits.

The international classification of the sector is provided by the United Nations Central Product

8. Press Information Bureau (PIB) (2012).
Values are converted from INR to $, exchange rate from 2004-05, INR 1 = $ 0.022 (period average), Exchange rate from 2009-10, INR 1 = $ 0.02 (period average). Extracted from historical exchange rates, Oanda Currency Converter, *http://www.oanda.com/currency/historical-rates/*.

9. *http://www.apeda.gov.in/apedawebsite/six_head_product/FFV.htm* (last accessed in June 2013).

10. Inputs from the Associated Chambers of Commerce and Industry of India (ASSOCHAM)

11. ASSOCHAM and Yes Bank (2012).

Classification (UNCPC). The latest UNCPC (version 2) classifies non-alcoholic beverages under food products, beverages and tobacco, textiles, apparel and leather products (CPC 2). This classification has evolved over time as shown in Annexure A-1.1.

In India, National Industrial Classification (NIC) 2008, is used to classify industries. Under this classification, food and beverages come under manufacture of beverages (Division 11), wholesale of food, beverages and tobacco (Group 463), retail of food, beverages and tobacco in specialised stores (Group 472) and food and beverages service activity (Division 56). From the perspective of manufacturing, the non-alcoholic beverage sector is classified as shown in Figure 1.1. Note that it excludes milk-based items (*kulfi*, ice cream and pouched milk) as well as coffee, tea and *maté* products.

A few market research organisations have tried to classify this sector. The most comprehensive classification is provided by Euromonitor.

I. *Bottled water*: Still bottled water, carbonated bottled water, flavoured bottled water and functional bottled water.

II. *Carbonated (sparkling) soft drinks*: All beverages in which carbon dioxide is dissolved. This includes all cola carbonated and all non-cola carbonated beverages, such as fruit-flavoured carbonated drinks, mixers and ginger ale. The beverages can be either normal or low calorie and can contain nutritive/non-nutritive sweetening agents.

III. *Fruit/vegetable juices*: 100 per cent juices, nectars (25-99% of juice content), juice drinks (up to 24% juice content) and fruit-flavoured drinks.

IV. *Fruit/vegetable concentrates*: Both liquid and powder concentrate.

V. *Ready-to-Drink (RTD) Tea*: Still RTD tea, such as RTD flavoured or normal tea (Nestea) and carbonated RTD tea.

VI. *RTD coffee*: Packaged ready-to-drink coffee (Georgia, Nescafe, etc.)

VII. *Milk-based beverages*: Contains normal or sweetened milk and milk-based beverages, such as *badam* milk, *lassi* and buttermilk.

VIII. *Functional drinks*: Sports and energy drinks.

(i). *Energy drinks*: Drinks with high levels of caffeine and amino-acid taurine designed to boost energy levels.

Figure 1.1

NIC 2008 Classification of the Non-alcoholic Beverage Sector

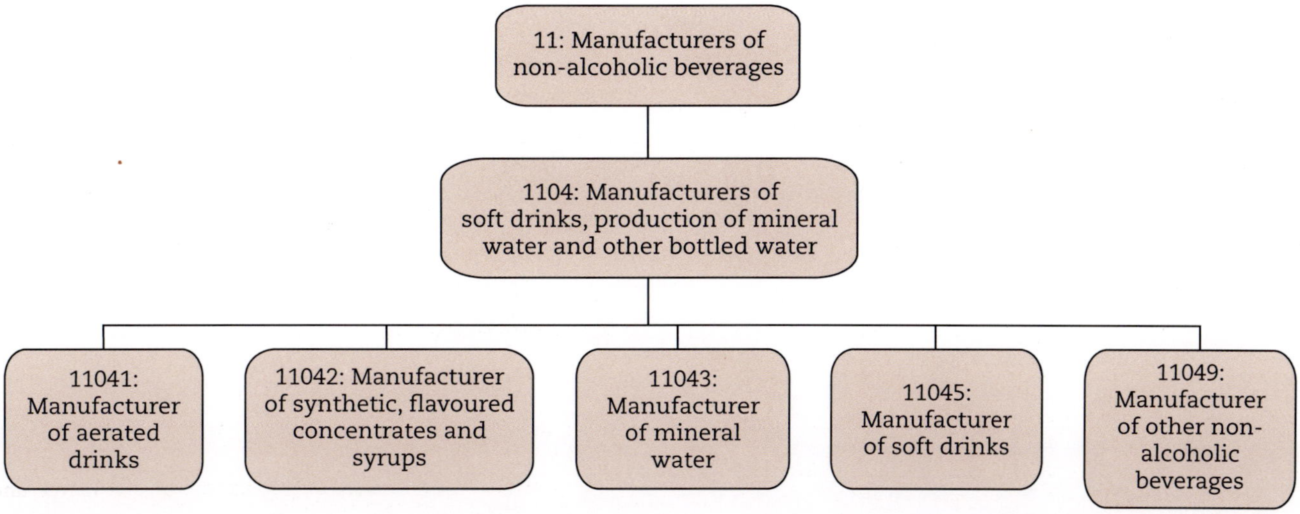

Source: Compiled from Central Statistics Office (CSO) (2008): 42. *http://mospi.nic.in/mospi_new/upload/nic_2008_17apr09.pdf* (last accessed in June 2013).

(ii). *Sports drinks*:

a. *Isotonic*: Contains 5-8 per cent carbohydrate. Usually they are used to replace lost body fluids and consumed during exercise or heat exposure.

b. *Hypotonic*: Contains less carbohydrate. This speeds up absorption and is therefore used during exercise.

c. *Hypertonic*: Stronger solution. Designed to maintain or replace energy levels during an exercise session of minimum one hour.

IX. *Asian specialty drinks*: Traditional drinks such as herbal organic tea, fruit, cereal/pulse-based drinks, such as soya bean drinks (commonly available in Asian countries).

In this report, non-alcoholic beverages will cover the sub-categories given in Table 1.1.

Table 1.1

Sub-categories of Non-alcoholic Beverages used in the Report

Sub-category	*Definition*	*Examples in India*
Bottled water	Includes mineral water, spring water, still water, flavoured and sparkling water	• Aquafina • Himalayan • TATA Water Plus • Kinley • Bisleri
CSDs	Any flavoured beverage containing dissolved carbon dioxide	• 7-Up • Coca-Cola • Fanta • Limca • Mirinda • Pepsi • Mountain Dew • Dukes Lemonade • Sprite • Thums Up
Energy drinks	Drinks that contain stimulants, such as caffeine, which boost energy levels	• Burn • Red Bull
Fruit-based drinks	Drinks that contain up to 20–30 per cent fruit juice with sugar, colour and flavour	• Maaza • Minute Maid Pulpy Orange • Nimbooz • Slice • Tropicana
Fruit juices	Contains some percentage of fruit pulp	• Real • Tropicana
Milk or yoghurt-based beverages	Ready-to-drink milk or milk-based beverages, such as *lassi* and buttermilk	• AmulKool • Safal
Organic/ayurvedic drinks	Drinks prepared from organic products	• Noni Juice • Patanjali
Sports drinks	Drinks used after exercise to replace lost body fluids	• Gatorade • Powerade
Tea/coffee-based drinks	Iced tea, lemon tea, iced coffee, etc.	• Georgia Cold Coffee • Fuze Tea • Lipton Iced Tea • Nestea
Vegetable juices	Contains some percentage of vegetable pulp	• Real • Tropicana
Vegetable or fruit concentrate/powder/syrup	Liquid and powder concentrates that can be dissolved in other liquids such as water	• Kissan • Rasna • Tang • Tropicana

Source: Authors' compilation.

In India a large part of the non-alcoholic beverage sector is in the traditional sector and is operated by a single person or family-owned businesses with no corporate management. For example, the neighbourhood juice seller makes and sells sugarcane juice. Therefore, a traditional retailer and manufacturer can be the same person. At the same time, there are large Indian companies such as Dabur India Limited and Anand Milk Union Limited (Amul) as well as global multinationals, such as Red Bull India Private Limited and Coca-Cola India and PepsiCo India. The corporate sector has professional managers, centralised quality control and sourcing and transparent accounting systems. Manufacturers and retailers can be in either the corporate/modern or the non-corporate/traditional segment. A corporate manufacturer may work with multiple contract manufacturers who can be both corporate as well as non-corporate players through the contract manufacturing model.

In terms of products, there are both branded and non-branded products; these can be either packaged or non-packaged. Branded products are manufactured by corporates or non-corporate manufacturers, who may be contract manufacturers of branded products; these products are sold through both traditional and corporate retailers.

1.3 Structure of the Report

Given this background, the flow of the remaining chapters is as follows:

Chapter 2 provides a global perspective on the non-alcoholic beverage sector. It describes how the industry has evolved, key features of global operating models and its contribution to the economy in some developed and developing countries. This helps us understand the Indian non-alcoholic beverage sector in the global context. The chapter then lists key regulations impacting this sector globally. Since India's regulatory structure is evolving, it helps to compare regulatory structures and how India can learn from global best practices. By presenting a comparative picture of India *vis-à-vis* some developed and developing countries, it sets the background for the next chapter—Chapter 3—that provides an overview of the growth and development of the non-alcoholic beverage sector in India. Chapter 3 also examines the governance structure and regulations in India. Since there is no organised system for collecting primary data on the non-alcoholic beverage sector, a primary survey was conducted. Chapter 3 describe the sampling framework and lays the ground for the primary survey.

The next three chapters—Chapter 4-6—cover the survey of manufacturers, retailers and consumers respectively. Chapter 4 deals with manufacturers of non-alcoholic beverages, both corporate and non-corporate. It describes their supply chain, forward and backward linkages, contribution to the economy in terms of employment generation and investment in research and development. It also summarises manufacturers' perceptions of the recent policy change that allows 51 per cent FDI in multi-brand retail.

The retail sector in India is evolving due to the entry of domestic corporate and foreign retailers, which is altering the linkages in the manufacturer–retailer supply chain. Chapter 5 captures this, along with the differences between corporate and non-corporate retailers. This chapter also presents the perceptions of retailers on various policies and regulations, which helps map their perceptions with those of manufacturers and consumers.

India is a large consumer market and Chapter 6 provides an overview of Indian middle-class consumers and their consumption patterns for non-alcoholic beverages based on a pilot survey. The survey focused on their purchase and consumption preferences, choice of retail outlets, perception of policies such as FDI in multi-brand retail and their awareness of consumer safety regulations and campaigns.

The last chapter, Chapter 7, summarises the barriers faced by different stakeholders in the non-alcoholic beverage sector in India and offers policy recommendations.

While some problems highlighted in this report are specific to the non-alcoholic beverage sector, the majority are more general and relate to the overall growth of the Indian economy and problems in manufacturing and the food processing sector. Hence, if the policy recommendations are implemented, they would not only enable the non-alcoholic beverage sector to grow but would also help the Indian economy through the growth of manufacturing, particularly in the food processing sector. Reforms would also help generate employment, upgrade skills, enhance the inflow of FDI and technology development, facilitate exports, and, by developing India as a production hub for agro-processing, they would link India with the global production network for agro-processed products.

2

The Global Non-alcoholic Beverage Sector

This chapter provides an overview of the global non-alcoholic beverage sector, focusing on the evolution of the sector, market structure and performance of the sector in some key developed and developing economies. It presents a comparative picture of the sector in India *vis-à-vis* other countries. This chapter also examines key regulations that impact the sector globally and the measures that companies have taken to comply with the regulations. Since the regulatory framework in India is evolving, the country can learn from global best practices.

The global non-alcoholic beverage market is large and is expected to grow. In terms of volume, the global sector was 457.37 billion litres in 2010,[1] and is expected to reach 522.84 billion litres in 2015, recording a growth rate of 14.3 per cent.[2] The major markets for non-alcoholic beverages are the developed countries, due to high incomes and the spending behaviour of consumers. The USA is the largest market,[3] followed by Europe. The fastest-growing markets are Asia Pacific and South America,[4] with emerging economies such as India, China and Brazil offering large and unsaturated markets for this sector.

The evolution of the non-alcoholic beverage sector is given in Box 2.1. Over the years, new varieties of carbonated and non-carbonated beverages have been created. Popular carbonated beverages include sparkling beverages such as aerated drinks (colas, tonic water and sodas). Non-carbonated beverages fall under a broader category that includes still beverages, such as fruit juices, fruit-based drinks, coffee, tea, packaged drinking water and regional drinks such as Asian specialty drinks.

Within the different segments of non-alcoholic beverages, CSDs have recorded remarkable growth in both the developed and emerging economies. The growth of CSDs can be attributed to the aggressive marketing and success of two brands—Coke and Pepsi. However, in the past 30 years, the demand for non-carbonated beverages such as fruit juices has risen due to growing health awareness.

The packaging techniques used for non-alcoholic beverages have also undergone changes. Since non-alcoholic beverages are perishable and carbonated beverages have to be stored carefully to keep the fizz intact, which is the unique selling point of the product, packaging has always been crucial. Initially, non-alcoholic beverages were sold in returnable glass bottles throughout the world. Keeping in mind consumers' preference for conveniently packaging and to reduce operating costs by minimising breakage during transportation, polyethylene terephthalate (PET) bottles, cans and aseptic packaging technologies such as multi-layered tetra paks were introduced. Packaging techniques also depend on the storage facilities available in different countries.

Box 2.1

Evolution of Non-alcoholic Beverages

The origin of the non-alcoholic beverage sector can be traced back to the 18th century, when non-carbonated drinks such as mineral water, which was known for its curative properties, became popular. In 1767, Jackson's Spa Water with curative properties was bottled and sold in Boston, USA. It was flavoured by adding ingredients such as lemon and honey. In 1810, the first US patent was issued for the "means of mass manufacturer of imitation mineral waters" to Simon and Rudnell of Charleston, South Carolina. In 1851, the bottled water brand 'Malvern' was created in London. Bottled water used to be imported into the USA from the United Kingdom (UK), but in 1871, the Mountain Valley spring bottled water plant was set up in the USA. Subsequently, there was a proliferation of brands and flavours in the bottled water segment.

The manufacture of juices from fruits and vegetables has been closely related to the development of agriculture. Through trial and error, people have learnt how to extract juice from various fruits and vegetables. Slowly, devices were invented to extract juice from fruits. The fruit juice-processing industry in the USA is said to have been started by Dr Thomas B. Welch and his son Charles in Vineland, New Jersey, in 1868. The first root beer was mass-produced for public sale in 1876 in Philadelphia, USA.

Carbonated drinks were first manufactured in Europe. In fact they were imported into the USA from Britain until 1800. In 1832, the apparatus to make carbonated drinks was invented and in 1886, a carbonated soft drink called Coca-Cola was invented in Georgia, USA, and in 1898, a variant called Pepsi-Cola was invented in North Carolina, USA. When the crown cork was invented in 1892, the marketing of carbonated drinks stepped up.

Source: Compiled from Hargitt (2006).

1. Rabobank (2012).
2. MarketLine (2011).
3. MarketLine (2011).
4. Rabobank (2012).

This industry clearly involves multiple processes and, given the size of the market, it has attracted a range of players, from global and domestic companies to medium and small-scale regional companies, along with a significant number of non-corporate players. This is discussed in the next section. We then discuss the key operations in the sector, followed by its contribution to the economy. The last section takes up the regulations in this sector, the main barriers and how stakeholders have tried to overcome these barriers.

2.1 Market Structure

The global market for non-alcoholic beverages contains both corporate and non-corporate players. Corporate players can be large global companies such as Del Monte Corporation, Kraft Foods Inc., Nestlé S.A., The Coca-Cola Company and PepsiCo Inc., or regional companies such as Britvic plc. (Europe) and Dabur India Limited (India). Non-corporate players are small and medium enterprises (SMEs) that manufacture and/or sell their own products or operate as contract manufacturers for large corporate players. Non-corporate players are predominant in emerging economies, such as India, China and Brazil.

The market structure for the non-alcoholic beverage sector varies across categories and geographies. For CSDs, energy drinks and sports drinks, companies usually require significant investments to set up production facilities, access raw materials and promote the product. These categories contain global brands such as Coke and Pepsi in CSDs and Red Bull in energy drinks. The markets for products such as CSDs are oligopolistic, with a few large players at the global level and very few regional players.

For fruit/vegetable juices and milk-based drinks, there are a large number of non-corporate players, especially in emerging economies. These players have easy access to raw materials that are locally available. Even if there are established brands in these markets, non-branded products are also popular. Hence, the markets for these categories are more competitive, with a large number of global corporate players as well as regional corporate and non-corporate players. Table 2.1 gives examples

Table 2.1

Global and Regional Players in the Non-alcoholic Beverage Sector

Category	*Global Players*	*Regional Players and their Markets*
Bottled water	• Nestlé S.A. • Groupe Danone • The Coca-Cola Company • PepsiCo Inc.	• Parle Bisleri Limited (India) • Nourish Co Beverages Limited (India) • Qingdao Laoshan Mineral Water Company Limited (China) • Britvic plc (Europe)
CSDs	• The Coca-Cola Company • PepsiCo Inc.	• Dr. Pepper Snapple Group Inc. (North America) • Britvic plc (Europe)
Fruit/vegetable beverages	• The Coca-Cola Company • Del Monte Corporation • PepsiCo Inc. • Kraft Foods Inc.	• Dabur India Limited (India) • Parle Agro Private Limited (India) • Malaysia Milk Sendirian Berhad (Malaysia) • Vita Food Factory Limited (Thailand)
Functional drinks (energy and sports drinks)	• Red Bull GmBH • PepsiCo Inc. • The Coca-Cola Company	• Frucor Beverages Limited (New Zealand and Australia)
Milk-based drinks	• Nestlé S.A. • Groupe Danone • International Dairy and Juice Limited (a PepsiCo Inc. and Almarai, Saudi Arabia joint venture)	• Mother Dairy Fruit and Vegetable Private Limited (India) • Lifeway Foods Inc. (USA) • General Mills Inc. (Europe and North America) • Philippine Carabao Center (Philippines)
RTD Tea/Coffee	• PepsiCo Inc. • The Coca-Cola Company • Nestlé S.A. • Suntory Holdings Limited • Unilever	• Dr. Pepper Snapple Group Inc. (North America) • Honest Tea, Inc. (USA) • Ito En, Limited (Japan)

Source: Compiled from stakeholder consultation.

of global and regional players in the global non-alcoholic beverage sector.

With the modernisation of retail, private labels[5] have emerged that compete with established brands. These products are manufactured by a small company and marketed under the corporate label. They are usually cheaper than established brands and offer corporate retailers higher margins and profitability. In mature markets for corporate retail, such as the USA, private labels offer strong competition to established brands and are popular among consumers. However, in a brand survey by Accenture (2012) that sampled more than 500 US consumers on their attitudes towards private labels *vis-à-vis* national brands, half the respondents felt that the quality of both brands was nearly the same. In emerging markets, such as India and China, private labels are a new concept, perhaps because consumers prefer to buy well-known brands.

2.2 Operations

The main operations of a global non-alcoholic beverage company are maintaining a supply chain network, creating consumer brand loyalty through marketing and product innovation and expanding market reach by venturing into new markets. The operations of global players and large companies differ from those of SMEs. Unlike local non-corporate manufacturers who have fragmented operations, global companies usually have integrated operations, from sourcing of raw materials to retailing the final products; in this way, they can control the supply chain, enjoy economies of scale and offer lower prices to consumers. Global companies take several initiatives to streamline their supply chain and increase their market reach.

In operations, global companies adopt different models. In vertically integrated operations,[6] the company buys out one component in the chain, which allows it to control a larger part of the chain. For instance, the bottling company, Groupe Danone, acquired the Alsatian brewer Kronenbourg as well as their largest customer, Evian mineral water; this enabled Groupe Danone to become a beverage manufacturer. In horizontally integrated operations,[7] the company buys a similar company to increase its market share. For example, The Coca-Cola Company bought Minute Maid Corp, which produces fruit juices, and PepsiCo Inc. bought the Lebedyansky and Wimm-Bill-Dann juice and dairy business in Russia. Companies may adopt different operations for different markets. While PepsiCo Inc. has adopted a vertically integrated operation model for CSDs in North America, in China, it has adopted a horizontally integrated operation model.[8] In new and emerging markets, companies frequently adopt a mixed model through a joint venture. This helps them capture the market and customise their products, since regional players know the local tastes and preferences. For instance, The Coca-Cola Company entered into a 50:50 joint venture with the State Light Industry Bureau (SLIB) to form Tianjin Jin Mei Beverage Company Limited in 1993 and launched a brand of tea, Tianyudi, in 1996 that became popular in China.[9]

Below, we describe the supply chain of a non-alcoholic beverage manufacturer and briefly discuss each component in the supply chain.

2.2.1 Supply Chain of Manufacturers

The supply chain of a non-alcoholic beverage manufacturer starts with the flow of raw materials from suppliers and extends until the final products reach consumers. Figure 2.1a shows a simple supply chain for a non-alcoholic beverage manufacturer, but they can be complex depending upon the number of processes attached with its manufacture. They also differ by product category, business model, type of operations, countries and even regions within the same country depending on the sourcing network. Two further examples of supply chains are given: Figure 2.1b shows the supply chain for fruit juice, using the case of orange juice, and Figure 2.1c depicts the supply chain for bottled water. In the case of orange juice, countries such as India import the oranges from Brazil. Small non-corporate players usually manage the entire supply chain themselves, but multinational companies work with different

5. Private label products are manufactured by one company and sold by another company under its brand name. For instance, Cott Beverages manufactures CSDs for Walmart, which Walmart then sells as Dr. Thunder.

6. When a company expands its business into areas that are at different points on the same production path, such as when a manufacturer owns its supplier and/or distributor. Source: *http://www.investopedia.com/terms/v/verticalintegration.asp* (last accessed in June 2013).

7. The acquisition of additional business activities that are at the same level of the value chain in similar or different industries. Source: *http://www.investopedia.com/terms/h/horizontalintegration.asp* (last accessed in June 2013).

8. *http://www.pepsico.com/PressRelease/Tingyi-Holding-and-PepsiCo-Enter-into-Agreement-to-Form-Strategic-Alliance-in-Ch11042011.html* (last accessed in June 2013).

9. *https://www.chinabusinessreview.com/public/0107/weisert.html* (last accessed in June 2013).

Figure 2.1a

Simplified Supply Chain for a Non-alcoholic Beverage Manufacturer

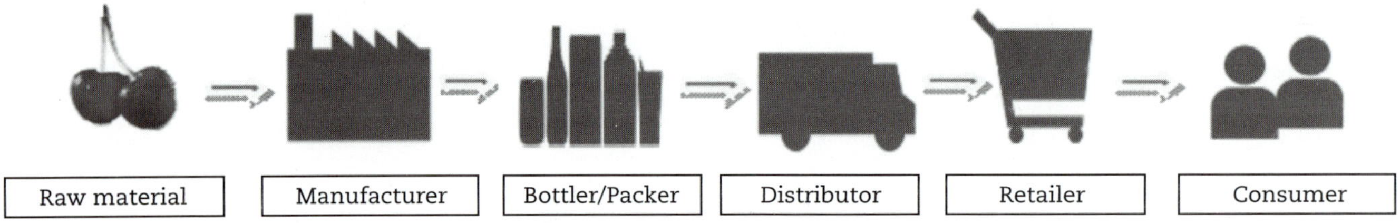

Source: Authors'compilation.

Figure 2.1b

Supply Chain for Juice

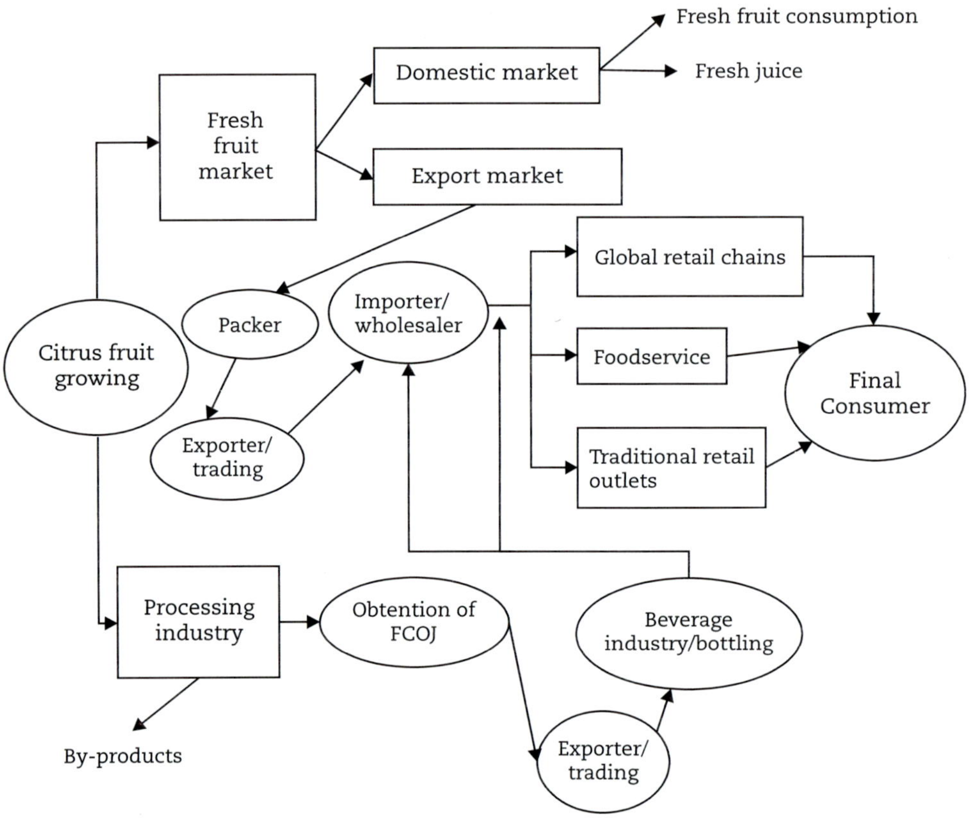

Note: FCOJ: frozen concentrated orange juice.

Source: *http://www.unctad.info/en/Infocomm/Agricultural_Products/Citrus-fruit/Marketing-chain/* (last accessed in June 2013).

Figure 2.1c

Supply Chain for Bottled Water

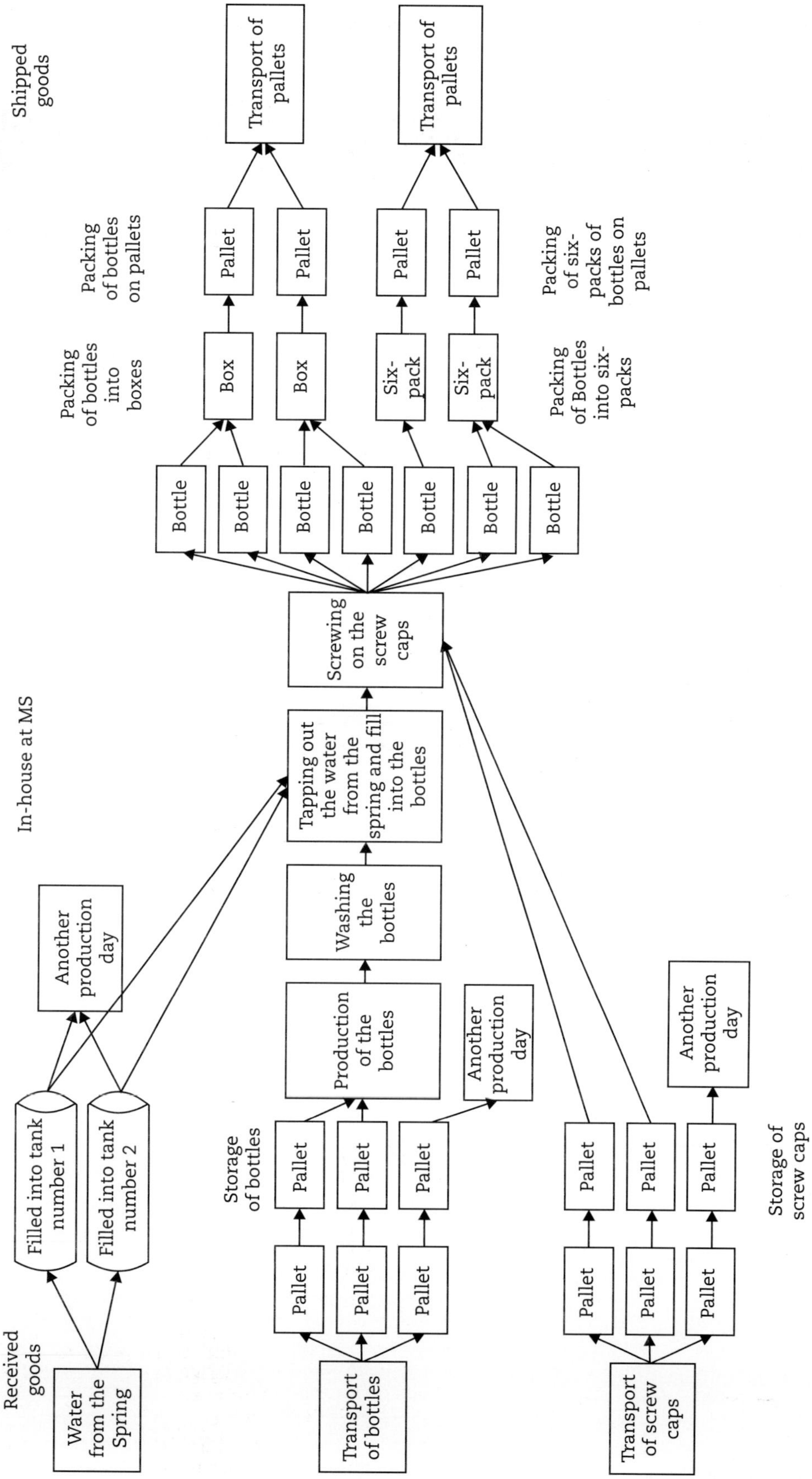

Sources: Karlsen *et al.* (2009).

segments such as farmers, contract manufacturers, packers and warehousing agents across the globe, especially in developing countries, to establish global supply chains.

Here, we describe the components of the supply chain.

Raw Material Procurement

The main raw materials for non-alcoholic beverages are water, sweeteners, soft drink or energy drink concentrates and agricultural raw materials, such as fruits, vegetables, milk, tea or coffee. Water is a key ingredient and companies generally depend on local water supply sources around the bottling locations. To mitigate water-related risks such as scarcity and hygiene, large global and regional/local players have come up with their own water sustainability programmes.

Concentrates are generally produced by the companies. Companies use different sweeteners in different markets depending on their availability and government regulations. For instance, while The Coca-Cola Company and PepsiCo Inc. use high fructose corn syrup as a nutritive sweetener in the USA, for other countries they use sucrose.[10] For milk-based drinks, the milk is generally sourced through a contract farming model. For example, the Gujarat Co-operative Milk Marketing Federation Limited (GCMMF) procures approximately 13 million litres of milk per day (peak period) from 16,117 village milk co-operative societies, 17 member unions covering 24 districts and 3.18 million milk producer members.[11] Nestlé Lanka PLC (Sri Lanka) paid approximately $31 million to the local farming community to procure raw materials, such as fresh milk and coconut, for its food and beverage products in 2012.[12]

The sourcing of agricultural raw materials such as fruit, vegetables or milk depends on quality, cost and assured supply. To enhance productivity and the quality of raw materials, multinational companies provide farmers with technical and financial support. Global companies liaise with global organisations such as the United Nations (UN), governments and non-governmental organisations (NGOs) for this purpose. For instance, Nestlé S.A. has a partnership with the United Nations Development Programme (UNDP) to promote better livestock management among 1,40,000 milk suppliers in Pakistan, including women (Pfitzer and Krishnaswamy, 2007).

Processes: Bottling, Labelling and Packaging

For bottling, labelling and packaging, global non-alcoholic beverage companies work with contract/franchise bottlers, packers, etc. Some companies set up their own integrated facilities, depending on the market. For instance, in 2009, PepsiCo Inc., China, entered into an agreement with Tingyi Holding Corporation, and Tingyi-Asahi Beverages Holding Company Limited (TAB) became a franchisee bottler for PepsiCo Inc. in China.[13] Similarly, packaging companies can enter the non-alcoholic beverage segment.

Distribution

When determining the distribution network for their products, global non-alcoholic beverage companies consider factors such as the shelf life of products, the market, consumer demand and cost of distribution. Based on these factors, companies either adopt direct store delivery[14] or work closely with both local and global third-party logistics (3PL)[15] and fourth-party logistics (4PL)[16] companies that can manage their distribution in a particular market. The advantage of working with local logistics service providers is that they understand the local market and have an established local network (Yadav *et al.*, 2013). For instance, in Poland, The Coca-Cola Company outsourced part of their warehousing and transportation networks to the Polish branch of DB Schenker Logistics, which has an established local network.[17] In the USA, Dr Pepper Snapple Group distributes nearly half its annual volume through the

10. *http://assets.coca-colacompany.com/79/be/d742827346398d224347d10205b4/10k_12_19.pdf* (last accessed in June 2013).
11. *http://www.amul.com/m/organisation* (last accessed in June 2013).
12. *http://www.nestle.lk/en/media/pressreleases/nestl%C3%A9-makes-highest-ever-contribution-to-local-farmers-in-its-history* (last accessed in June 2013).
13. *http://www.pepsico.com/PressRelease/Tingyi-Holding-and-PepsiCo-Enter-into-Agreement-to-Form-Strategic-Alliance-in-Ch11042011.html* (last accessed in June 2013).
14. In direct store delivery, manufacturers directly sell or distribute goods to retailers. The manufacturer avoids the logistics services provided by any third-party distributor or the retailers themselves.
15. A 3PL provider is a firm that provides logistics services to manufacturers for either part of or the whole supply chain.
16. A 4PL provider is a firm that assembles the resources, technology and capabilities of its own organisation and other organisations to design, build and run comprehensive supply chain solutions.
17. *http://www.3plnews.com/3pl/coca-cola-outsources-warehousing-of-finished-goods-to-db-schenker-logistics-in-poland.html* (last accessed in June 2013).

company-owned bottling and distribution network, while the remainder is done through third-party/licensed bottlers and distributors.[18]

To distribute their beverages in remote markets such as villages in emerging economies, companies also set up distribution centres and, thereby, provide direct and indirect employment. For example, when The Coca-Cola Company introduced the Micro Distribution Centre model in East Africa in 1999 to supply their beverages to remote African villages,[19] in the process, they provided employment to around 13,500 people and indirectly supported an estimated 48,000 dependents.[20] Del Monte Corporation, in an attempt to reduce the distance travelled by their products, introduced a model to set up plants and manufacturing near the final destination point; this model has been widely applied in the USA, helping the company to expand its business and establish nine strategically placed distribution centres that reach small villages.[21]

Retailers

Non-alcoholic beverages are sold through different modes, including business-to-business (B2B) and business-to-consumers (B2C) sales. B2B sales include sales to hotels, restaurants and other corporate sectors, such as offices, hospitals and educational institutes. B2C sales are done through different store and non-store retail formats.[22]

Retail formats vary widely between geographies, especially between developed and emerging markets. In developed markets, especially in the USA and Western Europe, food and beverages are sold mainly through corporate retail formats such as hypermarkets and supermarkets. In the USA, supermarkets and general merchandisers such as Walmart and Target account for 48 per cent of the total carbonated soft drinks sold.[23] In contrast, in emerging markets, there is a larger presence of non-corporate family-owned retail formats that are also called 'mom & pop' stores or traditional retailers. Though recent evidence shows that corporate retail formats are proliferating in emerging markets, the share of grocery expenditure in corporate formats still remains about 10 times higher in developed markets than in developing countries (Tandon *et al.*, 2011). Following this trend, non-alcoholic beverages in developed economies are sold mainly through corporate retail formats, whereas in developing economies such as India, they are sold mainly through non-corporate retail formats.

For greater consumer outreach and to optimise gains and minimise costs, non-alcoholic beverage manufacturers work closely with both corporate and non-corporate retailers and other retail sales points such as restaurants, bars, cafeterias, etc. To increase sales, companies continuously work to create new retail opportunities and design propositions that bundle service with product delivery. To attract retailers, companies also support them in managing storage, sales and promotions of the products (Yadav *et al.*, 2013).

Consumers

To expand market reach, global non-alcoholic beverage companies venture into new countries and new products. Based on factors such as a country's national and per capita income and consumers' tastes and preferences, multinationals and large domestic companies customise their products. For instance, The Coca-Cola Company introduced Xingmu (Smart), a line of carbonated fruit drinks that include green apple, watermelon and coconut flavours, in China in 1997.[24] Similarly, in 2011, PepsiCo Inc. introduced brands like Tropicana Pulp Sacs in China to meet local taste and beverage texture preferences.[25] Several large companies upon entering a new country also adopt merger and acquisition strategies with local firms in order to gain market access. For instance, in 2011, Nestlé S.A. acquired 60 per cent of Xiamen Yinlu Foods, which is a local

18. *http://www.drpeppersnapplegroup.com/company/operations/* (last accessed in June 2013).
19. *http://www.coca-cola.co.uk/community/micro-distribution-centres.html* (last accessed in June 2013).
20. *http://www.coca-cola.co.uk/community/micro-distribution-centres.html* (last accessed in June 2013).
21. *http://www.delmontefoods.com/cr/default.aspx?page=cr_distribution* (last accessed in June 2013).
22. Store formats include family-owned small-single shops or traditional outlets and corporate retail outlets (hypermarkets, supermarkets, convenience stores, etc.). Non-store formats include vending machines, direct selling and purchase through mail order, among others.
23. *http://www.foodpolitics.com/wp-content/uploads/SoftDrinkIndustryMarketing_11.pdf* (last accessed in July 2013).
24. *https://www.chinabusinessreview.com/public/0107/weisert.html*, July-August 2001 issue (last accessed in June 2013).
25. PepsiCo Inc. (2012).

Table 2.2

Estimated Market Size of the Global Non-alcoholic Beverage Sector

Name of Study	*Time Frame of Study*	*Coverage*	*Market Size ($ billion) (Year)*	*Market Size (billion litres) (Year)*	*Expected Market Size ($ billion) (Year)*	*Expected Market Size (billion litres) (Year)*
Soft Drinks: Global Industry Almanac	2010-2015	Retail sales of bottled water, carbonates, concentrates, RTD tea/coffee, smoothies	503.71 (2010)	457.37 (2010)	585.93 (2015)	522.84 (2015)
Soft Drinks: Global Industry Guide	2009-2014	Retail sales of bottled water, fruit-based drinks, carbonated soft drinks, RTD tea/coffee	440.3 (2009)	398.7 (2009)	511.6 (2014)	465.4 (2014)

Note: RTD, ready-to-drink.

Source: Compiled from MarketLine (2010, 2011).

Table 2.3

Estimated Share of Non-alcoholic Beverage Categories

Name of the Study	*Year*	*Top Categories*	*Percentage Share of Each Categories*
Rabobank-Global Beverage Outlook, 2012	2010	Bottled water CSD Fruit/vegetable juices	36.6 32.5 11.9
Soft Drinks: Global Industry Almanac	2010	CSD	40.6
Soft Drinks: Global Industry Guide	2009	CSD	42.5

Source: Compiled from Rabobank (2012), MarketLine (2010, 2011).

producer of RTD peanut milk, to penetrate markets in China.[26]

Consumer brand loyalty is a key factor for success in the non-alcoholic beverage business, but it is difficult to establish brand loyalty. In developing countries such as India and China, consumers experiment with new products, and in developed countries, consumer preferences have changed over time. For instance, with growing health consciousness, there is an increasing preference for health drinks such as low calorie/diet drinks and caffeine-free drinks. In keeping with this trend, companies have created low-calorie/health drinks. For instance, in 2010, Kraft Foods Inc. launched Crystal Light Pure Fitness, a low-calorie fitness drink mix, in the USA and Canada.[27]

Aggressive marketing techniques are a crucial part of global companies' operations to generate brand loyalty. These techniques could include the following elements:

- Advertising: It helps to increase product visibility and consumer reach.
- Brand positioning: It helps the company to create a distinct identity of the brand for the target customer. This helps increase consumer's preference for the particular brand in comparison to others.
- Product innovation and customisation: It helps a company expand its market by diversifying its product base and offering greater choices to its consumers. Companies can also customise their products to meet consumer tastes and preferences.

Consumer preferences for certain products in some markets act as an advantage for small and niche companies to survive and face competition from multinationals. This creates competition for multinationals that offer a wide range of products and brands. To compete with small local players and domestic companies, large multinationals have to adopt an appropriate pricing strategy and invest

26. Nestlé S. A. (2012).
27. *http://www.foodprocessing.com/vendors/products/2010/101.html* (last accessed in June 2013).

Table 2.4

Multinational Beverage Companies in the Fortune Global 500 List

Company Name	Total Revenue (in $ billion)[a]	Revenue from Beverages	Beverage Revenue as Part of Total Revenue (Percentage)	Country of Origin	Number of Countries where Company has Operations	Number of Countries where Products are Present	Number of Employees[b]
GroupeDanone	25.84	4.32	17	France	>120	>120	101,885
Kraft Foods Inc.	54.4	9.7	18	USA	~75	170	1,26,000
Nestlé S.A.	91.5	~27.5	~30	Switzerland	83	> 140	3,28,000
PepsiCo Inc.	66.50	34.25	52	USA	200	200	2,97,000
Red Bull GmbH	5.65	N.A	N.A.	Austria	164	164	8,294
The Coca-Cola Company	46.52	46.52	100	USA	>200	>200	1,46,200

Note: [a]: Numbers are as of December 31, 2011, from the company's annual reports.
[b]: The number of employees denotes the total number of people working in the company as per the company's annual report.
> : Denotes 'more than.'
N.A.: Data are not available.

Source: Compiled from company annual reports:
(a) GroupeDanone (2012).
(b) Kraft Foods Inc. (2012).
(c) PepsiCo Inc. (2012).
(d) Nestlé S.A (2012).
(e) *http://www.redbull.com/cs/Satellite/en_INT/Company-figures/001242939605518?pcs_c=PCS_Article&pcs_cid=1242937556133* (last accessed in June 2013).
(f) The Coca-Cola Company (2012a).

heavily in promotional and marketing activities. Most large companies also invest in innovation to develop new products for differentiation.

2.3 Size of the Sector

It is difficult to estimate the size of the global market for non-alcoholic beverages, because definitions and sector coverage vary across countries. Most countries do not record disaggregated data for the non-alcoholic beverage sector. Even the global association for the non-alcoholic beverage sector—International Council of Beverages Associations (ICBA)—does not have data on the size of the sector. One reason is that companies do not specialise in the production of non-alcoholic beverages (Krause Fund Research, 2012). For instance, PepsiCo Inc. manufactures and sells food items like potato chips and other snacks along with non-alcoholic beverages.

A few market research organisations have tried to measure the size of this sector, but they do not give comprehensive data for all countries, which makes cross-country comparisons difficult. Tables 2.2 and 2.3 present some estimates of the size of the global market and the size for different categories of beverages.

Table 2.4 presents the size of some global non-alcoholic beverage companies in the Fortune Global 500 List.[28]

2.4 Contribution to the Economy

The important indicators of the economic contribution of any sector are total production, employment creation and export generation. However, disaggregated data for the non-alcoholic beverage sector is often not available and the data do not clearly distinguish the contribution of this sector from other processed food sectors. The contribution of this sector to select economies—the USA, the UK and China—in terms of production, employment and exports are described below. The USA and the UK have been selected because the modern non-alcoholic beverage sector originated in these markets. China was selected because it is an

28. Fortune Global 500 is an annual ranking of the top 500 companies in the world based on revenues. The list is published annually by Fortune magazine.

emerging economy and one of the fastest-growing markets for the global non-alcoholic beverage sector. The data for India have been included so that its performance (as well as potential) can be viewed from an international perspective. We have used production and employment data from the UN database and the export data is compiled from the UN Comtrade database. Since the comparison is done across countries, the data was selected from the latest years in which the countries were listed in these databases. We have also tried to highlight the contribution of the sector in terms of higher income possibilities, FDI inflows, creation of infrastructure and R&D contribution, among others, based on country examples.

2.4.1 Output Generated in Terms of Total Sector Production

The total output generated by a sector helps us understand the sector's contribution to the GDP of an economy. It can be measured in terms of total production by a sector or total revenue generated by the sector. Figure 2.2 shows the output generated in terms of production by the beverage sector in select economies in 2008. Among the four countries, the beverage sector in the USA generated the highest output, but the sector's contribution to China's economy was very close. The Indian market was the smallest at $7.15 billion, because this industry is still at a nascent stage. However, this might suggest potential for growth, given the large size of the market.

Figure 2.2

Output Generated in terms of Total Production by the Beverage Sector, 2008

(in $ billion)

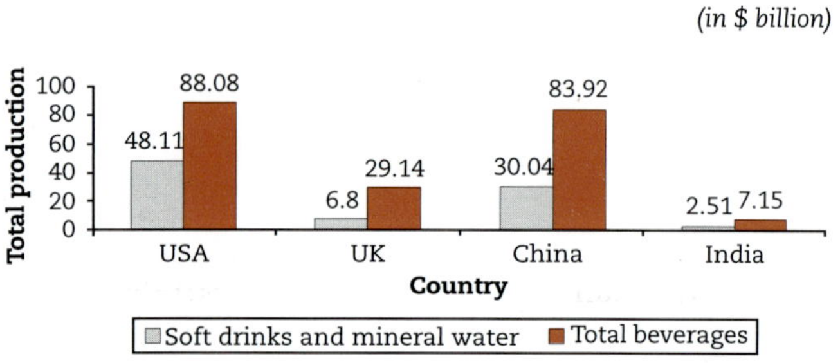

Source: Compiled from INDSTAT, UNDATA, *http://data.un.org/Data.aspx?d=UNIDO&f=tableCode%3a14%3bisicCode%3a155* (last accessed in June 2013).

2.4.2 Employment Generated

The creation of quality employment increases labour productivity and national income and provides livelihood to the population of a country. It also leads to higher per capita income and enhances the purchasing capacity of consumers and thereby creates widespread economic gains. Employment can be of two types: direct and indirect employment. Direct employment is employment in the beverage manufacturing companies, whereas indirect employment is employment created by the beverage manufacturing companies in allied sectors such as logistics and retail. The beverage sector has significant potential to create both direct and indirect employment. Figure 2.3 shows the direct employment generated by the sector in the USA, China and India in 2008. It shows that both the USA and India employ fewer workers than China.

Figure 2.3

Direct Employment in the Beverage Sector, 2008

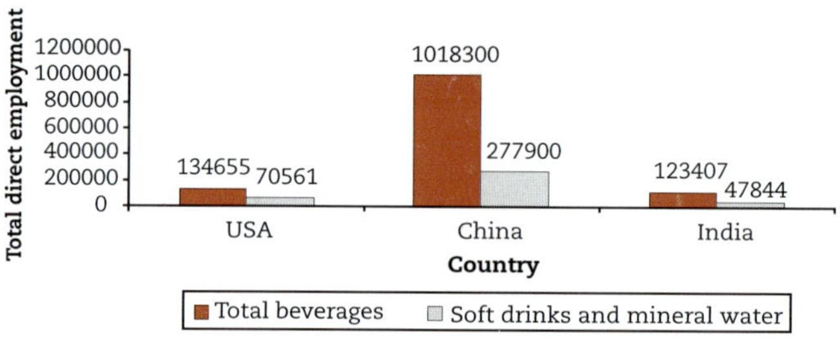

Source: Compiled from INDSTAT, UNDATA, *http://data.un.org/Data.aspx?d=UNIDO&f=tableCode%3a04%3bisicCode%3a155* (last accessed in June 2013).

The figures for direct employment do not capture the large number of people employed in this sector. Because of its forward and backward linkages, large numbers of people are indirectly employed in this sector—in packaging, transportation and retail. Several companies have designed initiatives to create self-employment opportunities for the rural poor. For example, in 2012, The Coca-Cola Company launched the '5by20' programme to provide self-employment opportunities to five million women entrepreneurs across their global supply chain. In this initiative, they collaborated with United Nations Women, the Bill and Melinda Gates Foundation, which is a charitable foundation, and Techno Serve, a company that provides business solutions to poverty.[29] PepsiCo India has a programme, PepsiCo EnAble, that provides equal employment opportunities to people with different abilities for which PepsiCo India won the prestigious Helen Keller Award.[30]

29. *http://www.coca-colacompany.com/stories/5by20* (last accessed in June 2013).

30. Inputs from the company.

2.4.3 Exports Generated

The non-alcoholic beverage sector has significant capacity to generate export revenue. Table 2.5 shows the sector's contribution to export revenues in the USA, the UK, China and India. The data show a huge difference between China and India. While China exported $1.83 billion worth of non-alcoholic beverages in 2011, India's exports were only $0.03 billion, despite the fact that India is the second largest producer of fruits and vegetables and the top producer of milk.[31]

Table 2.5

Export Revenue from the Non-alcoholic Beverage Sector, 2011

(in $ billion)

HS Code (as reported)	*Description*	*USA*	*UK*	*China*	*India*
2201	Waters, natural, etc., not sweetened, etc., ice and snow	0.11	0.05	0.14	0.0002
2202	Mineral water and aerated waters, sweetened and other non-alcoholic beverages except fruit and vegetable juice	0.91	0.59	0.45	0.007
2009	Fruit juices and vegetable juice, no spirits	1.31	0.08	1.22	0.018
0401	Milk and cream not concentrated or sweetened	0.06	0.47	0.02	0.005
0403	Buttermilk, yoghurt, *kephir*, etc., flavoured, etc., or not	0.11	0.75	0.007	0.0008
Total		2.50	1.94	1.83	0.03

Source: Compiled from UN Comtrade Database, *http://comtrade.un.org/db/* (last accessed in June 2013).

2.4.4 Other Contributions

The non-alcoholic beverage sector has the potential to make other contributions to an economy, such as generating higher income. Since there are no cross-country comparative data on these contributions, we present some examples to illustrate the point.

- *Income opportunities and secure livelihoods*: By working closely with farmers and SME suppliers, global manufacturers not only help in the percolation of technology but they also enable these farmers and SME suppliers to become a part of their global supply chain. This leads to higher income and secure livelihoods. One way in which farmers participate in the global supply chain is through contract farming.[32] For instance, Julie Juicer PLC (JJ plc), a UK-based juice-making company, entered into a sourcing agreement with 1,000 farmers in East African regions.[33] This helped the farmers to directly integrate into the supply chain of the company and thereby provided them with sustainable livelihoods. By reducing the number of intermediaries in the supply chain, farmers now have better earnings prospects. In 2012, Nestlé S.A. announced its partnership with local authorities in Morocco's Doukkala-Abda region with the aim of increasing regional milk production, enhancing the quality of fresh milk and increasing its sourcing of fresh milk from this region. This programme is expected to provide sustainable livelihoods to almost 10,000 farmers in the region by imparting training and expertise in milk supply, technical equipment and financial management.[34]

- *Foreign direct investment inflows*: Global companies bring in FDI in developing countries in manufacturing facilities, local infrastructure and supply chains. This not only creates employment opportunities, but also helps in the development of logistics infrastructure such as integrated cold chains. In developing countries, the logistics infrastructure is generally poor and fragmented and logistics costs are high. Investment by global multinationals helps to streamline the supply chain and improve the global competitiveness of the country's manufacturing sector in general. In 2011, The Coca-Cola Company announced an investment of $4 billion in China to be done in a phased manner over four years starting

31. *http://www.apeda.gov.in/apedawebsite/SubHead_Products/Dairy_Products.htm* and *http://www.apeda.gov.in/apedawebsite/six_head_product/FFV.htm* (last accessed in June 2013).

32. In contract farming, agricultural production is carried out according to an agreement between a buyer and farmers, which establishes conditions for the production and marketing of a farm product or products.

33. *http://www.ocr.org.uk/images/64862-question-paper-unit-f287-responsible-business-practices-in-today-s-global-market-case-study.pdf* (last accessed in June 2013).

34. *http://www.nestle.com/Media/NewsAndFeatures/Nestle-Morocco-Dairy* (last accessed in July 2013).

from 2012. This investment is expected to streamline the distribution chain in both urban and rural areas.[35] In 2010, PepsiCo Inc. also announced its plans to invest $2.5 billion in China in a phased manner over the next three years. This was in addition to their previous investment of $1 billion announced in 2008.[36]

- *Global research & development (R&D)*: Non-alcoholic beverage companies have substantial R&D spending. This leads to new product development, development of healthier beverage options, better storage development, etc. With changing tastes and preferences, companies are spending significant amounts on R&D to cater to customers' tastes and preferences. In 2009, the private expenditure on R&D in the UK food and beverage sector was $0.3 billion,[37] whereas this expenditure in China's food and beverage sector was $2.01 billion,[38] implying that companies in developing countries are spending more on R&D activities to enter countries that offer large markets for their products. For instance, in their 2012 Fact Sheet, Nestlé S.A., which already operates two R&D centres in Beijing and Shanghai, announced that it would open two more R&D departments in Greater China's Xiamen and Dongguan in 2013.[39] The facility at Xiamen will do specialised research on RTD beverages and support Nestlé S.A.'s partnership with Xiamen Yinlu Foods.

- *Consumer awareness initiatives*: Large multinational and domestic companies often design public outreach programmes to promote better lifestyles among children and youth. For example in 2007, The Coca-Cola Company launched a school outreach programme, Moderation-Balance-Variety, in Greece to teach students the importance of balanced nutrition and physical activity.[40] PepsiCo Inc. in Latin America supports Vive Saludable Escuelas, an initiative that teaches children to add physical activity to their daily lifestyles.[41]

2.5 Demand Trends around the World

With changing consumer behaviour, the demand for different categories of non-alcoholic beverages has altered. With globalisation, consumers now want more information before buying a product and hence they buy products based on rational decisions rather than impulse. Several factors influence their rational decisions including price, brand preference, impact on health and ingredients used in the products. In countries with high per capita income, such as the USA and the UK, consumers tend to buy beverages with higher aggregated values, such as 100 per cent juices, whereas countries with lower per capita income, such as Brazil, Russia, India, China and South Africa (BRICS) and Mexico, tend to consume more nectars and still drinks (Neves *et al.*, 2011).

Euromonitor provides data on different segments of non-alcoholic beverages (such as CSD, bottled water, etc.), which helps to analyse the consumption trends of non-alcoholic beverages in the USA and some select markets. In different categories of non-alcoholic beverages, the demand varies across markets. Figure 2.4 shows that in terms of sales volume, juices and CSDs recorded negative growth in the USA between 2006 and 2011 (–1% and –0.9%, respectively), unlike the Chinese market that witnessed high growth during the same period (13.2% and 5.6%, respectively). Demand for bottled water and energy drinks recorded high growth in both developed and developing countries.

Emerging economies show an interesting pattern in their growth rates for different product categories among non-alcoholic beverages. Energy drinks are popular in Brazil but not in China, and surprisingly, CSDs are the least popular category in both China and Brazil. In China, RTD tea is prevalent with 16 per cent volume growth, whereas in Brazil coffee is the fastest-growing category. This difference comes from the growing pattern of raw materials in the two countries; tea is grown in China, whereas coffee is

35. *http://www.chinadaily.com.cn/business/2012-03/24/content_14903726.htm* (last accessed in June 2013).
36. *http://www.pepsico.com/PressRelease/PepsiCo-to-Invest-25-Billion-in-China-Over-Next-Three-Years05212010.html* (last accessed in July 2013).
37. *http://stats.oecd.org/Index.aspx?QueryId=33210* (last accessed in June 2013).
38. *http://stats.oecd.org/Index.aspx?QueryId=33210* (last accessed in June 2013).
39. *http://www.nestle.com/asset-library/documents/library/documents/fact_sheets/facts-figures-nestle-china.pdf* (last accessed in July 2013).
40. *http://www.coca-colacompany.com/stories/promoting-healthy-lifestyles-in-greece* (last accessed in June 2013).
41. *http://www.pepsico.com/Purpose/Human-Sustainability/Partnerships-and-Community.html* (last accessed in July 2013).

Figure 2.4

Growth Rates of Different Product Categories, 2006-2011

(in percentage)

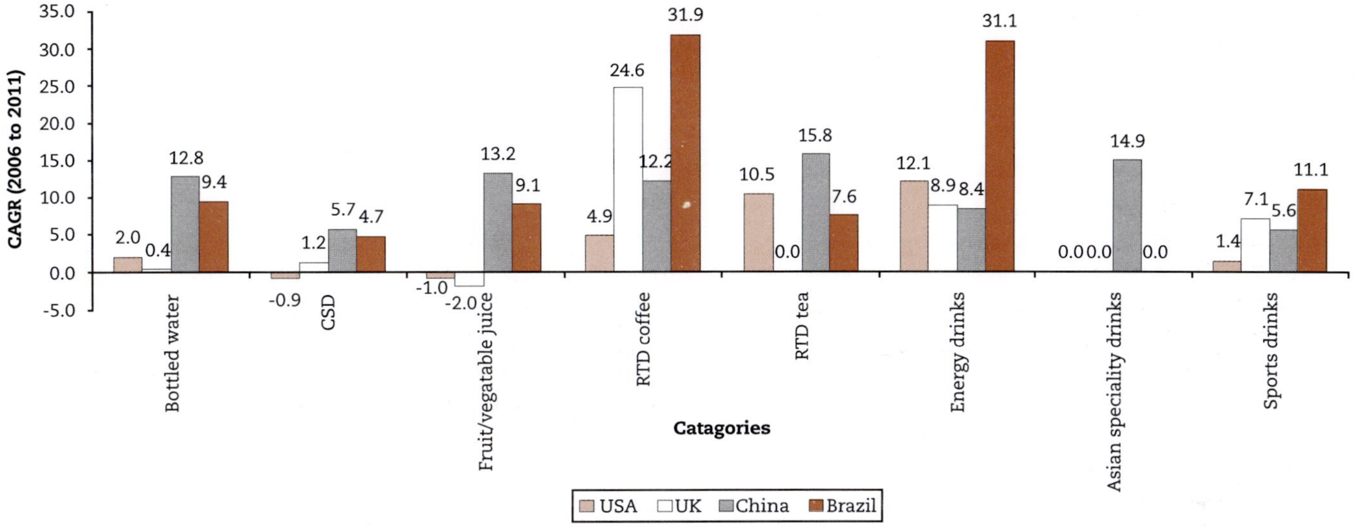

Source: Compiled from Euromonitor International.

grown in Brazil, which has also shaped consumer tastes.

2.6 Global Regulations and Lessons for India

This section discusses global regulations in the non-alcoholic beverage sector in two developed countries, the USA and the UK, and two developing countries, China and India. The regulations have evolved in developed countries and are evolving in developing countries such as India and China. These countries have been chosen with a view to put India's regulatory structure, which is relatively new and evolving, in a global perspective and to understand what India can learn from global best practices.

To the best of our knowledge, there are no specific regulations for the non-alcoholic beverage sector; instead, most regulations either cover both food and beverages or are applicable to the entire beverage sector (i.e., both alcoholic and non-alcoholic). Although regulations vary across countries, they are mainly based on international regulations. For instance, codes and standards are generally derived from the Codex Alimentarius Commission by the Food and Agricultural Organization (FAO) and the World Health Organization (WHO). These are accepted international standards for food safety that ensure fair trade and consumer protection at the global level and are recognised by the World Trade Organization (WTO). India also follows these international regulations.

Each country has its own food safety regulatory organisations, which work closely with the Codex Committee to set the guidelines that govern the food and beverage sector. Most regulatory guidelines are focused at the level of the ingredients used to manufacture and preserve the products, such as sweeteners and preservatives. Some guidelines are related to the labelling of the products. This ensures that complete information is passed on to consumers. The ICBA also participates actively in the Codex process. Like other countries, India has specific regulations for the food and beverage sector. To illustrate such regulations, Box 2.2 briefly describes regulatory guidelines in food safety and consumer protection in the USA, the UK and China along with that of India.

Although regulations are more stringent in developed countries than in developing countries, they are also more transparent and better implemented, which has helped companies grow. In particular, stringent implementation of food safety and consumer protection regulations enabled developed countries to control spurious products and brands and contaminated products, thereby benefitting consumers, on the one hand, and enabling genuine companies to grow, on the other. Apart from food

Box 2.2

Food Safety and Consumer Protection: Cases from Around the World

USA

Food Safety: The main regulatory body—the US Food and Drugs Administration (FDA)—is responsible for regulations related to food safety, ingredients used, packaging, labelling and food nutrition. The most important regulation guiding the sector is the Food Safety Modernisation Act (FSMA), which was announced on January 4, 2011. This act ensures the prevention of contamination as well as proper response to any outbreaks. The labelling requirements of food and beverage products are addressed under the Federal Food Drug and Cosmetic Act, 1938, and its amendments.

Consumer Protection: These laws are formulated and implemented by the Federal Trade Commission and the US Department of Justice. The acts are related to the information passed *via* beverage labels about the nutrition content of the beverage as in the Food Allergen Labeling and Consumer Protection Act (2004). There are also guidelines on advertising and marketing practices by companies under the Federal Trade Commission. Several states in the USA have adopted the Uniform Deceptive Trade Practices Act against fraud and deceptive trade practices.

UK

Food Safety: Guidelines for food processing are implemented by the Food Standards Agency, which was established under the Food Standards Act (1999). The Act aims "to establish the Food Standards Agency and make provision as to its functions; to amend the law relating to food safety and other interests of consumers in relation to food; to enable provision to be made in relation to the notification of tests for food-borne diseases; to enable provision to be made in relation to animal feeding stuffs; and for connected purposes."

As a member of the European Union (EU), the UK has to follow Union regulations as well as its own regulations. Basic minimum regulations are set by the Union laws. The main food laws that apply in the UK are:

- The Food Safety Act 1990 (as amended): This provides the framework for all food legislation in Great Britain.
- The General Food Law Regulation (EC) 178/2002, which provides the framework for general food safety.
- The General Food Regulations 2004 (as amended) provides for the enforcement of certain provisions of regulations under the General Food Law Regulation (EC) 178/2002.

Consumer Protection: Since the UK is a member of the EU, its consumer protection laws are based on EU guidelines. All consumer complaints are registered at the office of the Director General of Fair Trade after which it is taken up by the Office of Fair Trading. The Consumer Protection Act (1987) and its various amendments deal with consumer protection.

China

Food Safety: The Ministry of Health and the State Food and Drug Administration (SFDA) formulate and implement regulations that govern the safety of food, beverages, health food and cosmetics. They come under the State Council of the People's Republic of China. In 2004, the National Food Standards Development Plan 2004–05 was announced by several state bodies including the Standardization Administration of China, the Health, Agriculture and Commerce Ministries, the General Administration of Quality Supervision, Inspection and Quarantine and the SFDA. The plan specified the guiding principles for China's processed food sector. It aims to boost the overall standard of China's processed food, ensure safety and provide technical support to improve quality. In addition, several regulations guide food safety during manufacture and distribution:

- Regulation on the Management of Food Safety in Distribution (2006) by the Ministry of Commerce.
- Regulation on Food Hygiene License (2005) by the Ministry of Health.
- Regulation on Managing Hygiene in Food Additives (2002) by the Ministry of Health.
- Regulation on the Supervision and Administration of Sanitation for Imported and Exported Food (2006) by the General Administration of Quality Supervision, Inspection and Quarantine.

contd...

...contd...

Consumer Protection: The Consumer Rights and Benefits Protection Law (1993) under the State Administration for Industry and Commerce (SAIC) provides guidelines related to fraud and coercive practices by traders, the return and recall of defective products, impact analysis of a defective product on consumers, etc.

India

Food Safety: In India, the manufacturing, processing, distribution and sale of food and beverages are regulated by the Food Safety Standards Authority of India (FSSAI). This statutory authority was established under the Food Safety Standards Act (FSSA), 2006. This Act bundled together a number of central acts that were previously applicable to the food and beverage sector. These included the Prevention of Food Adulteration Act, 1954; Fruit Product Order, 1955; Solvent Extracted Oil, De-Oiled Meal and Edible Flour (Control) Order, 1967; Meat Food Products Order, 1973; Edible Oils Packing, 1998; Vegetable Oil Products Order, 1988; Milk and Milk Product Amendment Regulations, 2009 (MMPR-09) Division (MMPO, 1992, has been renamed MMPR, 2009)

In August 2011, the FSSAI implemented food safety regulations that were modelled under the FSSA, 2006. These are:

- Licensing and registration of food business regulations.
- Packaging and labelling regulations.
- Food product standards and food additives regulations.
- Regulations on prohibition and restriction on sale of food and beverages.
- Regulations on contaminants, toxins and residues used in food and beverages.
- Regulations governing laboratory and sample analysis of food and beverages.

These regulations cover all corporate and non-corporate food and beverage manufacturers, distributors and retailers.

Consumer Protection: The Consumer Protection Act (1986) and the Consumer Protection (Amendment) Act (2002), by the Ministry of Consumer Affairs provide guidelines for the protection of consumer interests and rights in India. These Acts also make provisions for the establishment of consumer councils and other similar authorities for the settlement of consumer grievances and disputes.

Source: Compiled from:

(a) *http://www.fda.gov/food/foodsafety/fsma/default.htm* (last accessed in June 2013).

(b) *http://www.fda.gov/food/labelingnutrition/FoodAllergensLabeling/GuidanceComplianceRegulatoryInformation/ucm106187.htm* (last accessed in June 2013).

(c) *http://www.ilga.gov/legislation/ilcs/ilcs3.asp?ActID=2357&ChapterID=67* (last accessed in June 2013).

(d) *http://www.legislation.gov.uk/ukpga/1987/43* (last accessed in June 2013).

(e) *http://eng.sfda.gov.cn/WS03/CL0757/61773.html* (last accessed in June 2013).

(f) *http://www.fssai.gov.in/* (last accessed in June 2013).

(g) *http://www.ncdrc.nic.in/1_1.html* (last accessed in June 2013).

safety and consumer protection, the non-alcoholic beverage sector also faces environmental regulations concerning water and packaging in most countries including India. To address these issues, global companies take several initiatives some of which are listed as follows.

- *Water usage*: To address water-related issues, companies have adopted water management programmes. For example, in their Water Stewardship programme of 2011, The Coca-Cola Company pledged to become water neutral by 2020,[42] after which in the same

42. The Coca-Cola Company (2011).

year they replenished 35 per cent of the water used in their finished beverages through their water recycling programmes.[43] Along similar lines, in 2007, PepsiCo Inc. set a global goal to reduce water usage by 20 per cent per unit of production by 2015 compared to a 2006 baseline. The company achieved the goal before time by improving their water usage efficiency by 20 per cent per unit of production in 2012 and was the recipient of the prestigious 2012 Stockholm Industry Water Award.[44]

- *Sustainable packaging*: To address environment sustainability issues, companies use sustainable, recycled packaging materials. Almost 70 per cent of Kraft Foods Inc.'s packaging materials in North America are recycled. In 2008 and 2009, they became official sponsors of Recyclebank, a company that rewards consumers for recycling packaging materials.[45] Del Monte Corporation has also committed to reduce its use of packaging materials by 15 per cent per pound of product by 2016, using 2007 as the baseline year. By 2016, the company aims to reduce the amount of natural resources used through the entire supply chain for producing packaging materials. By 2011, the company had already reduced packaging materials used per pound of product by 11 per cent.[46]

We can see that the global non-alcoholic beverage sector has evolved in its product variety and quality and the markets it caters to. This sector is growing, especially in emerging markets, and has significant potential in terms of economic contribution and the creation of forward and backward linkages.

43. The Coca-Cola Company (2012b).
44. *http://www.pepsico.com/PressRelease/PepsiCo-Receives-2012-Stockholm-Industry-Water-Award-at-World-Water-Week08282012.html* (last accessed in July 2013).
45. Kraft Foods Inc. (2011).
46. *http://www.delmonte.com/reduce-reuse-recycle.aspx* and *http://www.delmontefoods.com/cr/default.aspx?page=cr_packaging* (last accessed in July 2013).

3

The Indian Non-alcoholic Beverage Sector: An Overview

India, with a population of 1.2 billion and a large consumer base, is an attractive market for the non-alcoholic beverage sector. This sector has witnessed steady growth in India and is predicted to grow further. India has several advantages. There is an abundant supply of raw materials to manufacture a range of beverages from fruit and vegetable drinks, tea and coffee drinks, and speciality drinks, such as organic drinks, which are becoming increasingly popular around the world. India also has a huge pool of cheap and skilled labour. The government has identified the growth potential of the food processing sector, including the non-alcoholic beverage sector; it has allowed 100 per cent FDI in food processing and supply chains and has recently allowed 51 per cent FDI in multi-brand retail. It has also introduced a series of regulations including the Food Safety and Standards Act (FSSA), 2006, to streamline the regulatory process and to support the growth of the food processing sector.

Despite these advantages, the global perspective in Chapter 2 showed that India's performance on output/production, employment generation and exports in the non-alcoholic beverage sector is low compared to established markets such as the USA and the UK, as well as emerging markets, such as China. This suggests potential for growth within the country. Coupled with its strengths in raw materials and labour, India could also be developed into a manufacturing hub for non-alcoholic beverages.

This chapter provides an overview of the Indian non-alcoholic beverage sector. It uses the latest available data to analyse the economic indicators for production, FDI and exports; this shows the impact of the sector on the economy. The second half of this chapter covers government regulations and incentives for the food sector, which are also applicable to non-alcoholic beverage manufacturing, distribution and retail. Given this backdrop, we designed and conducted a survey of stakeholders in this sector (manufacturers, retailers, supply chain agents such as logistics service providers, consumers, etc.) to understand their perceptions of growth in this sector. The sampling frame is described in the final section of this chapter.

3.1 Evolution of the Sector

The non-alcoholic beverage sector in India used to be dominated by domestic non-corporate manufacturers that produced and sold non-branded beverages, such as *nimbu pani* (lime drink), *lassi* and fruit juices. Before independence in 1947, there were some domestic brands and a few established corporate players in this segment. For instance, RoohAfza was formulated by Hakeem Hafiz Abdul Majeed in 1906 in Ghaziabad (Uttar Pradesh) and is manufactured by Hamdard Laboratories; it still offers substantial competition to multinationals, showing that Indian entrepreneurs have the capacity to create brands in the non-alcoholic beverage segment. Among national companies, Parle Products Limited[1] was founded in 1929, and today Parle Agro Limited and Parle Bisleri Limited manufacture non-alcoholic beverages. Parle Agro Limited produces fruit drinks, nectars, juices, CSDs, packaged drinking water and confectionery. Its brands include Frooti, Appy Fizz and Bailley drinking water. The Bisleri brand of bottled water was introduced in Mumbai in 1965; Parle bought Bisleri (India) Limited in 1969, but retained the brand name.

In the 1956, The Coca-Cola Company entered the Indian market and launched its flagship brand Coke, which was the leading CSD brand until 1977 (Michael and Nedunchezhian, 2012). In 1977, it exited the Indian market, because the Indian government's closed-door policy forced the company to dilute its stake in favour of its Indian partners and reveal its secret concentrate formula as required by the Foreign Exchange Regulation Act (FERA), 1973 (for details, see Biswas and Sen, 1999). Thus, there was limited presence of multinationals between the 1950s and the 1970s and there were hardly any global brands.

During the 1970s, several Indian companies entered the CSD segment with their brands (e.g., Campa Cola, from Campa Beverages Private Limited). Indian companies also began to experiment with product variations. In 1977, Parle Products Limited launched Limca and Gold Spot and in the 1980s, it launched Thums Up (Michael and Nedunchezhian, 2012). This period also saw the entry and growing popularity of several fruit-based beverages into the Indian market. For instance, Pioma Industries launched the fruit concentrate Rasna and ParleAgro's mango-flavoured drink Frooti became popular (Biswas and Sen, 1999). Some regional brands became popular in certain parts of the country. For instance, Sabols, which is popular in South India, started by producing mineral water and then expanded to juice manufacturing and CSDs; Jagdale Foods launched Bejois, a non-

1. Parle Products Limited was split into three companies in 1984: Parle Products Limited (with brands such as Parle G and Melody), Parle Agro Limited (with brands such as Frooti and Appy) and Parle Bisleri Limited (with brands such as Bisleri).

carbonated drink, in 1986 as a natural fruit drink available in Tetra Paks in Karnataka. Overall, the 1970s and the 1980s witnessed the creation of brands in India and experimentation with different products.

From a closed-door economy, India started liberalising in the mid-1980s. In 1989, the multinational company PepsiCo Inc. entered the Indian market through a joint venture with Punjab Agro Industries Corporations Limited (PAIC) and Voltas India Limited. The government encouraged foreign investment in the early 1990s and The Coca-Cola Company re-entered the Indian market as Coca-Cola India. Since then, there has been significant growth in this sector. In the past two decades, foreign multinationals such as Red Bull GmBH, Groupe Danone and Del Monte Corporation have entered the Indian non-alcoholic beverage market, but domestic companies, such as Dabur India Limited and Mother Dairy Fruit and Vegetable Private Limited, have also entered this segment. With the entry of foreign and domestic companies, the non-alcoholic beverage sector experienced a proliferation of brands and the product categories diversified. After liberalisation, several domestic companies merged or set up partnerships with global players. For example, a regional brand of soda water, Duke, from Duke and Sons Private Limited in Mumbai was acquired by PepsiCo India in 1994; Duke has recently been re-launched by PepsiCo India.

At present, the sector has 8-9 broad product categories including bottled water, CSDs, fruit/vegetable beverages (juices and drinks), energy drinks, sports drinks, milk-based beverages and ready-to-drink (RTD) tea and coffee. There are several domestic and international brands in each category.

With growth in the Indian economy and rise in per capita income, the non-alcoholic beverage sector has evolved both in terms of product variety and the number and types of companies in this segment. CSDs and juices used to be the dominant products in the sector, but as the sector evolved, diversified products such as bottled water, energy drinks, sports drinks and milk-based drinks became popular. With product diversification and the growth of the sector, more players (both domestic and foreign) have entered the market. For example, in the past, CSDs were primarily manufactured by large corporate or organised manufacturers,[2] and juices were manufactured and/or sold primarily by small non-corporate or unorganised manufacturers (who could also have standalone stores). Although the manufacture of CSDs remains the niche area of large corporates because it requires large-scale investment, now both large and small manufacturers produce bottled water, energy drinks, sports drinks, milk-based drinks and juices. In all segments, there are branded and non-branded products, and the products of both corporate and non-corporate manufacturers are sold by corporate and non-corporate retailers. Corporate retailers have created in-house brands (e.g., Walmart's Great Value Pack) that offer competition to established brands. With the rise in health awareness, there is growing demand for organic products, bottled mineral water, etc. There has also been product customisation, whereby global players have customised their products to local tastes.

3.2 Market Structure and Operations

The market structure for non-alcoholic beverages varies by product category (Table 3.1). Both corporate players, such as Coca-Cola India, Dabur India Limited, Hindustan Unilever (HUL), Parle Agro Limited and PepsiCo India, and non-corporate players are present in the market. According to the Ministry of Food Processing Industries (MoFPI), almost 75 per cent of the non-alcoholic beverage sector is still dominated by non-corporate manufacturers. The presence of non-corporate players varies across sub-segments of non-alcoholic beverages, such as CSD and juices, depending on factors such as entry barriers (need for high investment, use of technology and high production and promotion costs), access to raw materials and consumer demand.

Most foreign players that entered the Indian market in the past two decades have created their own brands. Others have adopted the local acquisition strategy (Ray and Nagabhushana, 2012) and acquired popular domestic brands to enhance their market presence. For instance, Coca-Cola India acquired Thums Up from Parle Products Limited and PepsiCo acquired Duke from Duke and Sons Private Limited, Mumbai, using a horizontal integration strategy that multinationals commonly use in emerging markets (see Chapter 2). This strategy is also used by large Indian corporates. For instance CavinKare Private Limited, which is a Chennai-based fast-moving consumer goods (FMCG) company, acquired the Tamil Nadu-based fruit drink brand, Maa, from Maa Fruits

2. The terms 'organised manufacturers' and 'corporate manufacturers' are used interchangeably.

Table 3.1

Market Structure of the Indian Non-alcoholic Beverage Sector

Category	*Market Structure*	*Global*	*Domestic*
Bottled water	Competitive market; both corporate and non-corporate players	• Danone Food and Beverages India Private Limited • PepsiCo India • Coca-Cola India	• Parle Bisleri Limited • Tata Beverages • NourishCo Beverages Limited • United Breweries
CSD	Oligopolistic market dominated by a few large players	• PepsiCo India • Coca-Cola India	• Kali Mark Industries (in Tamil Nadu)
Fruit/vegetable beverages	Competitive market; both corporate and non-corporate players	• Del Monte Pacific Limited India • PepsiCo India • Coca-Cola India	• Dabur India Limited • Hindustan Unilever • Parle Agro Limited • Pioma Industries
Energy drinks and sports drinks	Oligopolistic market dominated by a few large players	• Red Bull India Private Limited • PepsiCo India • Coca-Cola India	• Goldwin Healthcare, JMJ Group
Milk-based drinks	Competitive market; both corporate and non-corporate players	• Danone Food and Beverages India Private Limited • Nestlé India	• Britannia Industries Limited • Mother Dairy Fruit and Vegetable Private Limited
RTD tea/coffee	Competitive market; both corporate and non-corporate players	• PepsiCo India • Nestlé India	• Café Coffee Day

Source: Authors' compilation.

Private Limited in 2008 in a bid to enter the fruit-based beverage market.[3]

The product and pricing strategies of large corporates are based on factors such as market structure, consumers' price sensitivity, local tastes and seasonal demand. Since per capita income in India is low, Indian consumers are price-sensitive. In response, several corporates have customised their product offerings. For instance, in 2001 Coca-Cola India launched 'Chhota Coke,' a 200 ml bottle priced at INR 5 especially for the Indian market.[4] Companies have also customised their products to Indian tastes. For instance, PepsiCo India launched Nimbooz, a lime-based drink to meet the demand for *nimbu pani* in India. Climatic variations across India affect the demand for cold beverages. Since the south of India is warmer throughout the year than the north, the demand for cold beverages is higher in the south and more uniform through the year.

Corporates in this sector have also changed their packaging techniques to suit changing lifestyles. A study by Technopak (2010) found that the consumption of 'out of home' and 'on the go' food and beverages is increasing in India. As a result, beverages sold in returnable glass bottles have been replaced by polyethylene terephthalate (PET) bottles, cans and Tetra Paks, etc.

Company operations vary, depending on their size and market reach. Small non-corporate players adopt labour-intensive operations that involve the entire family in production and distribution. The raw material is bought in bulk from local markets and prepared either at home or in the shops. They may have small shops/pushcarts near busy places, such as schools, colleges, markets and residential areas, which give them mobility since they can easily shift to a new location to access more customers. Large multinationals and domestic companies mainly use capital-intensive production technology. This ensures consistent product quality, reduces wastage and streamlines the supply chain. The broad operations of large corporates are outlined below, while a detailed survey-based analysis of their operations, distribution chain, etc., is given in Chapter 4.

3. *http://www.thehindubusinessline.com/todays-paper/tp-marketing/cavinkare-acquires-fruit-juice-brand-maa/article1617278.ece* (last accessed in June 2013).

4. Kashyap and Raut (2005).

- *Encouraging better farming techniques to improve productivity*: To increase productivity, ensure consistent supply of raw materials, reduce wastage and enhance the quality of farm produce, companies work closely with their suppliers—the farmers. They engage in organised farming through partnerships with farmers.[5] Large companies also work closely with cooperative producers' associations. They train farmers to adopt better farming techniques and use high-yielding varieties (HYVs) of crops. For instance, HUL plans to include 50,000 farmers in their food and beverage supply chain by the end of 2020, and will provide them with assistance to increase their productivity and improve the quality of the products.[6]

- *Managing Processes*. To manage processes such as bottling, packaging and labelling, companies can either have an in-house facility or outsource the processes to partners. The outsourcing may be either complete or partial, depending on the product category. For example, in the CSD business, companies usually work in a partnership or franchising model for bottling. In bottled water too, Indian companies work with outsourced bottlers and packers apart from their in-house facilities. For instance, Parle Bisleri Limited works with 33 co-packers along with 17 company-owned plants.[7]

- *Distribution*: To distribute non-alcoholic beverages in India, companies have adopted three types of models:

    - *Direct Distribution*: The company controls the entire distribution network. For instance, Dabur India Limited directly distributes all its products to retailers *via* stockists.[8]

    - *Indirect Distribution*: The company outsources its distribution process to other companies. For instance, Kalimark Industries distributes its CSD brand Bovonto to small retailers through dealers and wholesalers.

    - *Hybrid Model of Distribution*: The company may control part of its total distribution and outsource the rest to other companies. For instance, the distribution rights of Coca-Cola India brands are held by its wholly-owned subsidiary, Hindustan Coca-Cola Beverages, as well as its 13 authorised bottling partners.[9] PepsiCo India has also given the distribution rights of its brands to the 24 bottling plants owned by its three authorised partners apart from its own 14 plants.[10]

  In India, the distribution chain is fragmented, as there are few large corporates and a large number of small non-corporate manufacturers, logistics service providers and retailers who have fragmented operations. Also, the sector faces a considerable number of interstate barriers to the movement of goods, which makes it difficult to establish pan-India supply chains. The tax and regulatory framework requires fragmented operations. Companies also use different distribution models for traditional and modern retailers. This is because the requirements of traditional retailers are small and these can be met through wholesalers and distributors. Large retailers prefer to have centralised bulk-sourcing models. Modern or corporate retailers have their own distribution centres and prefer to source non-alcoholic beverages directly from the producers.

- *Marketing*: Marketing and promotion of non-alcoholic beverages is largely done by corporate manufacturers and/or retailers. CSDs have substantial spending on media advertising, but even juice brands such as Frooti are advertised using similar techniques. Some marketing and promotion techniques are given as follows:

    - *Advertisements*: Large corporate companies advertise non-alcoholic

---

5. An agricultural production system that involves an agreement between a buyer and farmers and establishes conditions for the production and marketing of farm products.
6. *http://www.hul.co.in/sustainable-living/betterlivelihoods/* (last accessed in June 2013).
7. *http://www.bisleri.com/#/About_Us/Future/Team* (last accessed in July 2013).
8. Simchi-Levi *et al.* (2007).
9. *http://www.coca-colaindia.com/ourcompany/coca_cola_system.html* (last accessed in June 2013).
10. Inputs from PepsiCo India.

beverages through popular media, such as television and radio, as well as hoardings and pamphlets. To reach the youth, several companies use celebrities such as film stars and sports personalities to endorse their brands (Singh and Agrawal, 2012). In a recent trend, some corporates use social media such as Facebook and Twitter to advertise their products.

- *Personal Selling*: Personal selling uses direct marketing techniques such as 'pull marketing.'[11] Red Bull India Private Limited used this technique; they targeted young college students and office-goers for their energy drink, directly approached their target customers, talked about their energy drink and encouraged customers to try the drink. This popularised the brand in India.[12]

- *Sales Promotion*: Companies give their customers discounts, free gifts, etc., to promote their brands and/or products. These promotional offers are also extended to retailers and distributors, who are offered credit assistance and facilities, such as cooling equipment, to build good relations (Biswas and Sen, 1999).[13]

- *Publicity and Public Relations*: To publicise their brands, large companies often sponsor events. For instance, Red Bull India Private Limited sponsors sports events, such as car and bike races, which gives them visibility among Indian youth,[14] and PepsiCo India sponsored the Indian Premier League (IPL), which is the biggest cricket tournament in the sub-continent.

3.3 Size of the Sector

It difficult to estimate the sales and revenue of the Indian non-alcoholic beverage sector because of the large non-corporate or unorganised sector. Also, the Indian government does not record data separately for the non-alcoholic beverage sector, but considers it part of the food and beverage sector. Multinationals such as PepsiCo India, which is not listed in India, do not declare their revenues publicly. Hence, it is difficult to estimate the actual size of the Indian non-alcoholic beverage sector. Some market research companies have estimated the size of the sector, but their figures differ due to variations in the definition and coverage of the sector (Table 3.2). Even though growth projections vary, the estimates indicate that the sector has been growing rapidly. Thus, this sector exhibits a lot of potential within the food processing sector for the generation of manufacturing capabilities and employment.

3.4 Contribution of the Sector to India's economy

Global studies show that the non-alcoholic beverage sector can contribute substantially to GDP, employment, investment and exports. The sector also generates significant backward and forward linkages, since companies work closely with farmers, distributors, small retailers, etc., to reach consumers. Therefore, the sector makes both direct and indirect contributions to the economy.

3.4.1 Contribution to GDP

Despite variations in estimates, it is clear that the non-alcoholic beverage sector has recorded a double-digit growth rate (refer to Table 3.2). Consequently the sector's share in GDP has also increased. Disaggregated data on the contribution of this sector to the GDP is not available. However, the food processing sector, of which the non-alcoholic beverage sector is a key component, accounted for 9.3 per cent of the total manufacturing GDP and 1.5 per cent of the total GDP in 2009-10. In that year, the beverage manufacturing sector (both alcoholic and non-alcoholic beverages) accounted for 1.1 per cent of the total manufacturing GDP.[15] In absolute terms, the beverage sector's contribution to India's GDP increased from \$0.8 billion to \$1.6 billion between 2004-05 and 2009-10 (Figure 3.1). The figure corroborates our observation that the sector's contribution to the GDP is increasing.

11. Pull marketing involves heavy advertising and consumer promotion of a new product before it is actually available for retail distribution. This builds consumer demand for the product once it is available for retail distribution.
12. *http://businesscasestudies.co.uk/red-bull/engaging-consumers-through-word-of-mouth-marketing/introduction.html#axzz2KaVhJ9RP* (last accessed in June 2013).
13. Examples of how large companies work with retailers are given in Chapter 4.
14. *http://www.redbull.in/cs/Satellite/en_IN/Sports-en_IN/Red-Bull-India-F1/001243080406694* (last accessed in June 2013).
15. Calculated from MoFPI (2012) and National Accounts Statistics (2011).

Table 3.2

Size of the Indian Non-alcoholic Beverage Sector

Study and Time-frame	*Coverage*	*Market Size ($ billion)*	*Market Size (billion litres)*	*Growth Rate (in percentage)*
Ministry of Food Processing Industries (2006-2015)	Fruit beverages, squashes, syrups, fruit juices and concentrates	0.12-0.22	NA	AAGR 10
	Soft and aerated drinks	1.05-NA	NA	AAGR 6–7
Nielsen Retail Audit (2009-2012)	Carbonated soft drinks	2.87	3.95	CAGR: 11 by value
	Bottled water	0.52	3.04	CAGR: 3 by value
	Juices	0.08	0.05	CAGR: 20 by value
	Juice drinks	0.05	0.05	CAGR: –11 by value
	Sports/energy drinks	0.01	0.00	CAGR: 26 by value
	Dairy/soy	0.08	0.11	CAGR: –9 by value
IS Advisors: Non-Alcoholic Beverage Industry in India (2011-2015)	Bottled and carbonated water, milk beverages, juices, tea, coffee, energy drinks	10-NA	3.15-6.29	CAGR: 20
AM Mindpower Solutions: Indian Non-Alcoholic Beverage Market Outlook to 2015 (2005-2015)[a]	Overall sector	NA	6.77-20.25	CAGR: 11.9
	Bottled water		2.89-6.49	
	Carbonated soft drinks		2.79-3.62	
	Fruit-based drinks		0.2-0.4	
	Functional drinks including energy and sports drinks		0.013-0.048	
	Tea and coffee beverages with no alcohol content		NA	
Business Monitor International: India Food and Drink Report (2009-2015)	Carbonated drinks, juices, bottled water, RTD tea/coffee, functional drinks including energy and sports drinks	2.17-5.18	4.49-7.9	CAGR: 9.6 by volume, 11.7 by value
Federation of Indian Chambers of Commerce and Industry (FICCI), Ministry of Food	Fruit juices and fruit-based drinks	1.13-NA	NA	AAGR 35-40
	Carbonated drinks	1.36-NA	NA	AAGR 10-12
	Tea	1.8-NA	NA	AAGR 1.2
Processing Industries and Technopak (2008-2014)	Functional beverages including energy and sports drinks	NA-0.35	NA	NA
	Packaged water	0.34-NA	NA	CAGR: 40

Note: NA: Data not available in the report.
AAGR: average annual growth rate.
CAGR: compound annual growth rate.
[a] : The category-wise market shares are from 2005 to 2010.

Source: Compiled from the following sources:
(a) *http://mofpi.nic.in/ContentPage.aspx?CategoryId=547* and *http://mofpi.nic.in/ContentPage.aspx?CategoryId=548;* (last accessed in June 2013).
(b) IS Advisors (2012).
(c) AM Mindpower Solutions (2011).
(d) Business Monitor (2011).
(e) FICCI and Technopak (2008).
(f) AC Nielsen (2012).

The sector's performance was assessed by analysing the Index of Industrial Production (IIP) for the food and beverage sector.[16] Figure 3.2 shows that from 2007-08 to 2010-11 both manufacturing and the food and beverage sectors exhibited a fall in the IIP, but the manufacturing sector performed better. However, if we look at the change between 2010-11 and 2011-12, we find that the food and beverage sector is experiencing a rapid recovery, whereas the manufacturing sector is again experiencing a dip. This is, therefore, a high potential sector within the manufacturing sector and can be viewed as a sunrise industry.

16. *http://mofpi.nic.in/images/File/DataBank_SectoralDatabaseFPIs_140212.pdf* (last accessed in June 2013).

Figure 3.1

Contribution of the Beverage Sector to India's GDP

(in $ billion)

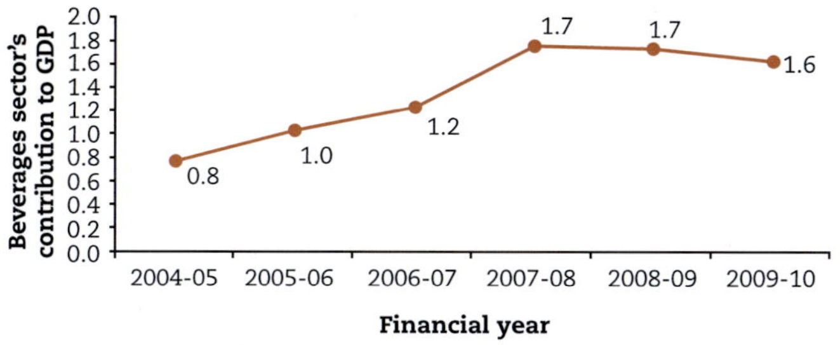

Source: Compiled from MoFPI (2012), *http://mofpi.nic.in/images/ar11-12.pdf* (last accessed in June 2013).

Figure 3.2

Trends in Total Manufacturing Sector vs. Food & Beverage Sector, using Percentage Change in IIP (base 2004-05 = 100)

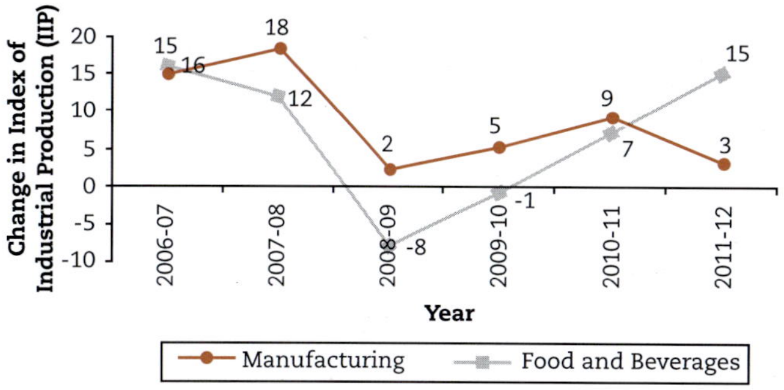

Source: Compiled from CSO (2013), *http://mospi.nic.in/mospi_new/upload/t2_new.pdf* (last accessed in June 2013).

3.4.2 Employment Generation

The non-alcoholic beverage sector has the potential to generate employment through its backward and forward linkages. According to a study by the National Council of Applied Economic Research (NCAER) (2001), the extra production of 1,000 cases of CSDs generates extra employment of 410 person-days.[17] The Ministry of Statistics and Programme Implementation (MoSPI) in the Annual Survey of Industries (ASI)[18] shows that in 2009-10, the overall beverage sector employed 1,03,647 people directly, and UN estimates for 2008 put the figure at 1,23,407 people.[19] The annual reports and websites of companies also give data on employment. In 2011-12, Coca-Cola India and PepsiCo India together employed around 31,400 people directly and approximately 3,50,000 people indirectly.[20] Indian companies such as Dabur India Limited and Britannia Industries Limited directly employ 8,856, and 1,987 people, respectively.[21]

3.4.3 Foreign Direct Investment

According to the Department of Industrial Policy and Promotion (DIPP) under the Ministry of Commerce and Industry, the food processing sector attracted FDI worth $2.6 billion between 2000 and 2011, which is 1.78 per cent of the total FDI ($147.08 billion) India received during this period.[22] In 2011, the non-alcoholic beverage sector attracted approximately $19.44 million as FDI under the automatic route,[23] but there is no disaggregated data available for the other foreign investment routes [Foreign Investment Promotion Board (FIPB) and the acquisition of shares]. Large non-alcoholic beverage companies have huge investment plans for India. In 2011, Coca-Cola India announced that it would bring a total investment of $2 billion in India over the next five years starting from 2012.[24] In 2008, PepsiCo India announced investments plans of more than $500 million in the Indian beverage business in a phased manner.[25]
In 2009, FieldFresh Foods Private Limited, the joint venture between Del Monte Pacific Limited India and Bharti Enterprise, announced an investment of INR 1,000 million ($21.8 million) to set up manufacturing plants and a backward supply chain in India.[26]

17. *http://www.coca-colaindia.com/ourcompany/company_history.html* (last accessed in June 2013).
18. It should be noted that the sample is limited to organised manufacturing.
19. *http://data.un.org/Data.aspx?d=UNIDO&f=tableCode%3a04%3bisicCode%3a155* (last accessed in June 2013).
20. *http://www.coca-colaindia.com/ourcompany/company_history.html and http://pepsicoindia.co.in/company/about- pepsico.html* (last accessed in June 2013).
21. Dabur India Limited (2012); Britannia Industries Limited (2012).
22. *http://pib.nic.in/newsite/subpdfdisplay.aspx?docid=96* (last accessed in June 2013).
23. The DIPP states that FDI in Indian industries can enter through three routes: the FIPB route, the automatic route and through acquisition of shares. FDI is allowed under the automatic route without prior approval from the government or the Reserve Bank of India (RBI) in all activities/sectors specified in the consolidated FDI Policy, issued by the Government of India. FDI in activities not covered under the automatic route requires prior approval from the government, which is then considered by the FIPB.
24. *http://www.coca-colaindia.com/ourcompany/message_from_leadership.html* (last accessed June in 2013).
25. *http://pepsicoindia.co.in/media/Press-Releases/release_09_21_08.aspx* (last accessed in June 2013).
26. *http://www.fieldfreshfoods.in/pressreleases/view/7* (last accessed in July 2013).

3.4.4 Contribution to Exports

India is the largest producer of milk and the second largest producer of fruits and vegetables in the world. Thus, India has significant potential to develop as an export hub for non-alcoholic beverage raw materials as well as finished products (PHD Chamber and Yes Bank, 2012). India's non-alcoholic beverage exports increased from $6.3 million to $26.5 million between 2001 and 2011 (Figure 3.3).[27] Exports of fruit and vegetable juices are the highest; between 2001 and 2011, they increased from $4.2 million to $18.0.[28] This increase in exports of fruit and vegetable juices can be attributed to changes in production patterns. In recent years, there has been a shift in agricultural production from food grains to high-value agricultural commodities including fruits and vegetables; there is also increased processing of horticultural products such as fruits and vegetables and increased trade in processed fruits and vegetables compared with traditional agricultural commodities (Sharma and Jain, 2011). In contrast, exports of milk and milk-based beverages like buttermilk have not increased due to the fragmented dairy sector, lack of promotion of high-value-added dairy products and lack of technological innovation, upgrading and quality management.

Figure 3.3

Exports of Non-alcoholic Beverages

(in $ billion)

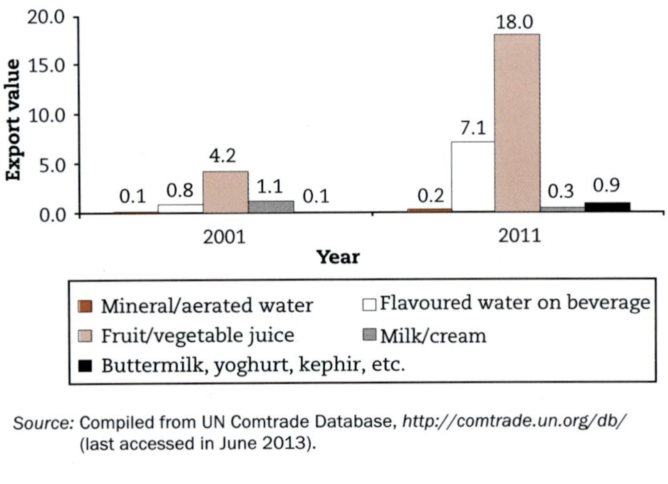

Source: Compiled from UN Comtrade Database, *http://comtrade.un.org/db/* (last accessed in June 2013).

27. *http://comtrade.un.org/db/* (last accessed in June 2013).
28. *http://comtrade.un.org/db/* (last accessed in June 2013). Despite the availability of raw materials, India is a net importer in this sector. This issue is discussed in Chapter 7.

3.5 Governance Structure, Regulations and Incentives

Over the years, there have been changes in the regulatory structure and policies for the non-alcoholic beverage sector in India. Their current status is given below.

3.5.1 Governance Structure

Due to the quasi-federal structure of India, with responsibility distributed between the central and state governments, the governance structure is complex. Multiple ministries and departments are responsible for enacting and implementing numerous acts (Figure 3.4).

Agriculture is a state subject. The central government provides broad guidelines for various acts, but implementation is largely at the discretion of state governments. The states play a significant role in decisions on product sourcing, taxes and interstate mobility of agriculture products.

Non-alcoholic beverages are subsumed under the food processing industry, which is governed by several ministries/departments at the centre, state and local/municipality levels. At the centre, the MoFPI regulates the food processing sector including the non-alcoholic beverage sector. This ministry works closely with the Ministry of Agriculture, which governs the agriculture sector and implements policies and programmes related to agriculture and allied activities. The Food Safety and Standards Authority of India (FSSAI) under the Ministry of Health and Family Welfare regulates the implementation of the FSSA (2006), thereby affecting the manufacture, distribution and retail standards of non-alcoholic beverages. Other ministries such as the Ministry of Commerce and Industry regulate manufacturing and foreign trade, and the DIPP under this ministry regulates foreign investments in India. In addition, the Central Board of Excise and Customs (CBEC) under the Ministry of Finance regulates the customs clearances required in the trade of food and raw materials (such as concentrates used to manufacture non-alcoholic beverages). The Central Pollution Control Board under the Ministry of Environment and Forests regulates the use of packaging materials and disposal of packaging waste by the industry. The Planning Commission lays down the broad policy framework and budget for the sector through its five-year plans. There are also nodal agencies/autonomous bodies such as the Agricultural and Processed Products Export Development Authority (APEDA), under the Ministry of Commerce

Figure 3.4

Governance Structure of Non-alcoholic Beverage Sector in India

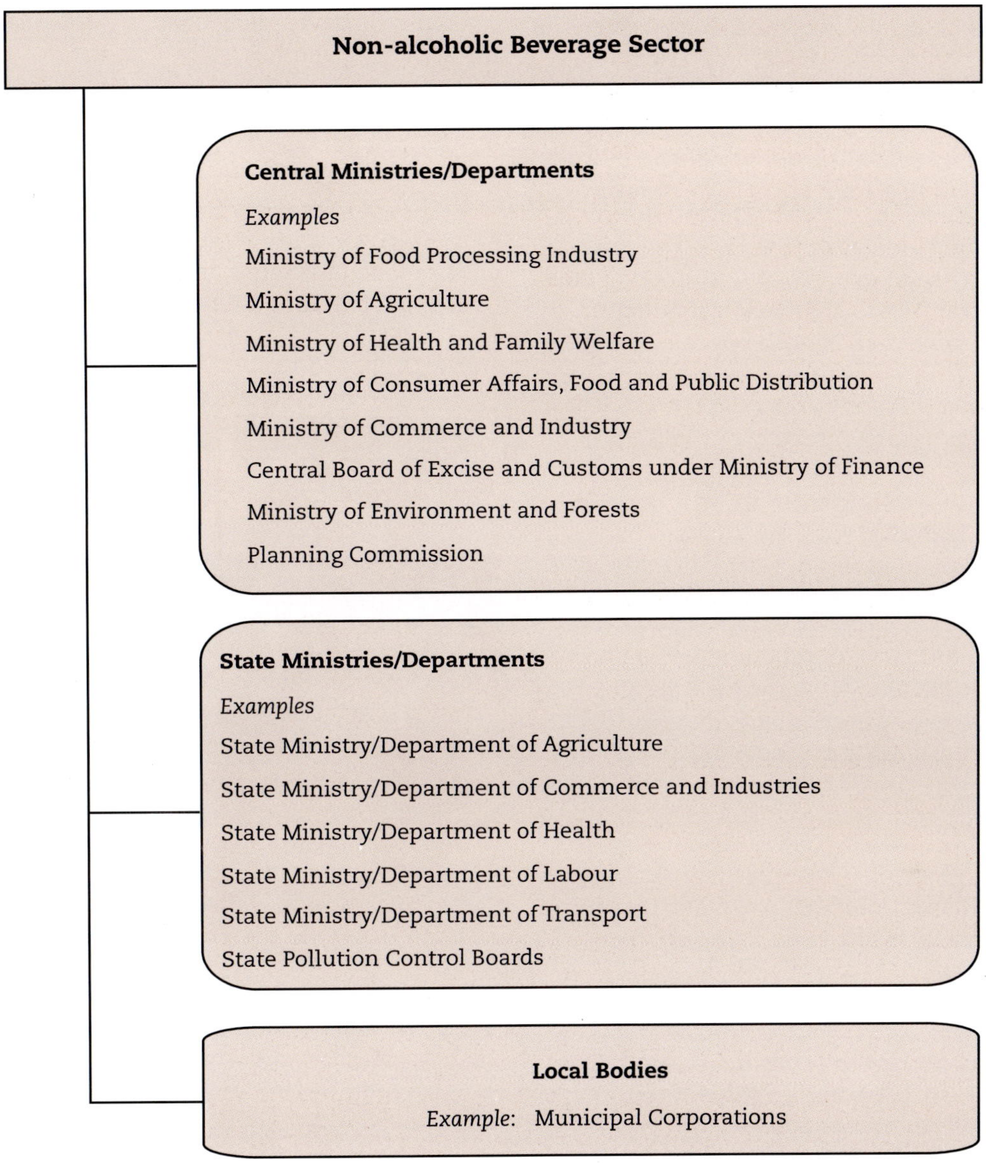

Source: Authors' compilation.

and Industry, that regulate the export of processed food, including non-alcoholic beverages.

3.5.2 *Regulations*

The regulations that impact the non-alcoholic beverage sector are discussed under FDI regulations, other acts and regulations and trade-related regulations. The FDI regulations are liberal in manufacturing and there is no discrimination between Indian and foreign companies in manufacturing. There are FDI restrictions in retail and foreign companies face discrimination *vis-à-vis* domestic companies in the retail sector.

3.5.2.1 FDI Regulations

The Indian government has relaxed FDI norms in food and beverage processing, supply chain and retail. This is expected to encourage global companies to invest in agro-processing, set up distribution chains and develop supply chains and logistics infrastructure. Some of the norms for FDI are listed as follows:

Food Processing

- Hundred per cent FDI under the automatic route is allowed in the non-alcoholic beverage sector, including milk and milk products.
- Hundred per cent FDI through the automatic route is allowed in coffee processing.
- Hundred per cent FDI with approval from the FIPB is permitted in the tea sector, including plantations, subject to disinvestment of 26 per cent equity in favour of the Indian partner within five years and prior approval of the state government if there is any change in future land use.

Supply Chain

- 100 per cent FDI is allowed under the automatic route in storage and warehousing, which includes warehousing of agricultural products with refrigeration.

Distribution and Retail

- Hundred per cent FDI is allowed in the wholesale cash and carry segment through the automatic route, subject to certain conditions.
- Hundred per cent FDI is allowed in test marketing under the government/FIPB route. In August 2013, the Indian government changed the conditions for FDI in test marketing. Previously, investment in test marketing was only allowed for items for which the retailer had approval for manufacturing and the manufacturing facility needed to be set up simultaneously with the commencement of test marketing for the product; moreover, test marketing was only allowed for a period of two years. Under the reviewed policy, the Indian government has withdrawn all these conditions.[29]
- Hundred per cent FDI is allowed in single-brand retail and 51 per cent FDI in multi-brand retail, subject to certain conditions. From August 2013, the entry routes for FDI in single-brand retail have been modified. Previously, FIPB approval was required for 100 per cent investment, but now up to 49 per cent investment is allowed under the automatic route; only investments exceeding 49 per cent require FIPB approval.
- In September 2012, the Indian Cabinet allowed 51 per cent FDI in multi-brand retail, subject to certain conditions, which was cleared by the Parliament in December 2012. These conditions were further explained and to certain extent modified in August 2013 through DIPP Press Notes 5 and 6 (see Annexure A-3.1 for the new FDI policy).

3.5.2.2 Other Acts and Regulations

The acts that regulate the food processing sector and, in turn, the non-alcoholic beverage sector are listed in Table 3.3, together with the stage and supply chain to which they apply. The key act is the FSSA (2006), which was implemented in 2011 (see Box 3.1).

Box 3.1

Food Safety and Standards Act (FSSA), 2006

- Came into effect in August 5, 2011.
- It is compulsory in all states.
- It establishes the FSSAI to set scientific standards for articles of food and to regulate their manufacture storage, distribution, sales and import.
- It consolidates a series of laws relating to food.
- Food business operators are responsible for the supply of safe food to consumers with the help of food testing laboratories that would be upgraded to the National Accreditation Board for Testing and Calibration Laboratories (NABL) standards.
- All corporate and non-corporate manufacturers and retailers are covered under this act.

Note: The act does not cover farmers whose farming technology, use of pesticides, etc., play a key role in farming standards.

Source: *http://www.fssai.gov.in/portals/0/pdf/food-act.pdf* (last accessed in June 2013).

29. 'Consolidated FDI Policy (effective from April 5, 2013),' DIPP, Ministry of Commerce and Industry, Government of India and Press Note.6, DIPP, Ministry of Commerce and Industry, Government of India.

Table 3.3

Select Acts and Regulations that Impact the Non-alcoholic Beverage Sector

Act/Regulation	*Description*	*Regulatory Authority*	*Production Stage*	*Processing Stage (Packaging and Labelling)*	*Distribution Stage*	*Retail Stage*	*Export/ Import*	*Voluntary/ Mandatory Implementation at State Level*
Food Safety Standards Act, 2006	Lays down standards for articles of food and beverages and regulates their manufacture, storage, distribution, sale and import to ensure availability of safe and wholesome food for human consumption.	Ministry of Health and Family Welfare	✓	✓	✓	✓		Mandatory
Agriculture Produce and Marketing Committee Act, (reformed in June 2008)	Regulates and administers marketing of agricultural produce at the state level. Direct marketing and contract farming are regulated under this act.	State governments			✓			Voluntary
Essential Commodities Act, 1955	Regulates production, supply and distribution in the domestic market and trade and commerce in international market of certain commodities (essential commodities whose irregular supply can affect normal life).	State governments/ Union Territories	✓		✓			Mandatory
Drugs and Cosmetics Act, 1940	Regulates production and distribution of dietary supplements in India.	Ministry of Health and Family Welfare			✓	✓		Mandatory
The Warehousing (Development and Regulation) Act, 2007	Regulates storage of non-alcoholic beverages, by controlling and regulating development of warehouses.	Ministry of Consumer Affairs, Food and Public Distribution		✓				Mandatory
Warehousing Corporation Act, 1962	Sets up state and central warehousing committees to undertake the establishment of warehouses in India			✓				
Shops and Establishments Act, 1953	This is a state act and each state has framed its own rules under the act. It provides statutory obligation and rights to employees and employers in shops and establishments	State governments			✓			Mandatory
Grading and Marketing Act, 1937	Non-alcoholic beverages are graded under 'Agmark' standards under this act.	Directorate of Marketing and Inspection (DMI) under Ministry of Agriculture		✓				Voluntary
Bureau of Indian Standards' (BIS), 1987 Regulations	Accredits non-alcoholic beverages according to standards set for products meant for consumption. It ensures that the product is edible and has no harmful effects.	Ministry of Consumer Affairs, Food and Public Distribution	✓	✓				Voluntary
Export Quality Control Inspection Act, 1963	Standardises non-alcoholic beverages according to international standards—Codex Alimentarius.	Export Inspection Council (EIC), Ministry of Commerce	✓	✓				Mandatory

contd...

...contd...

Act/Regulation	*Description*	*Regulatory Authority*	*Production Stage*	*Processing Stage (Packaging and Labelling)*	*Distribution Stage*	*Retail Stage*	*Export/ Import*	*Voluntary/ Mandatory Implementation at State Level*
Legal Metrology Act, 2009	Lays down guidelines for packaging and labelling non-alcoholic beverages and regulates the contents of non-alcoholic beverages. It protects consumers and regulates the distribution of safe products.	State government, Directorate of Weights and Measures under the Ministry of Food and Civil Supplies	✓	✓	✓			Mandatory
Plant Quarantine (Regulation of Import into India) Order, 2003 and amendments	Regulates the imports of plant-based raw materials used to manufacture non-alcoholic beverages and also other non-alcoholic beverages, such as organic beverages that are prepared from plant extracts.	Ministry of Agriculture					✓	Mandatory
Livestock Importation Act, 1898	Regulates the imports of livestock-based raw materials used to manufacture non-alcoholic beverages.	Ministry of Agriculture					✓	Mandatory
Agricultural and Processed Food Products Export Cess Act, 1985	Implements cess on exports of non-alcoholic beverages.	Ministry of Food Processing Industries and Ministry of Agriculture					✓	Mandatory
Agricultural Produce Cess Act, 1940	Implements cess on exports of raw materials to be used to manufacture non-alcoholic beverages.	Ministry of Food Processing Industries and Ministry of Agriculture					✓	Mandatory
SEZ Act, 2005	Regulates operations of companies operating in SEZs and AEZs.	Ministry of Commerce and Industry	✓					Mandatory
Land Acquisition Act, 1894	Regulates ownership of land and protects rights of landowners.	Ministry of Rural Development	✓					Mandatory

Source: Government of India websites.

The FSSA applies to the food processing industry. It consolidates several existing acts and orders, with the objective of effective implementation, transparency and accountability. The implementation of this act is compulsory in every Indian state, which was not the case with several other acts. For instance, the model Agriculture Produce and Marketing Committee (APMC) Act, 2003, is not implemented in states such as Uttar Pradesh (UP).

3.5.2.3 *Trade-related Regulations*

Various regulations govern the import of processed food items into India. The EIC along with the union government has laid down guidelines, acts and regulations on imported commodities. These are based on international standards—Codex Alimentarius. The EIC monitors imports of food items and checks the condition of the hold in which the goods are being transported, the visual/physical appearance of the goods and the labelling of the products. Customs officials check the consignments of edible/food products imported through ports, inland container depots, air cargo complexes, container freight stations and land customs stations. The port health officer checks the samples of imported food products. In addition, every imported food item at the time of its import is examined to have a valid shelf life of not less than 60 per cent of its original shelf life;[30] food articles that do not meet this condition cannot be sold in the domestic market. There are various packaging and labelling requirements for imported products. The Bureau of Indian Standards (BIS) sets standards that safeguard the quality of processed food items imported into the Indian market.

3.5.3. Incentives for Domestic and Foreign Players

Since the reforms of the 1990s, the food processing industry has been progressively liberalised and various incentives and schemes have been extended to this sector to attract domestic and foreign investment; these schemes also apply to the non-alcoholic beverage sector. However, in the case of fiscal incentives, compared to other food processing sectors, non-alcoholic beverage segments like CSD and bottled water still face discrimination in the form of higher taxes.

In 1999, the food processing industry was listed as a priority sector for bank lending. The MoFPI envisioned a growth plan for the food processing industry and drafted the Vision 2015 document; the benefits are certain to trickle down to the non-alcoholic beverage industry. The plan aims to increase the processing of perishables from 6 per cent to 20 per cent, increase value addition from the present level of 20 per cent to 34 per cent and the share in global trade from 1.6 per cent to 3 per cent, thus tripling the size of the processed food industry by 2015. The infrastructure incentives are described below and the fiscal incentives are given in Box 3.2.

Infrastructure Incentives

Export Processing Zones and Industrial Parks. The Indian government implemented a scheme to promote food parks under the 10th Five Year Plan (FYP) (2002-2007). This scheme was extended and reformulated into the Mega Food Parks[31] Scheme under the 11th FYP (2007-2012) to upgrade the existing infrastructure for the industry and particularly to streamline the supply chain for the food processing industry. It is based on a cluster approach. The scheme will be demand-driven and would help food processing units meet environmental, safety and social standards.

The Indian government also introduced a policy allowing Agro Export Zones (AEZs) to be established under the Export Import (EXIM) Policy, 2001-02. These are special export zones that focus on improving food processing techniques in order to reduce wastage, increase marketability and help farmers enjoy higher profits. It is based on the cluster approach of identifying potential products and the geographic region in which these products are grown and adopting an end-to-end approach of integrating the entire process from the stage of production until it reaches the market.

To encourage private sector investment in agriculture and reduce wastage in transporting agriculture produce, including non-alcoholic beverages, the Ministry of Agriculture has set up terminal market complexes (TMCs) in collaboration with the state governments in Bihar (Patna), Orissa (Sambalpur), Tamil Nadu (Perundurai), Maharashtra (Nagpur and Nasik) and Gujarat (Ahmedabad and Surat). The TMCs in Ahmedabad and Surat operate on a hub-and-spoke format, in which they form the hub and will be linked to several collection centres (spokes) located at key

30. *http://www.sethassociates.com/food-and-drug-industry-in-india.html* (last accessed in June 2013).

31. Food parks are food processing clusters that contain several units. They have in-built storage and distribution facilities and are designed so that all supporting industries are located within one park. The idea is to increase efficiency by reducing timelines.

Box 3.2

Fiscal Incentives for the Food Processing Industry

Income Tax Relief

1. Under the Income Tax Act, 1961, income tax rebate is given for 100 per cent of the profits for five years and 25 per cent of the profits in the next five years to new agro-processing industries set up to package and preserve fruits and vegetables.
2. Deduction is allowed for expenditure incurred on investment in capital for setting up items related to food processing. The deduction amount is 150 per cent of the expenditure from April 1, 2013. The specific businesses include setting up and operating a cold chain facility and warehousing facilities to store agricultural produce and sugar.

Excise Duty

1. Excise duties on various processed food items have been reduced or waived. For instance, excise duty has been reduced on aerated drinks from 24 per cent to 12 per cent and fully waived on dairy machinery.
2. Processed food items, including flavoured milk, attract a concessional rate of 2 per cent duty, subject to non-availment of Central Value Added Tax (CENVAT) credit or 5 per cent with CENVAT credit.
3. Zero excise duty on conveyor belt systems used in cold storage facilities.

Customs Duty

1. Import duty on capital goods and raw materials used in units that are 100 per cent export-oriented has been completely waived.
2. Customs duty on various products has been reduced or completely waived. For instance, customs duty on food processing machinery has been reduced from 7.5 per cent to 5 per cent, the duty on packaging machines has been reduced and dairy machinery is completely exempt from central excise duty
3. Project Imports, 2011, is an innovation to help set up and expand industrial projects; the benefits have been extended to cold storage, cold rooms and industrial projects for preservation, storage and processing of agricultural, horticultural, dairy products, etc. All imported goods related to food processing, irrespective of their tariff classification, are entitled to uniform assessment at concessional basic customs duty of 5 per cent.
4. There is no import duty on capital goods and raw material for 100 per cent export-oriented units. Earnings from export activities are exempt from corporate tax.

Other facilities

1. External commercial borrowings are available for investment in cold storage facilities.
2. Schemes have been launched to modernise abattoirs and promote terminal markets.
3. Subject to de-canalisation, exports of some milk-based products are freely allowed, provided these units comply with the compulsory inspection requirements of the concerned agencies, such as the National Dairy Development Board and Export Inspection Council.

Source: Extracted from MoFPI (2013) and *http://mofpi.nic.in/ContentPage.aspx?CategoryId=137* (last accessed in June 2013).

production centres in Gujarat; growers will have easy access to the nearest terminal market. The two TMCs also provide extension support and advisory services to farmers either at a nominal cost or without any direct service charges.

Some state governments have permitted contract farming in the agriculture sector. For instance, the Punjab government has allowed Bharti-Walmart to engage in contract farming with farmers in Punjab. This has helped farmers grow high-quality fruits and vegetables with assistance from the company at each stage of cultivation. This initiative is intended to reduce inefficiencies in the supply-chain mechanism, since manufacturers can procure raw materials directly from the farmers, thereby reducing the cost of production.

Other Government Support for Infrastructure. The MoFPI has set up the National Mission on Food Processing to improve co-ordination between the state and central governments for the speedy implementation of the schemes. The ministry has also set up an Innovation Fund and a Venture Capital Fund for food processing to promote innovation and technology development. Under the 12th FYP, the ministry is working to set up a network of efficient food-testing laboratories, both government and private, by providing incentives and is strengthening the existing institutes.

3.6 Primary Survey

It is evident from the above that the non-alcoholic beverage sector in India has evolved significantly over the past two decades. While the growth of the Indian economy has led to the growth of the sector, the sector has also contributed to the Indian economy in terms of output, employment, investments and exports (Figure 3.5).

Figure 3.5

Linkages between the Non-alcoholic Beverage Sector and the Indian Economy

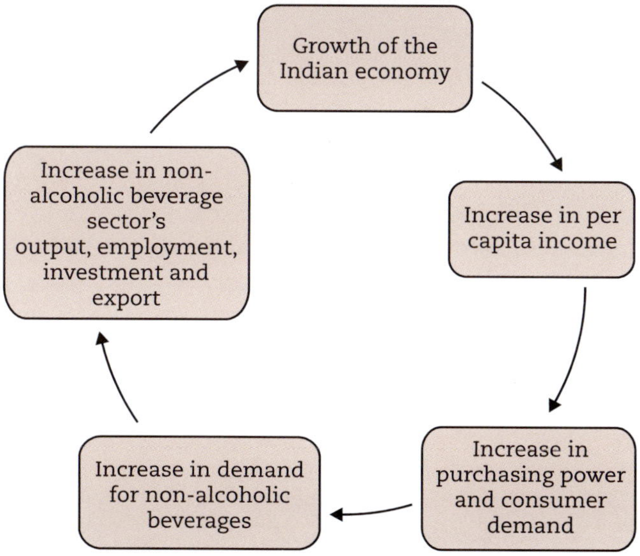

Source: Authors' compilation.

Despite this, the sector faces various barriers to growth. To understand the future potential of the sector, its linkages with the economy and the obstacles to its growth, an in-depth survey covering all key stakeholders including manufacturers, exporters, importers, supply chain service providers, retailers and consumers was conducted.

The objective of the survey was to understand the backward and forward linkages generated by the agro-food processing sector, particularly the non-alcoholic beverage sector, and identify the potential as well as the barriers for the sector. The following indicators were used.

- Current size and growth projections of the non-alcoholic beverage sector.
- Contribution of the sector to employment generation, skill development, collaboration with SMEs, percolation of technology, FDI inflows and development of India as a sourcing hub.
- Dynamics of the sector to bring out key differences and similarities between the corporate and non-corporate sectors (both retailers and manufacturers)
- Impact of policy changes on the non-alcoholic beverage sector.
- Key barriers to growth for stakeholders and what they want from the government.

The participants were 440 randomly selected stakeholders (Table 3.4) including manufacturers, retailers, traders, consumers, associations and policymakers, and semi-structured questionnaires were used. Separate questionnaires were designed for each respondent category. In addition, closed-door discussions were conducted with policymakers and associations. The key areas covered were: growth trends and recent developments in the non-alcoholic beverage sector; its contribution to the economy in terms of employment generation; training imparted to employees; growth across different categories of non-alcoholic beverages; brand penetration; the impact of changes in regulations such as FDI in retail policy and the FSSA, 2006; factors affecting the growth of corporate retail; key barriers affecting the sector; and future scenario for growth. Some questions were common across different stakeholders such as manufacturers, retailers and consumers to understand differences in perception.

The field survey was conducted by Dun & Bradstreet Tangram Advisory Services Private Limited between August 2012 and January 2013. The survey of consumers and retailers was conducted in four cities: Delhi (NCR), Mumbai, Bangalore and Kolkata. These cities were selected because of the presence of retail stores in different categories, such as corporate retailers (hypermarkets, supermarkets, discount stores and speciality stores), non-corporate retailers, and cash & carry outlets. The survey of manufacturers and supply chain agents was conducted across several cities and states.[32]

Table 3.4

Sampling Frame

Type of Respondent	*Number of Respondents*
Corporate manufacturers of non-alcoholic beverages	18
Non-corporate manufacturers of non-alcoholic beverages	70
Importers of non-alcoholic beverages	5
Exporters of non-alcoholic beverages	5
Supply chain agents	22
Corporate retailers	16
Non-corporate retailers	79
Consumers	220
Farmers	5
Total	440

A pilot survey was first conducted for all the categories, which covered around 10 per cent of the sample, to check the feasibility of the questionnaires and make necessary changes. Further, in light of the cabinet approval to allow 51 per cent FDI in multi-brand retail, a section to map perceptions of the same was added to the questionnaire after the pilot survey.

The survey data and information was analysed to answer key questions:

- Despite the numerous incentives given to the non-alcoholic beverage sector, why are Indian companies locating their manufacturing bases abroad?
- Which is a bigger reform for the agro-processing sector: allowing FDI in retail or implementing the Goods and Services Tax (GST)?
- What can be done to reduce agricultural price inflation and wastage in the supply chain?
- How can India attract investment in the food processing sector and how can the non-alcoholic beverage sector become more corporatised, with better job quality and higher salaries?

The survey does have some shortcomings. First, the sample size is small. Second, some corporates did not want to share financial information. Thus, while the survey does shed light on the growth potential of this sector, one cannot do exact projections based on these data. Third, there is limited awareness about various government policies among some stakeholders, especially in the non-corporate sector. Fourth, there is a sample bias in some categories, such as consumers [where only Socioeconomic Classification (SEC)[33] A and SEC B category have been interviewed] and retailers (only four metros were considered). Despite these limitations, the survey provided useful information that is described in the chapters that follow.

32. The cities and states covered by the survey are: Delhi (NCR), Bangalore (Karnataka), Mumbai (Maharashtra), Kolkata (West Bengal), Hyderabad (Andhra Pradesh), Lucknow (Uttar Pradesh) and Indore (Madhya Pradesh).

33. Originally developed by IMRB International (formerly Indian Market Research Bureau) as a way to understand market segments and consumers, it was standardised and adopted by the Market Research Society of India in the mid-1980s as a measure of socioeconomic class and is now commonly used as a market segmentation tool in India. The two parameters used to categorise consumers are Occupation and Education of the chief wage earner (Head) of the household (Annexure A-3.2).

4

Survey of Manufacturers

The non-alcoholic beverage sector in India involves several stakeholders such as manufacturers, retailers, supply chain agents, importers and exporters. This chapter provides an overview of manufacturers of non-alcoholic beverages based on a primary survey.

Manufacturers in this sector can be divided into corporate and non-corporate manufacturers. Non-corporate manufacturers are small businesses owned by a single person or a family in a particular region. They usually have a single manufacturing unit, and sourcing and distribution is done locally. Corporate manufacturers are those who have professional management, a centralised accounting system, centralised sourcing and quality control. Most corporate manufacturers have pan-India operations and their scale of operations and reach are much larger than those of non-corporate manufacturers.

Manufacturers can also be classified by other labels, such as organic manufacturers and contract manufacturers. Organic manufacturers use organic farming techniques and natural/organic/ayurvedic ingredients to manufacture non-alcoholic beverages. Contract manufacturers are those that manufacture branded or non-branded beverages under a contract with a firm. These contract manufacturers could be either corporate or non-corporate businesses. In India, corporate manufacturers may work with several contract manufacturers; corporate manufacturers either outsource a part of the process or the complete process to their contract manufacturers.

The non-alcoholic beverage sector in India is dominated by non-corporate manufacturers in terms of numbers (almost 75%) and by corporate manufacturers in terms of volume of sales and revenue. The number of non-corporate manufacturers varies across different product categories. For instance, in the case of fruit juices and milk-based beverages such as *lassi*, where production is possible with low initial investment, there are a large number of non-corporate manufacturers. However, for beverages such as CSDs and energy drinks, where production may require significant initial investment, the sector is dominated by corporate manufacturers and their contract manufacturers. The survey tried to ensure a representative distribution of both corporate and non-corporate manufacturers in this sector.

4.1 Research Objectives, Methodology and Sampling Frame

4.1.1 Objectives

To understand the contribution of non-alcoholic beverage manufacturers to the Indian economy, both corporate and non-corporate manufacturers were asked about various aspects of their operations and their perceptions of recent policy changes. The survey gathered the following specific information:

- The size of the sector and that of individual manufacturers surveyed; their revenues and growth projections across product categories; share of domestic and international trade; investments; location; level of mechanisation and other operations-related information.
- The potential of the sector to generate employment and its contribution to skill development, investment and tax revenue.
- The manufacturing processes followed by the sector, including their packaging techniques and pricing models.
- The backward linkages or the procurement channel for raw material and the sourcing of semi-finished and finished products.
- The forward linkages, which were identified through questions on meeting demand expectations and customer outreach.
- Other activities of the manufacturing process such as R&D, waste management, water conservation techniques and corporate social responsibilities.
- Perceptions of recent policy changes, such as Food Safety and Standards Act (FSSA), 2006 and allowing FDI in retail.

The information was used to identify key problems for manufacturers and then make recommendations to policymakers who are looking into the growth of this sector (see Chapter 7).

4.1.2 Selection

The survey tried to cover manufacturers in the different product categories. While some manufacturers were engaged in the manufacture of more than one category, others specialised in a single product category.

The survey covered 18 corporate manufacturers selected by a random process. The references of corporate manufacturers were obtained from industry associations and all of them were members of industry chambers and associations such as the Indian Beverage Association (IBA), Federation of Indian Chambers of Commerce and Industry (FICCI), Confederation of Indian Industry (CII) and PHD Chamber of Commerce. The respondents were managers or senior staff, who were well-informed about the company's operations and market trends. Since non-corporate players are not registered with industry associations, the survey team selected manufacturers in different cities and towns using the random sampling technique. In total, 70 non-corporate manufacturers were interviewed. The respondents were the owners or senior managers. In most cases, the survey team sat with the company representatives and asked them questions based on a semi-structured questionnaire. An average interview lasted for nearly an hour. In some instances, the survey team shared questionnaires with the company representatives, which they later completed and sent back.

All the corporate manufacturers were located in large cities, such as Delhi, Bangalore, Mumbai and Kolkata. The non-corporate manufacturers were selected from these four cities as well as smaller cities such as Indore and Lucknow (Figure 4.1).

Figure 4.1

Locations of Manufacturers in the Survey

(in percentage)

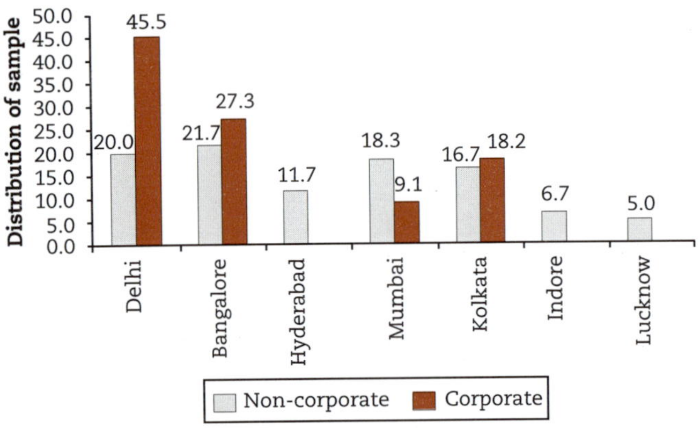

At the end of the survey, there were 88 completed questionnaires: 70 from non-corporate manufacturers and 18 from corporate manufacturers. The ratio of 80:20 reflects the structure of the sector. This was confirmed in our interviews with industry chambers, such as ASSOCHAM (The Associated Chambers of Commerce and Industry of India), IBA and FICCI.

4.2 Key Findings of the Survey

In this section, we describe the scale of operations, growth potential, employment generation capability and contribution to skill development, investment in the sector and tax revenues.

4.2.1 Scale of Operations

The scale of operations in terms of annual sales is much larger for corporate manufacturers than for non-corporate manufacturers. In 2010-11, the average sales of corporate manufacturers were around INR 26.6 billion, whereas it was around INR 3.6 million for non-corporate manufacturers (Figure 4.2). Growth in sales is also much higher for corporate manufacturers than non-corporate manufacturers. Between 2009-10 and 2010-11, sales grew by 46.3 per cent for corporate manufacturers and by 14.3 per cent for non-corporate manufacturers. Between 2008-09 and 2010-11, the compound annual growth rates (CAGRs) for the sample of corporate and non-corporate manufacturers were 30.4 per cent and 12.6 per cent, respectively. Although growth rates vary across companies and between the corporate and non-corporate sectors, the survey found that non-alcoholic beverage sector is a fast-growing sector in India, with a double-digit growth rate even during the years when the global economy was facing an economic downturn.

4.2.2 Growth Forecasts

The survey respondents were asked about the growth potential of the sector. Both corporate and non-corporate retailers said that this is a fast-growing sector that would continue to grow at a double-digit rate for the next 10 years. In the short run, i.e., in the next three years, corporate manufacturers expect to grow at an annual rate of 16.5 per cent, and non-corporate manufacturers said that they would grow at an annual rate of 19 per cent. These growth projections are based on a GDP growth of 7 per cent.

The companies were then asked to give reasons for their high growth projections. The most important reason is that the Indian market is large and unsaturated. The second reason is that consumers are becoming more receptive to packaged drinks; such drinks are becoming convenient for women

Figure 4.2

Distribution of Annual Sales by Type of Manufacturer (2010-11)

(in percentage)

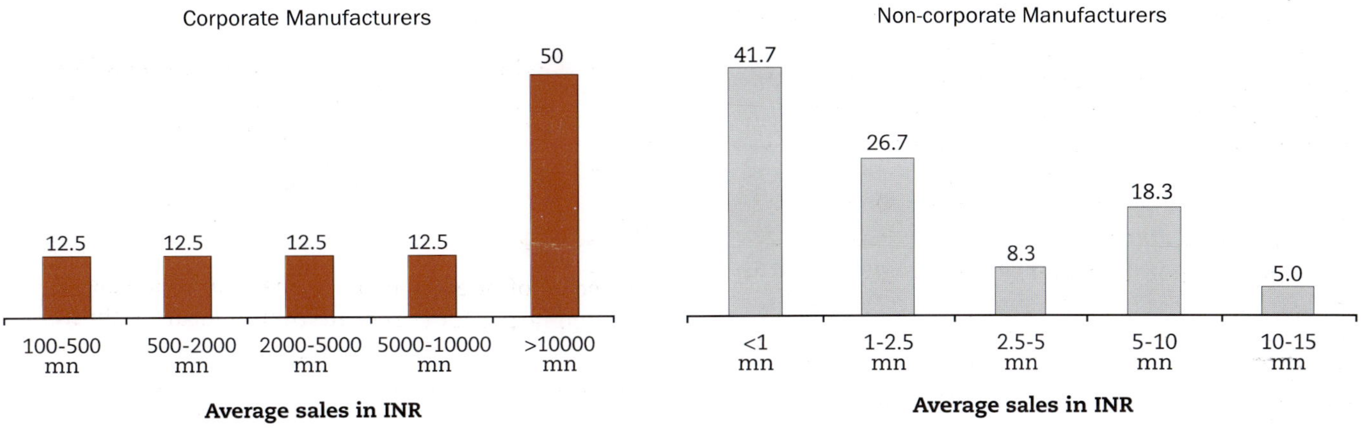

entering the workforce and young people working away from home. The companies also said that their growth projections would depend on factors such as the GDP growth rate, rise in per capita income and reduction in food inflation. They pointed out that non-alcoholic beverage manufacturing will grow at more than double the GDP growth rate, but rising food inflation may force consumers to move to necessity purchases (basic food such as rice, potatoes and onions) and reduce their ability to purchase non-alcoholic beverages.

Respondents were also asked to identify the fast-moving product categories within non-alcoholic beverages. Although it is difficult to estimate growth trends across different product categories because both corporate and non-corporate manufacturers do not operate across all product categories and their growth rates vary, the survey found that juices and energy drinks are the fastest-growing products (Table 4.1); this finding is corroborated by other studies (Table 3.2 in Chapter 3). It can be attributed to growing health-consciousness and the willingness to try new products. To meet the growing consumer preference for fruit-based drinks, corporate manufacturers are diversifying their products and experimenting with fizzy, fruit-based drinks. There is also a growing demand for bottled water due to rising health-consciousness and the lack of clean and safe drinking water.

The survey found that the growth projections for the next three years (2012-13 to 2014-15) are lower than actual growth rates for 2008-09 to 2010-11, because of the economic slowdown and food inflation. This may be due to the timing of the survey, which was conducted during the economic slowdown. Nevertheless, since the size of the Indian middle class is growing, per capita income is rising and Indian consumers are experimenting with new products, this sector is expected to grow at a high rate. The growth forecast by corporate manufacturers in different product categories is given in Table 4.1.

Table 4.1

Growth Forecasts by Corporate Manufacturers for Product Categories (in percentage)

Product category	2012-13	2013-14	2014-15
CSDs	16.0	14.0	12.0
Vegetable juices	20.0	20.0	20.0
Fruit-based juices	19.0	19.0	20.0
Vegetable/fruit concentrate/ fruit powder syrup	20.0	15.0	15.0
Milk/yoghurt-based beverages	14.0	18.0	10.0
Energy drinks	27.5	25.0	25.0
Sports drinks	NA	NA	NA
Bottled water	13.0	13.0	15.0
Ayurvedic/organic drinks	NA	NA	NA
Tea-based drinks	20.0	15.0	15.0
Coffee-based drinks	20.0	15.0	15.0

Note: NA: respondents did not provide information.

4.2.3 Employment Generation

The non-alcoholic beverage sector has significant employment potential.

4.2.3.1 Types of Employment

The sector generates three types of employment: direct, indirect and self-employment.

Direct Employment. Due to the large variation in the sizes and scale of operations of different units (both corporate and non-corporate) in the sector, their direct employment potential varies significantly. The survey found that within the sample of manufacturers, on average, corporate manufacturers employed almost 100 times more people than the non-corporate sector (Table 4.2). However, in terms of absolute numbers, the divisions with the largest number of employees in both sectors are the same, namely, processing, marketing and supply chain. This implies that these three activities are very important and form the core of the business.

Table 4.2

Average Number of Employees in Corporate and Non-corporate Sectors

Average Sales of the Unit (in INR)	*Corporate Manufacturers >100 million*	*Non-corporate Manufacturers <2.5 million*
	Average No. of Employees	
Division/process		
Processing	1,051	8
Supply chain	225	4
R&D	56	3
Marketing	462	6
Administration	118	2
Other (utility and periphery, finance, information technology (IT), human resources, etc.)	868	2
Total	2700	25

Indirect Employment. The sector generates indirect employment through three main channels:

- Working with several contract manufacturers.
- Outsourcing manufacture of packaging materials, such as containers, caps, straws and labels.
- Working with third-party logistics (3PL) service providers to reach consumers across India.

According to survey respondents, the sector has the potential to create four indirect employments for every direct employment, which is similar to the software industry.

Self-employment Opportunities. Since the non-alcoholic beverage sector operates in every stage from farm to final consumers, it provides opportunities for self-employment. Non-corporate players such as owners of corner juice shops pointed out that the sector offers them self-employment opportunities. For some respondents, this is the only source of income for the family.

Large corporate manufacturers in the sector source agricultural raw materials such as fruits, vegetables and milk from rural farmers *via* partnership farming models. In the process, they provide better income opportunities to these farmers. Corporate manufacturers also work closely with non-corporate retailers for the distribution of their beverage brands and thereby increase the earning potential of these retailers.

Global multinationals gave estimates of their potential to create employment. For example, PepsiCo India pointed out that at any given point of time, at least 25,000 people are engaged in the total supply chain, and for every crate[1] of bottles, 35 people get employment. Similarly, for every million crates sold, Coca-Cola India said that it creates employment for 1,100 people. Thus, there is a difference in how companies estimate their indirect employment contributions.

4.2.3.2 Wages and Salaries

In the case of direct employment, the research shows that there is a huge wage differential between the corporate and non-corporate sector,[2] and corporate manufacturers pay higher wages across all types of employment. The survey also found that across all age groups, the average salary paid by corporate manufacturers is higher by almost 40 per cent compared to non-corporate manufacturers. In the sample, the average monthly salary paid by non-corporate manufacturers was INR 5,500 and by corporate manufacturers, it was INR 8,800 (Figure 4.3).

1. Each crate contains 24 bottles.
2. Karan and Selvaraj (2008).

Figure 4.3

Average Salary Paid by Corporate and Non-corporate Manufacturers by Age Group

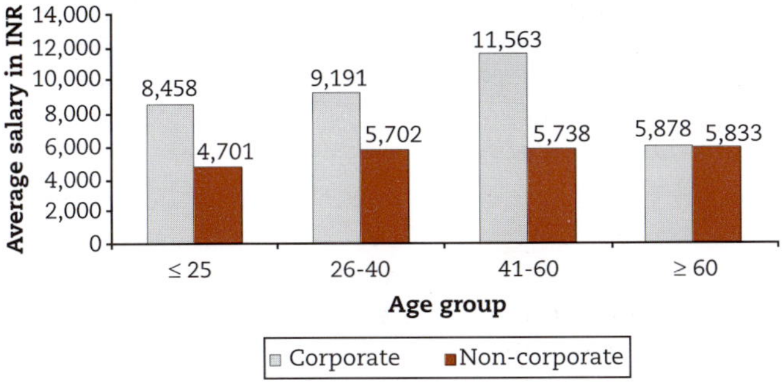

It is difficult to compare salary scales across corporate and non-corporate manufacturers because different factors affect the salaries. Salary is highly correlated with skill level, educational qualifications, years of experience, quality of employment, etc. For instance, the skill level required by manufacturers varies with the level of mechanisation in the manufacturing units. Across corporate manufacturers, all the respondents pointed out that 70 per cent of the output is produced using machines; the same is true of contract manufacturers. In contrast, non-corporate manufacturers and organic beverage manufacturers produce 70 per cent of the output using labour. The demand for skilled labour is higher in units that use capital-intensive techniques of production, and skilled labour gets higher wages. Thus, one reason for the higher wage is the higher skill requirements in the corporate sector.

Second, human resource (HR) managers in corporate manufacturing units, during in-depth interviews, said that they strictly follow all labour market regulations and offer employee benefits, such as overtime compensation and holidays. The non-corporate manufacturers pointed out that they do not have to strictly adhere to labour regulations or compensate employees for overtime, etc. Hence, there is a difference in wages between the corporate and non-corporate sectors.

4.2.3.3 Training and Skill Development

Non-alcoholic beverage manufacturers, especially corporate manufacturers, provide training and help in skill development of not only their own employees but of all the other stakeholders involved in the supply chain, such as farmers, raw material suppliers, logistics service providers, distributors and retailers. Skill development in the food processing sector as a whole is a major challenge with lack of skills at the floor level. Hence, initiation by companies becomes very important to carry on processes adopting new technology [Institute of Applied Manpower Research (IAMR, 2012)]. Corporate manufacturers spend substantially and contribute significantly to skill development. During the survey, corporate manufacturers pointed out that skills are upgraded at broadly three levels as shown in Figure 4.4. They train their employees and even educate contract manufacturers about appropriate techniques to be used in the outsourced processes.

Several Indian and foreign companies work with producers to develop their skills and output. Two of these cases—Amul's Animal Nutrition initiative and Coca-Cola India's Unnati project—are described in Box 4.1.

4.2.4 Investment

The survey found that due to its large consumer base and abundant raw material and labour supply, India attracts significant investment from both global and domestic non-alcoholic beverage companies. This, in turn, contributes to the economic growth of the country.

The investment is made across all stages in the supply chain, including infrastructure, technology upgrading, marketing and distribution. In 2010-11, FieldFresh Foods Private Limited, a joint venture between Del Monte Corporation and Bharti enterprises, invested INR 125 crore ($27.25 million) to set up manufacturing and distribution channels in India. In 2011-12, Parle Bisleri Limited invested INR 100 crore ($20.7 million) to install plants and machinery across India and INR 150 crore ($31.05 million) in marketing and advertisement of its brands. In view of the growing competition, companies have also stepped up investment in R&D, brand building and product innovation.

In addition to the investment by non-alcoholic beverage manufacturers, ancillary industries, such as manufacturers of packaging materials, also invest in India. Bericap India Private Limited, which manufactures caps and closures for non-alcoholic beverages, invested INR 44.45 crore ($9.69 million) in India in the year 2010-11.

Despite the attractiveness of India as an investment destination, the survey also noted that several global and Indian companies are shifting their manufacturing bases to neighbouring countries

Figure 4.4

Skill Development at Different Levels

Supplier and contract manufacturer training	• At the contract manufacturing level, training is given in product manufacturing and perfection training. • At the supplier level, there is training in how to increase the productivity of raw material. • Amul India Dairymen Training. This programme builds the managerial skills of progressive farmers who have more than five milch animals to bring greater success in their dairy husbandry.
In-house employee training	• Companies invest in in-house employee training. • Del Monte Corporation conducts training for in-house trainees at all levels on both the management and technical side of operations. The firm uses both in-house and local training institutions to train workers. • PepsiCo India introduced the 'WorkSmart' and 'ManageSmart' programmes in 2010 under the LearnSmart training pack to enhance the productivity and efficiency of its employees. • Dabur India Limited has a Career Development Centre that identifies and grooms future talent. The process has enabled the company to assess and upgrade nearly 1,000 employees.
Retail-level training	• Companies design specific training programmes at the sales level to increase company sales. • Hindustan Unilever (HUL) has implemented 'Project Shakti' to strengthen their reach in the Indian villages. Under this programme, they have already employed 45,000 women in the rural areas of 15 Indian states and trained them in distribution and retail.

Box 4.1

Working with Producers/Farmers

Amul and Animal Nutrition

Gujarat Co-operative Milk Marketing Federation Ltd. (GCMMF) spurred India's White Revolution, which made the country the world's largest producer of milk and milk products. In the beginning, to take care of the nutritional requirement of cows and buffaloes owned by the milk producers, Amul, which is a subsidiary of GCMMF, procured and distributed cotton seeds. The Cattle Feed Plant of Amul was set up with the assistance of Oxfam International under the Freedom from Hunger campaign of the Food and Agriculture Organization (FAO) to produce 50 million tonnes (Mt) of balanced cattle feed. The plant since has grown to become Asia's largest cattle feed plant, producing more than 1,100 Mt of feed daily. Amul has plans to expand its capacity in the coming years. To ensure that the feed supplied to the farmers is cost-effective, raw materials are procured during the season from all over India. As feed constitutes 70 per cent of the cost of milk, reducing the cost of feed while ensuring its nutritive value contributes significantly to improving the income of milk producers. With this animal nutrition programme, Amul has helped dairy farmers sustain their dairy farming.

Coca-Cola and Project Unnati

Coca-Cola India and Jain Irrigation launched Project Unnati in 2011. This is a partnership with farmers to demonstrate and enable the adoption of the ultra-high density plantation (UHDP) practice for mangoes. Through UHDP, nearly 600 trees instead of only 40 trees can be planted in an acre and mango orchards attain their full potential in 3-4 years. During the first phase of this project, 200 demonstration farms between 1 and 3 acres used the UHDP technique for mango cultivation while also using the benefits of drip irrigation. This improved the annual income of farmers by improving yield per acre and simultaneously decreased the quantity of water used per kilo of mango. The first phase of the project has an investment outlay of more than $2 million, which will be shared equally by Coca-Cola India and Jain Irrigation. These demonstration farms will be used to showcase and train farmers on the techniques and adoption of UHDP in a joint capability-building programme under the aegis of Jain Irrigation and Coca-Cola University.

Source: Compiled from the survey and company websites.

and investing in the food processing sector there. For instance, Dabur India Limited has invested in building manufacturing units in Nepal and Sri Lanka. When probed for the reasons behind their relocation, companies pointed out that India lacks a conducive investment climate due to the lack of governance, the presence of multiple regulations, lack of coordination between different ministries and the incidence of large-scale corruption. Additionally, the tariff structure in India is not favourable for importing agricultural raw materials such as fruits and vegetables. All these factors have compelled companies to shift their bases to neighbouring countries where the investment climate is more conducive (see Chapter 7).

4.2.5 Tax Contribution

Companies were asked about their tax contributions, but the majority did not share this information. Some companies' annual reports have income tax data, but it is difficult to estimate the direct and indirect tax contributions. Even the Government of India's (GoI) budget does not have commodity-wise revenue data for non-alcoholic beverages. The National Council of Applied Economic Research (NCAER) (2001) shows that while the contribution of the CSD sector to total excise revenue was 0.9 per cent in 1999-2000, it increased to 1.1 per cent in 2000-2001.

4.3 Manufacturing Process

The manufacturing process of a non-alcoholic beverage manufacturer is fairly complex. It involves several processes, starting from product innovation to its delivery to the final consumers, and generates significant backward and forward linkages (Figure 4.5).

While the operations of the majority of non-corporate manufacturers are integrated and involve manufacture as well as retail, most corporate manufacturers are only involved in manufacturing beverages. To distribute their brands to consumers across India, corporate manufacturers enter into partnerships with both corporate and non-corporate distributors and retailers. The survey noted that some corporate manufacturers such as Haldiram's manufacture and sell non-alcoholic beverages; at the same time, they sell different brands of CSDs and bottled water.

The manufacture of non-alcoholic beverages can be done either in-house or outsourced. A basic manufacturing process involves procuring raw material from different sources, followed by washing, cleaning, preparing and mixing raw materials, and extracting the pulp (in the case of fruits and vegetable juices). This is followed by filtration, sterilisation and conversion into concentrates. The concentrates are either bottled in-house or sent to outsourced bottling units. For instance, Dabur India Limited packages its fruit juice brand, Real, in-house. In contrast, Coca-Cola India has outsourced manufacture under a franchisee model; the company supplies concentrates, syrups, beverage bases and powdered beverage mixes manufactured in their wholly-owned subsidiaries (WOS) to the franchisee. The concentrate

Figure 4.5

Key Business Activities that Require Engagement with Various Stakeholders

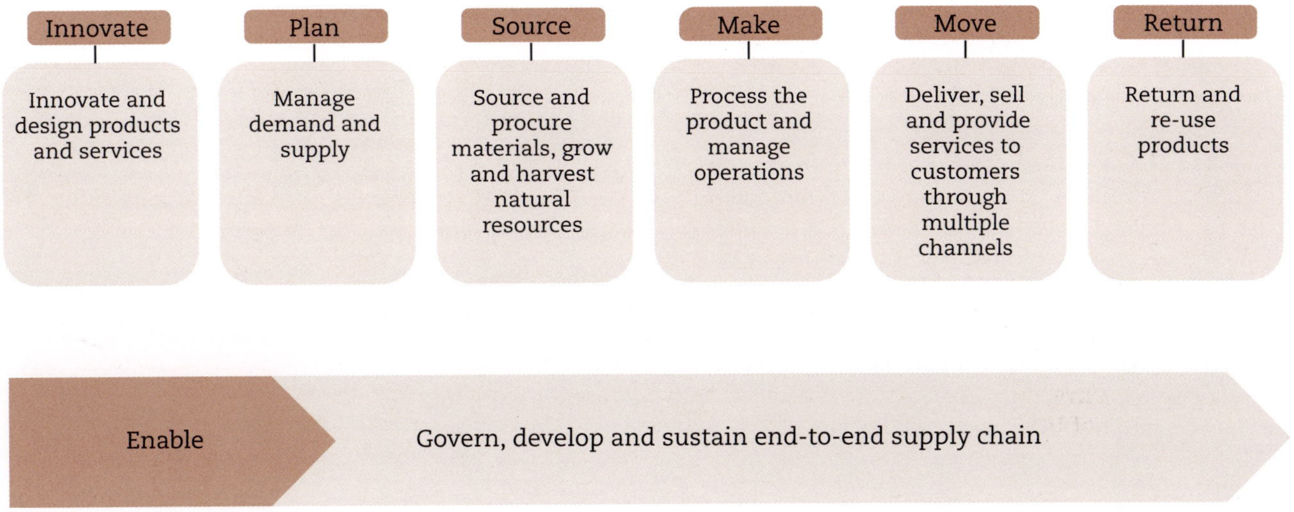

formula, especially in the CSD category, is patented and companies such as Coca-Cola India and PepsiCo India supply the concentrate to their contract manufacturers.[3] At the bottling stage, the concentrate is combined with raw materials, such as treated water and sweeteners, blended and carbonated. The finished product is sent for grading, packaging and labelling. The survey found that almost 50 per cent of processes such as grading, bottling and packaging are handled by small and medium enterprises (SMEs).

Two key activities of the manufacturing process of a non-alcoholic beverage producer, namely, packaging and pricing, are discussed below and section 4.4 focuses on the entire supply chain.

4.3.1 Packaging

Packaging plays a crucial role in the operations of manufacturers for several reasons:

- To increase the life span of the product: Since non-alcoholic beverages are perishable, they need to be packaged appropriately to avoid wastage and to preserve the freshness of the product. Also, the packages have to be clean and hygienic.
- Consumer preferences: Packaging preferences depend on the purpose of consumption. For example, there are different packaging preferences for party packs and travel packs.
- To adhere to norms and standards: Government norms and international packaging standards have to be met.
- To ensure proper storage: Climatic conditions govern the material used. Transit storage conditions and facilities as well as retailers' storage and display conditions affect the choice of packaging.

While non-corporate manufacturers consider freshness of the beverages as the most important factor that determines product packaging, followed by ease of carrying, corporate manufacturers consider ease of carrying and disposal as the most important factors, followed by the freshness of the beverages.

According to the majority of the respondents, polyethylene terephthalate (PET) bottles are the preferred packaging, followed by Tetra Pak; glass bottles seem to be the least favoured packaging (Table 4.3). The shift from glass to PET picked up in the past 12 years because the transportation of glass bottles poses major challenges for companies. Infact, one multinational pointed out that to counter the risk of transporting glass bottles, they had to set up additional manufacturing units, each of which covers an area of 300 km.

The survey found that a few non-corporate manufacturers still use returnable glass and around 55-60 per cent of packaging is done in returnable glass bottles in the Indian industry. This is still lower than countries such as the Philippines where 70 per cent of the packaging is done in returnable glass. In contrast, PET bottles and cans dominate in the USA market.

Table 4.3

Packaging Preference by Type of Manufacturer

(in percentage)

Packaging Preference	*Corporate Manufacturers*	*Non-corporate Manufacturers*
PET bottles	67	67
Tetra Pak	33	30
Glass bottles	None	3

Respondents highlighted that packaging and labelling regulations under the Food Safety and Standards Act (FSSA), 2006, have imposed restrictions on packaging sizes that will restrict the ability of companies to develop innovative package sizes. For instance, to promote new products in non-alcoholic beverages, manufacturers offer an extra quantity commonly using Tetra Paks. Respondents highlighted that this would no longer be possible. Respondents said that this move would adversely affect the industry, and would promote the use of cans over Tetra Paks, despite the latter being more environment friendly. Moreover, since procurement and moulding of packaging material for non-alcoholic beverages is done at least one year in advance, the new packaging regulations would affect companies that have invested in the old packaging sizes.

4.3.2 Pricing Products

Companies have come up with a variety of price points and sizes to cater to Indian consumers.

3. The formula of the concentrate is not shared with the contract manufacturers; instead, the companies supply the concentrate to the contract manufacturers.

Due to the competitive market, in segments such as juices, milk-based drinks and CSDs, corporate manufacturers have similar prices for products of the same size. The pricing strategy of any company is usually driven by factors such as input costs, inflation, consumer needs and other market dynamics. However, in India, despite the rise in prices of raw materials such as sugar, companies cannot change beverage prices since consumers are price-sensitive and there is competition even within the oligopolistic structure of CSDs. The high price elasticity is due to factors such as relatively low brand loyalty compared to developed countries.

4.4 Supply Chain

Supply chain activities are critical in the operations of a non-alcoholic beverage manufacturer, as they transform the raw materials into the final beverages that are then distributed to consumers. The supply chain consists of two distinct processes—the backward chain, which involves procurement and processing of the raw materials, and the forward chain, which involves distributing the processed beverages to consumers.

Figures 4.6 and 4.7 depict the supply chains of non-corporate and corporate manufacturers respectively. These are illustrative and do not cover all product categories. Also, these figures do not depict the supply chains of contract manufacturers, who have to adhere to the strict quality guidelines of the parent company. Contract manufacturers procure raw materials either directly from parent companies or from designated sources vetted by the parent companies.

The survey found that corporate manufacturers provide infrastructure support, help upgrade quality standards and transfer knowledge of best practices at various levels in the supply chain. The objective is to reduce wastage and enhance operational efficiency. For instance, in 2012, Nestlé S.A. announced that it was setting up its first coffee demonstration farm in India to help farmers improve quality, productivity and sustainability in Karnataka, Kerala and Tamil Nadu.[4] Nestlé S.A. aims to provide farmers with high-yielding, disease-resistant plantlets developed by its R&D teams.

4. *http://www.nestle.com/Media/NewsAndFeatures/Nescafe-Plan-India* (last accessed in June 2013).

The next section describes each component of the supply chain for a non-alcoholic beverage manufacturer.

4.4.1 Backward Linkages: Procuring Raw Material

Non-alcoholic beverage manufacturers procure raw materials from several stakeholders including farmers and farmer cooperative societies, wholesalers, commission agents/middlemen and retailers. In the process, they create strong backward linkages that relate to the spill-over benefits generated by the sector.

The three basic raw materials for the non-alcoholic beverage industry—milk, sugar, and fruits and vegetables—are procured in different ways.

Procuring Milk. In the case of dairy/milk-based beverages, all corporate manufacturers and the majority of non-corporate manufacturers said that they procure milk directly from dairy farmers. These farms are usually located close to the manufacturing units. For instance, Dodla Dairy Limited in Bangalore procures milk from dairy farms in south India. Similarly, Mother Dairy Fruits and Vegetables Private Limited that supplies dairy beverages to north India procures milk from dairy farms in Uttar Pradesh (UP) and Punjab. The concentrates and flavours added to raw milk are either imported from countries such as China or procured domestically from states such as Maharashtra and Tamil Nadu.

Procuring Sugar. Since sugar is an essential commodity, two factors govern its procurement — volumes and location. The procurement channel for sugar in India is highly fragmented and sugar is traded in different ways. Farmers usually sell their sugarcane produce to the traders through state-controlled *mandis*. The traders in turn sell the sugarcane to sugar mills, which process it and distribute the sugar for retail or other purposes. In some instances, farmers may also have tie-ups with sugar mills and directly sell their produce to them. In both cases, farmers receive an assured minimum support price (MSP) for their produce. In UP and Punjab (that have abundant sugarcane production), the state governments fix the state support price (SSP) for essential commodities such as sugar. This SSP is higher than the central government's MSP. While non-corporate manufacturers procure sugar from local retailers or distributors, most corporate manufacturers procure the sugar from sugar mills. Despite the large number of sugar mills in India, not all sugar mills process the quality of sugar

Figure 4.6

Supply Chain of Non-Corporate Manufacturers

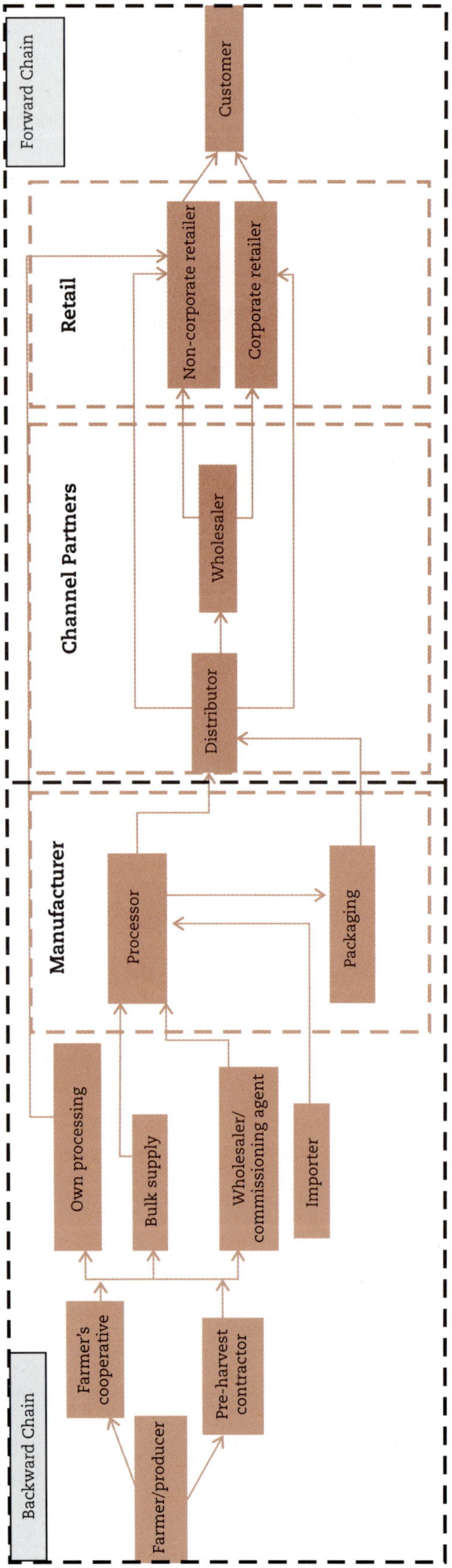

Figure 4.7

Supply Chain of Corporate Manufacturers[a]

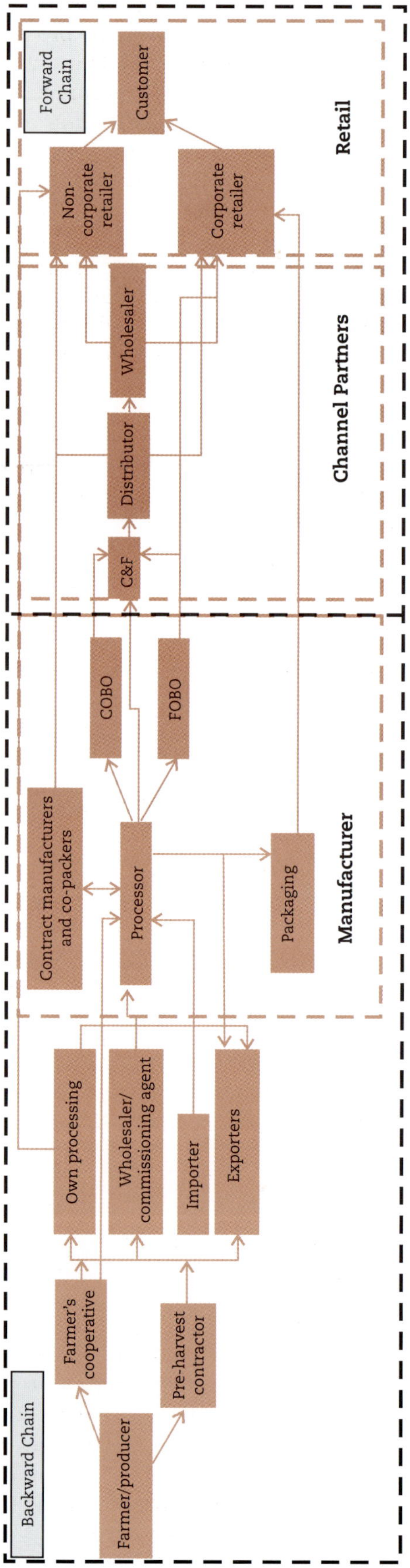

Note: 'a' shows the supply chain of a corporate CSD manufacturer.
COBO: company-owned bottling operations;
FOBO: franchise-owned bottling operations;
C&F: clearing and forwarding.

required for processing non-alcoholic beverages. One respondent pointed out that his company procures sugar from only 30 of the 500 sugar mills in the country, because they produce the appropriate grade of sugar. Some corporate manufacturers import sugar from countries such as China. However, imports are sporadic because the government sometimes implements non-tariff barriers such as import quotas or imposes a high import cess. Another issue highlighted by corporate manufacturers was that despite excessive controls and erratic supply, sugar cannot be replaced with imported artificial sweeteners because their imports are restricted in India.

The shortage of sugar can be a major concern for CSD manufacturers, but is less so for manufacturers of fruit/vegetable-based drinks since sugar constitutes 1-2 per cent of their total ingredients.

Procuring Fruits and Vegetables. The procurement of fruits and vegetables is highly fragmented for two reasons. First, a large number of farmers with fragmented land holdings across India are involved in the cultivation of fruits and vegetables and the quality of produce varies, and second, the produce is highly perishable with very limited shelf life.

The survey found that small manufacturers procure fruits and vegetables directly from neighbouring corporate and non-corporate retailers or from the *mandis*. The large and medium-scale non-corporate manufacturers procure from middlemen; the number of middlemen varies, depending on their location. If their units are located close to the farms, they procure from the aggregators, and if further away, they procure from large traders or distributors. Hence, the further the manufacturing unit is from the farms, the greater is the number of middlemen in the supply chain.

For corporate manufacturers, the procurement of fruits and vegetables is more elaborate and dynamic. They procure fruits and vegetables in one of the four ways:

- *Contract farming/partnership agreement/procurement from cooperatives*. A few corporate manufacturers in this sector have engaged in contract farming and, hence, directly procure the pre-determined produce from the farmers. The term 'contract farming' cannot be used in many states and thus production arrangements between farmers and manufacturers have different names in different states (such as partnership agreements in West Bengal). Fruits and vegetables can also be procured from co-operatives. For example, the Andhra Pradesh Mango Farmers' Co-operative Society sells mangoes directly to Coca-Cola India for the production of Maaza. Respondents highlighted that they prefer doing business in states such as Punjab, Andhra Pradesh and Maharashtra that allow contract farming, unlike UP that restricts it. This leads to the diversion of business from states rich in the cultivation of fruits and vegetables and deprives farmers and SMEs that can benefit from being associated with corporate manufacturers in terms of technology and skill upgrading.

- *Pre-harvest agreements*. Several corporate manufacturers and even aggregators enter into pre-harvest agreements with farmers 3-4 months before the harvest. They usually choose farmers with large holdings and high yields to assure the supply of products. Unlike vegetables, the gestation period for fruits is much longer as most trees take several years to bear fruit. Hence, while there are plenty of small farmers engaged in producing vegetables, there are relatively fewer large farmers growing fruits. Hence, both contract farming and pre-harvest agreements are means of reducing the risk and assuring supply.

- *Procurement through middlemen*. Corporate manufacturers procure fruits and vegetables from 'aggregators' (known as *Seths*, *Thakurs* and *Chowdharies*).[5] According to the survey, unlike sugar, fruits and vegetables are procured from farmers at prices below the MSP. Gandhi and Namboodiri (2002) found that in the case of fruits and vegetables, farmers sell their produce at one-third to one-half of the final price, because they fear a loss if their products are not procured by the aggregators. The aggregators supply the produce to large traders and corporate manufacturers for two purposes: value addition/food processing and for final consumption. The manufacturers channel the produce to their processing units for the

5. Aggregators are middlemen who have monopolised the procurement of fruits and vegetables from farmers in states such as UP, Bihar (for *litchis*), Madhya Pradesh (for red guavas), Karnataka and Andhra Pradesh (for mangoes).

manufacture of non-alcoholic beverages. Companies such as HUL and Reliance Industries Limited follow this model. The survey found that the traceability of fruits and vegetables is a challenge in India. Although some consignments of fruits and vegetables sourced from Agriculture Produce and Marketing Committee (APMC) *mandis* have stickers that are used for branding by large distributors, these stickers do not have codes and, hence, the origin of the products cannot be traced. Thus, under the FSSA, 2006, manufacturers and retailers are accountable for the quality of agricultural commodities, whereas farmers are not accountable. This is despite the fact that pesticides and fertilisers used by farmers can play a key role in food safety and standards.

- *Imports*. Corporate manufacturers import fruit pulp as well as fruits, such as lemons from Argentina and cranberries from Nepal. Most non-alcoholic beverage companies import oranges from Brazil, where orange cultivation is more organised, leading to an output of 16.8 tonnes per ha. China has emerged as a leading source for apple imports. The import duties are as high as 37 per cent. Manufacturers who import fruits and vegetables have to export agriculture commodities of an equivalent value as per the present policy. To meet this condition, a corporate manufacturer pointed out that it exports spices procured from Kerala. Respondents who import fruits and vegetables pointed out that even though India has abundant fruits such as oranges, their quality fails to meet the standards required for processing. One reason is that farmers are not well-equipped or trained in horticulture. Further, average farm sizes in India (at 2 acres) are too small for mechanisation, unlike Europe where farm sizes are 30-40 acres.

Other procurement. The key concentrates used to manufacture non-alcoholic beverages are manufactured in India as mandated by Indian laws. In the case of carbonated and treated water used as raw materials, the sourcing is usually done locally by both corporate and non-corporate manufacturers or is treated in-house.

During and after procurement, manufacturers have to consider two criteria: ensure the quality of raw materials and ensure their proper storage.

4.4.1.1 Ensuring Quality of Raw Materials

Corporate manufacturers said that to maintain uniform quality in their beverages, they have to adhere to strict quality standards in their procurement process. This is a challenge because there are multiple agents in the supply chain. The poor infrastructure in agriculture and transportation delays procurement, which can impact the quality of agricultural raw materials. Box 4.2 presents the procurement norms of corporate manufacturers, using the examples of one Indian and two global companies.

4.4.1.2 Ensuring Proper Storage

Cold storage facilities are an integral part of the supply chain. Raw materials have to be stored properly in appropriate cold storage facilities while they are moved from one stakeholder to another in the supply chain. Since the raw materials are perishable, the storage and transportation facilities have to be well-equipped to preserve them. However, according to respondents, cold storage facilities and logistics laws in India pose a challenge to this sector. Government facilities are ill-equipped to meet standard requirements for preserving raw materials, which leads to wastage, and private facilities present several problems. The government recognises this barrier and mentions that:

> Consequently, the investment in food processing infrastructure is abysmally low in the country, especially in the rural areas, making the sector subject to fragmented and unreliable supply chain, which further corrodes the profitability and in turn makes the sector relatively unattractive for large investments. To address this key concern, during the 11th Plan the Ministry had come out, with four schemes addressed at correcting this imbalance *viz.*, Mega Food Parks Scheme, Scheme for Cold Chain, Value Addition and Preservation of Infrastructure and Scheme for Modernisation of Abattoirs. In addition, the proposed outlay of this industry in the 12th plan was also raised to INR 5,225 crores for infrastructure development.
>
> — 12th Five Year Plan Working Group Report on Food Processing Industry

The Mega Food Park scheme has been promoted to encourage companies to set up their processing plants and storage infrastructure in the same place. This will help manufacturers consolidate their operations and save wastage and logistic expenses by addressing storage and logistics issues. However, corporate non-alcoholic manufacturers argue that the

Box 4.2

Procurement Norms of Companies

Domestic Company

Dabur India Limited follows strict quality checks for suppliers of raw materials, including fruits and vegetables, for their beverages. The quality checks include:

- Strict vendor certification guidelines to ensure quality and reliable service.
- Regular testing and technical analysis of commodities.
- Maintaining supplier diversity through a dual system of centralised procurement for bulk commodities and decentralised purchases for greater flexibility.

A new vendor for Dabur India Limited needs to fill out a vendor profile form that asks detailed questions on the plants and machinery of the vendor, their quality control systems and the storage and packaging materials used to transport the product. The company also obtains a sample from the supplier for quality assurance. Quality parameters for the raw materials are strictly adhered to in the procurement process.

Since Dabur India Limited's 'Real' brand of juices has no preservatives, the company uses double-seal spill-proof caps that retain the freshness of the beverages and extend their shelf life.

Global Companies

Coca-Cola India has strict norms for their raw materials as well as packaging. For example, the quality norms for the procurement of carbon dioxide (CO_2) include:

- Bottlers are required to procure CO_2 that meets International Society of Beverage Technologists (ISBT) standards. India produces two grades of CO_2— beverage grade and industrial grade—but Coca-Cola India buys only beverage grade.
- CO_2 suppliers are authorised after due diligence is done by the Coca-Cola India quality team based on purity, storage conditions and source validation.

Similarly, PepsiCo India has a robust seven-step supplier quality assurance (SQA) process that is followed before procuring any ingredient from potential vendors. The SQA processes ensure that all ingredients and packaging material meet PepsiCo's quality, food safety and local statutory norms and are procured only from approved vendors. Each material procured is then tested against specifications and approved for use only after ensuring conformance to food safety and quality requirements. A monthly review process is in place to review vendor performance and approval status.

Source: Compiled from:
(a) *http://www.dabur.com/Suppliers-Access%20to%20Supply*
(b) *http://www.daburfoodservices.com/berman_tavern.html*
(c) Primary survey.

plot size that the food parks are willing to allocate to corporate manufacturers is too small for their requirements and is more suited to small-scale manufacturers.

The other issue highlighted was the policy incentive of a five-year income tax holiday on setting up a cold storage facility. The incentive is not viable because the returns are low and there is hardly any income during the first five years. Some respondents feel that if they invest in setting up cold storage facilities on a large scale, they may not have enough volumes to store. As a result, most private players in this sector are not keen on investing in cold storage facilities.

This conflicts with the popular belief that given appropriate tax incentives and subsidies, private participation especially at the grass-roots level in this sector will induce competition, improve efficiency and contribute to reducing wastage and food inflation. To attract private investment, it is important to understand the business model and streamline taxes rather than giving *ad hoc* subsidies. These issues are discussed in Chapter 7.

Figure 4.8

Types of Customers/Channels in the Supply Chain

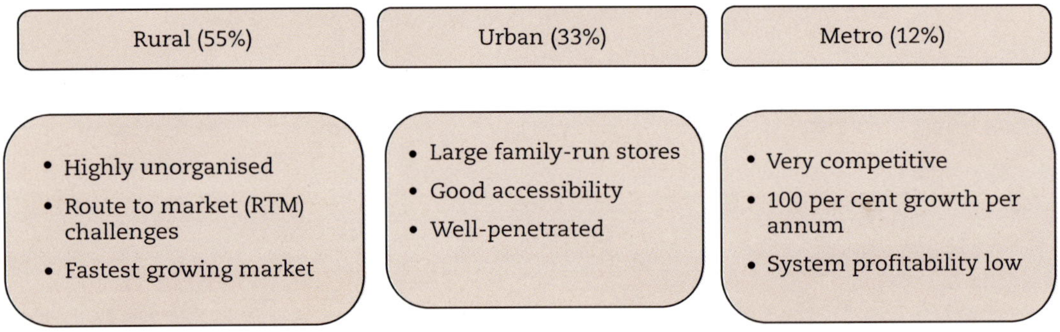

Overall, the operations of manufacturers in the non-alcoholic beverage sector generate strong backward linkages and they benefit stakeholders in the sector and allied industries. The survey found that the rising demand for non-alcoholic beverages in India and growing health-consciousness among consumers have led to a sharp rise in the demand for fruit and vegetable juices, replacing CSDs. This has contributed to the growth of the agriculture sector in terms of both quality upgrading and volumes.

4.4.2 Forward Linkages: Reaching the Final Consumer

The forward supply chain of the non-alcoholic beverage sector includes several intermediaries, namely, distributors/stockists, C&F agents, wholesalers and retailers.

The key contribution of the sector can be measured in terms of meeting the market demand for non-alcoholic beverages. The survey found that both domestic and foreign corporate manufacturers mainly cater to the domestic market and there are limited exports from India; this is especially true of dairy products and bottled water. Some corporate manufacturers, such as Dabur India Limited and Britannia Industries Limited, export fruit and vegetable juices to the USA, Saudi Arabia, Singapore and Bangladesh. Survey participants pointed out that India has the potential to develop as a manufacturing hub for non-alcoholic beverages if appropriate policy incentives are provided and if India is able to produce fruits and vegetables of processing quality.

Most corporate manufacturers, such as Britannia Industries Limited, Coca-Cola India, Dabur India Limited and PepsiCo India, have a pan-India presence and cater to both urban and rural areas. Figure 4.8 shows the different channels in a forward supply chain.

Non-alcoholic beverages are transported from manufacturing units through C&F agents to distributors who further sell them to wholesalers or stockists[6] who finally sell it to retailers in the market. According to the survey (Figure 4.9), among corporate manufacturers, about 75 per cent of their produce is sold to distributors and super-stockists,[7] around 15 per cent is sold directly to retailers and only 10 per cent is sold to business entities such as restaurants and hotels. In the case of non-corporate manufacturers, most of their produce is sold directly to retailers, indicating a direct manufacturing—retailer relationship. The retailers are mainly based in neighbouring areas. By selling directly to retailers, these manufacturers can sell at lower margins. Non-corporate manufacturers have fewer channel partners, because their market reach is limited to a specific area. In some instances, the same person can be the manufacturer and retailer as is the case with the neighbourhood juice seller.

The survey noted that the forward supply chain in India is more fragmented than the supply chain of developing countries such as Brazil due to the large presence of non-corporate retailers and state-level barriers that impact interstate movement of goods.

6. A retailer or distributor who has stocks of a certain type of item for sale.

7. Super-stockists keep stocks of products to pass them on to the next steps in the supply chain such as wholesalers, dealers, retailers and finally to customers.

Figure 4.9

Forward Linkages Generated by Manufacturers

(in percentage)

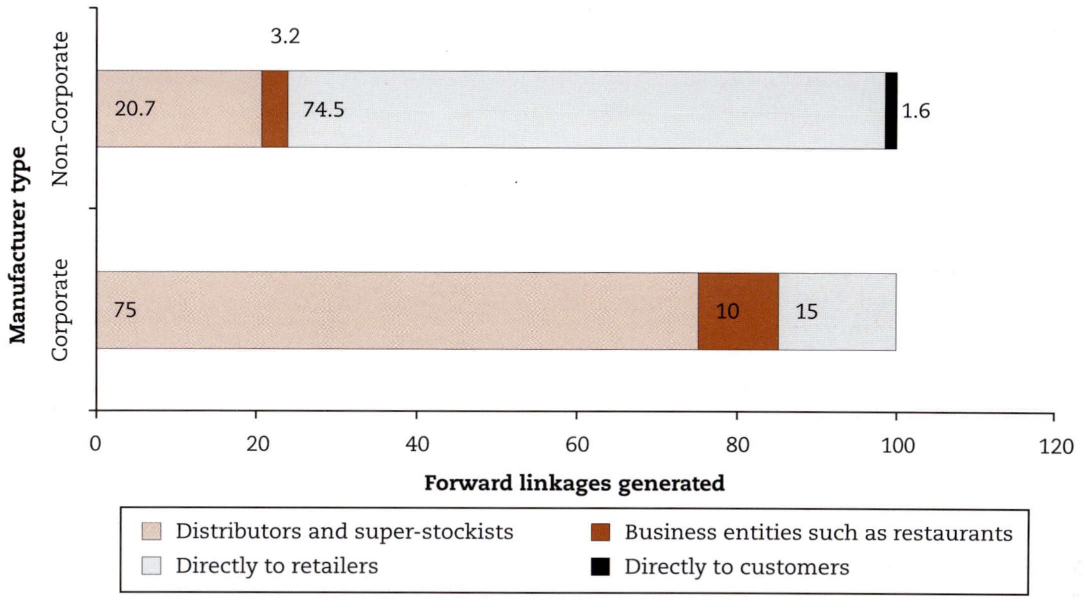

The fragmented supply chain increases the cost of distribution and leads to logistics inefficiencies. Since non-alcoholic beverages are perishable and most non-corporate retailers lack proper storage facilities, corporate manufacturers often have to work closely with non-corporate retailers to train them to store products properly and even provide them with refrigerators and storage facilities. Once companies have been able to manage the supply chain and reach consumers in remote areas, they have the advantage of a large consumer base.

The key factor governing the split between direct procurement and supply through intermediation is the total volume that needs to be procured. The Indian retail sector is dominated by small and medium-sized non-corporate retailers. Their demand in terms of volume varies during the year and is usually low. As a result, the distribution of non-alcoholic beverages through middlemen—distributors, C&F agents and wholesalers—is more effective than direct procurement.

In contrast to streamline the supply chain and ensure timely supply of products, large corporate retailers such as Reliance India Limited procure directly from various corporate manufacturers. This helps them control the storage and transportation of non-alcoholic beverages to reduce wastage and increase operational efficiency. Moreover, due to their greater bulk-buying capacity compared to non-corporate retailers, corporate retailers have higher bargaining power.

4.5 Other Activities of Manufacturers

Apart from manufacturing processes and the supply chain, other activities form part of the operations of non-alcoholic beverage manufacturers, especially in the corporate sector. These include R&D, waste management, water conservation and corporate social responsibility (CSR) initiatives.

4.5.1 Research & Development (R&D)

R&D activities are particularly important in an emerging market such as India where the consumer base is large, products have to be customised and market requirements are dynamic. For a non-alcoholic beverage manufacturer, the development of new products involves the following steps:

- Understanding customer needs through regular interactions with the marketing team.
- Designing new concepts, products and delivery formats to suit customer requirements and establishing the image of the beverage brands.

This requires heavy investment and regular interactions with stakeholders at all levels—raw material suppliers, contract manufacturers, ancillary industries, distributors and retailers. The survey found that global companies share best practices from other countries when developing new products. Among Indian companies, the R&D divisions in non-alcoholic beverages are well-established. For instance, the R&D division of Hamdard (Wakf) Laboratories dates to the early 1900s when the founder of the company invented RoohAfza, a non-alcoholic beverage concentrated squash made of fruits, herbs and vegetables. Currently, the company has research divisions in India, Pakistan and Bangladesh.

The R&D teams of corporate manufacturers also work with central government departments such as the Food Safety and Standards Authority of India (FSSAI) and Bureau of Indian Standards (BIS), and industry bodies, such as Federation of Indian Chambers of Commerce and Industry (FICCI) and CII, to ensure that the quality of their products adheres to the specifications laid down by the Food Safety and Standards Regulations.

Companies also invest in processes such as waste management. According to the survey, around 70 per cent of the corporate manufacturers and 8 per cent of non-corporate manufacturers have invested in R&D activities for product and process development, waste management and water conservation.

4.5.2 Waste Management

Corporate manufacturers (especially multinationals) emulate global standards as well as requirements in India for effective waste management and emphasise the use of green technology. They have altered their packaging standards and techniques after the Indian government banned the use of plastic packs. Indian corporates such as Dabur India Limited continuously monitor their waste to adhere to government pollution control norms. The company has initiated a Carbon Footprint Study at the unit level with the aim of becoming a carbon-positive company. The global packaging company, Tetra Pak India, along with non-alcoholic beverage companies, such as Amul, Dabur India Limited and Parle Agro Limited, have launched environment friendly initiatives in which they invite ragpickers to collect used TetraPak cartons and sell them back to the packaging company to be recycled. Companies are also adopting community waste management programmes to fulfil their pledge to environmental sustainability. For instance, PepsiCo India has adopted the 'Waste to Wealth' programme in six municipalities in Tamil Nadu, Andhra Pradesh and Haryana. The programme not only aims to educate the community on recycling waste, but also provides livelihood to more than 600 green ambassador members of the community.

Within the non-corporate sector, those who manufacture for global brands and are contract manufacturers for large companies are more likely to adopt these initiatives.

4.5.3 Water Conservation

Water is a key input for non-alcoholic beverages. The survey found that around 50 per cent of the corporate manufacturers have taken steps to conserve water in one way or another, against around 17 per cent of the non-corporate manufacturers. For instance, Coca-Cola India has reduced its water usage ratio by more than 25 per cent between 2004 and 2009. PepsiCo India has had a positive water balance since 2009; the company recharges more water than it consumes in its operations and has reduced its water consumption per litre of finished beverage by 24 per cent since 2006.

Some initiatives for water conservation are:

- Water balance operations such as rainwater harvesting,
- Reduced consumption of ground water by adopting water-efficient technologies,
- Laser levelling of agricultural fields and
- Community water recharge projects.

4.5.4 CSR Initiatives

The survey found that 91 per cent of the corporates have undertaken initiatives under CSR, especially after the Indian government's regulation of December 2012, which stated that both public and private companies with net profit or net worth above INR 5 billion have to set up a CSR committee and invest at least 2 per cent of their average profit of three years in CSR activities. For instance, Parle Agro Limited has started Frooti Foundation, which partners with non-governmental organisations (NGOs) such as Akanksha Foundation in Mumbai and Udavum Karangal in Chennai, to distribute their mango drink among less fortunate children.

4.6 Manufacturer's Perceptions of Recent Policy Changes

There have been two recent policy changes that impact the food processing sector: FSSA, 2006, and permission for 51 per cent FDI in multi-brand retail.

4.6.1 Perceptions of FSSA, 2006

The key act regulating the food processing sector, FSSA, 2006, was brought into effect in August 2011. The survey found that corporate manufacturers are well aware of the act, but there is lower awareness among non-corporate players.

Overall, manufacturers are positive about this act. At the same time, they pointed to problems such as lack of supply chain traceability and lack of synergy with global classifications, categorisations and additive approval standards. The licence application process is complicated, with separate licences for the central and state level, and there is a dearth of qualified testing laboratories and trained food inspectors. These issues are discussed in Chapter 7. The manufacturers said that if these issues are addressed, this act would be beneficial, because it would enable manufacturers and retailers to maintain proper quality and safety standards in the processed food and beverage sector in India.

4.6.2 Perceptions of FDI in Multi-brand Retail

In the year 2012, the government allowed 51 per cent FDI in multi-brand retail subject to certain conditions, which were modified by the government in August 2013. Overall, manufacturers were positive about the impact of FDI in multi-brand retail. The responses of manufacturers on the impact of FDI in multi-brand retail are given in Table 4.4.

Although manufacturers perceive that large retailers would give more discounts and schemes, there is less likely to be price reduction (as perceived by the government) since the cost of agricultural raw materials is rising and there are multi-layered taxes and other barriers.

Manufacturers highlighted a few concerns. The majority said that it would lead to the proliferation of brands and, since multi-brand retail outlets are expected to stock a wider range of products and brands, consumers would purchase brands they prefer rather than brands that are available. In addition, it would be easier for corporate manufacturers to push new products or new variants of existing products through corporate retailers; for new entrants, it might be difficult to convince non-corporate retailers to give shelf space. Around 80 per cent of the corporate manufacturers and 70 per cent of the non-corporate manufacturers perceive that the policy would benefit consumers, who would get more product choices at competitive prices. However, some manufacturers said that their bargaining power might be reduced. Also, since global retail chains have their own brands, manufacturers would face competition from in-house brands. Further, packaging needs might change and manufacturers would need to have packaging sizes as per the requirements of retail chains.

Table 4.4

Responses of Manufacturers on the Impact of FDI on Multi-brand Retail

Pameters	*Percentage of Response*
More product choices	75
Margins of small and medium manufacturers will reduce	45
Margins of large manufacturers will reduce	54
Organised retailers would have to improve customer service/make more investments	58
Business of unorganised retailers will decrease	32
Increased buying from organised retailers	83
Skill upgrading	89
More options to sell	87
More discounts/schemes	78
Reduction in prices	51

Note: This is a multiple-choice question.

4.7 Conclusion

The survey found that the non-alcoholic beverage manufacturing sector is dominated by non-corporate manufacturers in terms of the number of firms, but the corporate sector dominates in terms of contribution to total output, employment generation, percolation and use of technology and economic development. There are similarities and differences in the operations and contributions of corporate and non-corporate manufacturers, but the contribution of corporate manufacturers in terms of backward and forward linkages seems to be higher and more significant. Their scale of operations helps them develop a more streamlined supply chain, and they are capable of investing in infrastructure and storage facilities to support the supply chain. This reduces wastage and losses in transit. The survey also highlighted that there are strong linkages between corporate and non-corporate manufacturers. Corporate manufacturers work closely with contract manufacturers, who can be the owners of both corporate and non-corporate businesses, which gives them training, input and technology. In addition to generating strong forward and backwards linkages, non-alcoholic beverage manufacturers, especially in the corporate sector, invest in other activities such as R&D, water management and waste treatment.

In terms of sector growth, since the market is unsaturated, both corporate and non-corporate manufacturers foresee good possibilities in the future. This is despite the effect of the global slowdown and the slowdown of economic growth in India. With the growth of the economy and increase in demand for non-alcoholic beverages, the sector will further contribute to the Indian economy.

Finally, the survey found that non-alcoholic beverage manufacturers face several barriers in establishing their manufacturing facilities and supply chain networks. More positive efforts by the government and industry representation in policymaking bodies would certainly help eliminate some of these barriers (see Chapter 7). In a globalised world, as India enters into trade agreements and global production networks, it is important for the manufacturing sector to be globally competitive, productive and efficient or else the country will not get investment. In the modern manufacturing scenario, the scale of operations, efficiency, productivity and skills upgrading are important. This is feasible with an increase in corporate presence within the sector. Incentives, therefore, should focus on enabling SMEs to grow and become a part of the global supply chain network rather than limiting their scale of operations.

5

Retailers: Bridging the Gap between Manufacturers and Consumers

Retailers are a critical link between manufacturers and consumers—they enable manufacturers to access their consumers. In a modern market economy, an efficient retail infrastructure reduces wastage of products by removing intermediaries and through just-in-time delivery of products to the consumers. Thus, they help to streamline the supply chain. The retail sector also provides producers with much-needed information about consumer demand patterns, which enables them to match the demand with supply, lower the requirements for maintaining inventories, modify production schedules and categories, etc. For the consumer, retailers not only provide a wide variety of products, but also often offer complimentary services (such as home delivery); this gives consumers more informed choices and greater convenience in buying.

India has one of the largest retail infrastructures in the world. However, the bulk of the retail business is in the non-corporate sector and corporate retail only accounted for 8 per cent of total retail in the year 2012. Retail is one of the fastest-growing sectors in India and the overall retail market is expected to grow at a compound annual growth rate (CAGR) of 19 per cent by 2015. The food and grocery retail sector is the largest retail segment in India, and in 2012, it was valued at INR 17,120 billion. It is expected to grow at an annual rate of 17 per cent by 2015. With the modernisation of the Indian economy, modern food and grocery retail is growing at a rapid pace. In 2012, it constituted only 1.4 per cent of the total food and grocery retail market. However, it is expected to grow at a CAGR of 30 per cent by 2015.[1]

The non-alcoholic beverage retail market is a key segment in the total food and grocery retail sector. Though there is no separate data on this particular segment, as a part of the food and grocery retail sector, it is expected to grow at a rapid pace.

In terms of structure, non-alcoholic beverage retail as in the case of food retail comprises two distinct market segments: non-corporate and corporate retail. Non-corporate retail comprises direct manufacturers and sellers, such as hawkers and street vendors. They also include family-owned convenience stores called *kirana* stores. They are conveniently located for neighbourhood residents, offer personalised service and credit facilities, carry smaller sizes in products (for single use and emergencies) and are open for longer hours (Joseph *et al.*, 2008). They also include small restaurants owned by a single person or family that sell beverages as part of the meal. Non-corporate retailers sell both branded and non-branded non-alcoholic beverages.

The corporate retail segment consists of various store formats that differ in size, product range, pricing, etc. Some of these include:

- Hypermarkets/Supermarkets: These are large (20,000 square feet plus) self-service stores that sell a variety of products at discounted prices. Supermarkets tend to be located in key residential markets and malls, and offer competitive prices due to economies of scale in logistics and purchasing. An example in India is Big Bazaar.

- Convenience stores: These are retail businesses of less than 5,000 square feet with the primary emphasis on providing the public with a convenient location to quickly purchase an assortment of food and other consumable products. They are usually open seven days a week for extended hours. Twenty Four Seven is an example of a chain of convenience stores.

- Discount stores or fair price stores: These are general merchandise retailers that offer a wide variety of merchandise, limited services and low prices. An example is KB's Fair Price Store.

- Food and beverage chains such as McDonald's and Café Coffee Day.

- Stores set up with government assistance: Mother Dairy Fruit and Vegetable Private Limited (a wholly-owned subsidiary of the National Dairy Development Board) and Kendriya Bhandar (cooperative society) that sell food and beverages.

Some corporate retailers sell their private labels along with branded products; for instance, the food and grocery retailer Nature's Basket has its own brand, B Natural, that it sells along with other brands such as Tropicana and Snapple.

There is also a close link between corporate and non-corporate manufacturers and retailers. Many non-corporate retailers and manufacturers have expanded and become corporate retailers after economic liberalisation. Some of these family-owned

1. Images (2013).

businesses in the food segment, such as Haldiram's, have expanded to the point that they have a pan-India presence and export their products. With liberalisation, the sector has become attractive and several Indian corporates have entered the food and grocery retail sector; examples are the RPG Group (Spencer's, Spencer's Retail Private Limited), Aditya Birla Group (More, Aditya Birla Retail Limited) and Reliance Industries Limited (Reliance Mart, Reliance Retail Limited). Many of them have diversified their business from manufacturing to retail. The growing Indian market has also attracted foreign retailers, but given the restrictions on multi-brand retail until recently, they operate under different agreements. Auchan, the hypermarket chain, has a franchise agreement with Max Hypermarket India Private Limited (Landmark Group). Starbucks, the US-based beverage chain, has opened outlets in India through a 50:50 joint venture with Tata Global Beverages in the food catering and chain restaurant segment. Global multi-brand food and grocery retailers (Walmart, Metro AG and Tesco PLC) operate in India in the wholesale cash and carry format.

With the entry of Indian and foreign players in the manufacture and retail of non-alcoholic beverages, there has been a proliferation of brands and product categories. CSDs and fruit juices have had a long presence in India, but energy and sports drinks are a recent addition.

Against this background, this chapter goes on to examine the retail segment in the non-alcoholic beverage sector through a survey of retailers. It describes the characteristics of corporate and non-corporate retailers and their operations to understand their backward linkages with manufacturers and their forward linkages with consumers. Since recent government policy changes (such as the policy of allowing FDI in multi-brand retail) impact the retail sector, the survey also tried to tap their knowledge and perceptions of changes in specific policies.

5.1 Research Methodology and Sampling Frame

The survey covered both corporate and non-corporate retailers. Since corporate retail is prevalent in larger cities, four metros—Delhi, Mumbai, Kolkata and Bangalore—were selected for the survey. A set of semi-structured questionnaires was sent to both corporate and non-corporate retailers. Of the 100 questionnaires administered to 80 non-corporate and 20 corporate retailers, 79 completed questionnaires were received from non-corporate retailers and 16 from corporate retailers, bringing the total to 95. Table 5.1 shows the distribution of retailers who provided completed questionnaires for the survey.

The sample selection was based on a stratified random sampling method and four categories of retail outlets were selected: (a) outlets that sell both alcoholic and non-alcoholic beverages, (b) outlets that sell only non-alcoholic beverages, (c) outlets that sell food and beverages and (d) outlets that sell food, beverages and other items such as fast-moving consumer goods (FMCGs). In terms of the products that are sold, food and beverage retailers may sell only branded or non-branded products or both, and some retailers also sell private labels. This is shown in Table 5.1.

Table 5.1

Distribution by Type of Retailer

(in percentage)

	Branded	*Private Label*	*Non-brand*	*Branded*	*Non-brand*
Only beverages (alcoholic and non-alcoholic)	0	0	0	1.1	3.3
Only non-alcoholic beverages	11.1	7.4	3.7	66.3	34.8
Food and beverages	14.8	7.4	3.7	70.7	41.3
Food, beverages and other items	55.6	14.8	29.6	39.1	17.4

In addition, the survey team held in-depth interviews with three global retailers.

5.2 Characteristics of the Non-alcoholic Beverage Retail Sector

This section describes key characteristics of non-alcoholic beverage retailers: sales and employment. It also examines their use of technology, because it can enhance efficiency in operations such as billing and stock-keeping.

5.2.1 Annual Sales

Respondents were asked about their average annual sales in the past three years. As expected, the figures are lower for non-corporate than corporate retailers. Almost half the non-corporate retailers have an annual turnover below INR 1 million and only about 10 per cent have a turnover above INR 5 million. In contrast, the majority of the corporate retailers (almost 55%) have an annual turnover above INR 10

Figure 5.1

Average Annual Sales of Retailers

(in percentage)

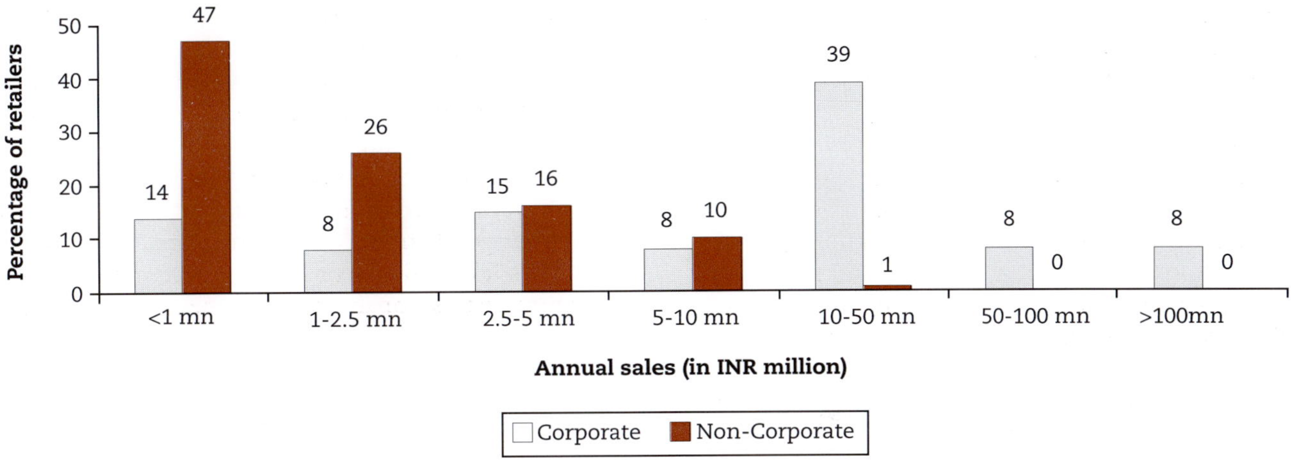

million, of which 16 per cent have an annual turnover above INR 50 million (Figure 5.1). This is similar to the pattern for corporate manufacturers versus non-corporate manufacturers presented in Chapter 4.

5.2.2 Sales Growth

The retailers were asked to give their growth projections for different categories of non-alcoholic beverages (such as CSDs and vegetable and fruit juices) for the next three years. Since not all retailers sell all types of non-alcoholic beverages, their projections are limited to the products that they sell. Both corporate and non-corporate respondents perceived that the non-alcoholic beverage sector would experience double-digit growth. Thus, retailers, like manufacturers, consider this to be a fast-growing sector. Their optimism is based on the following perceptions: the Indian market is unsaturated, there is scope for market penetration and the demand for and acceptability of packaged food and drinks is increasing in India. In terms of product categories, CSDs are projected to have high growth, along with fruit-based juices, bottled water and tea/coffee-based drinks. Although energy drinks have a small presence in India, retailers expect this product category to grow at a rapid pace, especially in large cities.

5.2.3 Employment and Emoluments

The number of employees on the shop floor in corporate retail is almost five times higher than in non-corporate retail stores. For corporate retailers, the average number of employees is 21, whereas the average number of people employed in a non-corporate retail store is 4, of which 1-2 people are owners and their immediate family.

It is difficult to compare salaries in corporate and non-corporate retail, since they depend on factors such as age, qualification and experience. The average monthly salary for employees in non-corporate retail and corporate retail are INR 5,900 and INR 6,700, respectively, in the age group of 26-40 years. Thus, average salaries in the corporate retail sector are higher by at least 10 per cent. The higher salaries may be due to the higher and more specialised skills required in the corporate sector, such as customer service, stock-keeping/ merchandising and inventory management. Often, corporate retailers train their employees in these skills, but in the non-corporate sector, individuals largely gain experience on the job without any formal training (Mukherjee and Goyal, 2012).

The survey found that the quality of employment is better in the corporate than in the non-corporate sector for three reasons: the corporate sector strictly adheres to labour laws, which provides job security; employees get benefits, such as provident fund and overtime; and employees have greater learning opportunities due to the use of technology. Corporate retailers also give their employees one day off in a week. In contrast, of the 35 per cent non-corporate retailers in the survey who keep their outlets open 7 days a week, more than half do not provide a weekly day off to their employees.

Figure 5.2

Use of Technology for Billing

(in percentage)

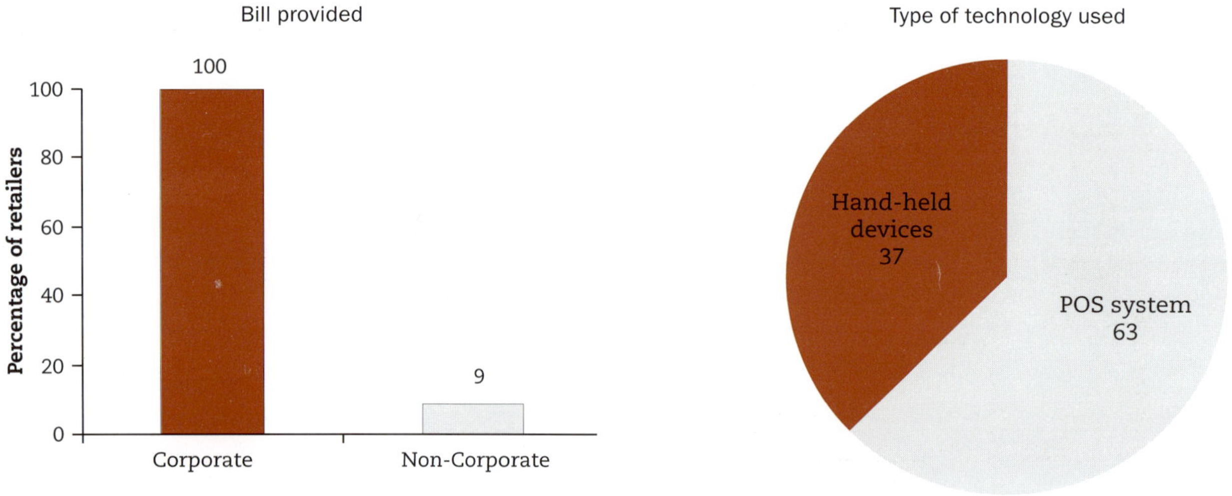

Note: POS refers to point-of-sale billing.

5.2.4 Technology Used

The level of technology adoption differs across corporate and non-corporate retailers. Technology enables retailers to have efficient operations through better inventory tracking and management, consumer profiling, transparent accounting and billing, etc. However, it involves an additional investment, which small retailers may not be able to afford.

Technology enables retailers to provide electronic bills to their customers. This system of electronic billing increases transparency in billing and helps the government in tax collection. The survey found that all corporate retailers give their customers electronic bills, but only 9 per cent of the non-corporate retailers provide electronic bills to customers (Figure 5.2). The retailers who use an electronic billing system mainly use hand-held devices[2] (63%).

Only 5 per cent of the non-corporate retailers use technology for stock-keeping; in contrast, all the corporate retailers have adopted technology for stock-keeping, which has reduced wastage and increased profitability by keeping a check on pilferage and spoilage (Figure 5.3). However, as shown in Figure 5.3, even in the corporate sector, the use of technology such as Radio Frequency Identification (RFID) is low.

2. Hand-held devices are used to scan product prices and generate an itemised bill for customers.

5.3 Linkages: Backward and Forward

Since retailers are in the middle of the supply chain, their backward linkages to manufacturers and their forward linkages to consumers are critical. Some of the linkages were discussed in Chapter 4 and this section adds to that information.

5.3.1 Backward Linkages: Getting the Products

When getting the products, retailers have to manage both their sourcing and the storage.

Sourcing

The food and beverage supply chain involves the primary producers or farmers, the manufacturers or processors who manufacture/process the raw food, intermediaries such as wholesalers and traders, and the retailers, who source a range of such products and sell them to the final consumer.

The sourcing procedure varies between non-corporate and corporate retailers. More than 80 per cent of non-corporate retailers source non-alcoholic beverages from both wholesalers and distributors, of which 55 per cent is sourced from distributors. Interestingly, Figure 5.4 shows that 34 per cent retailers source bottled water and 8 per cent source milk-based beverages directly from manufacturers. This indicates disintermediation or direct sourcing from manufacturers among these retailers, which reduces wastage in the supply chain. The direct sourcing is mainly from small local manufacturers

Figure 5.3

Use of Technology for Stock-keeping

(in percentage)

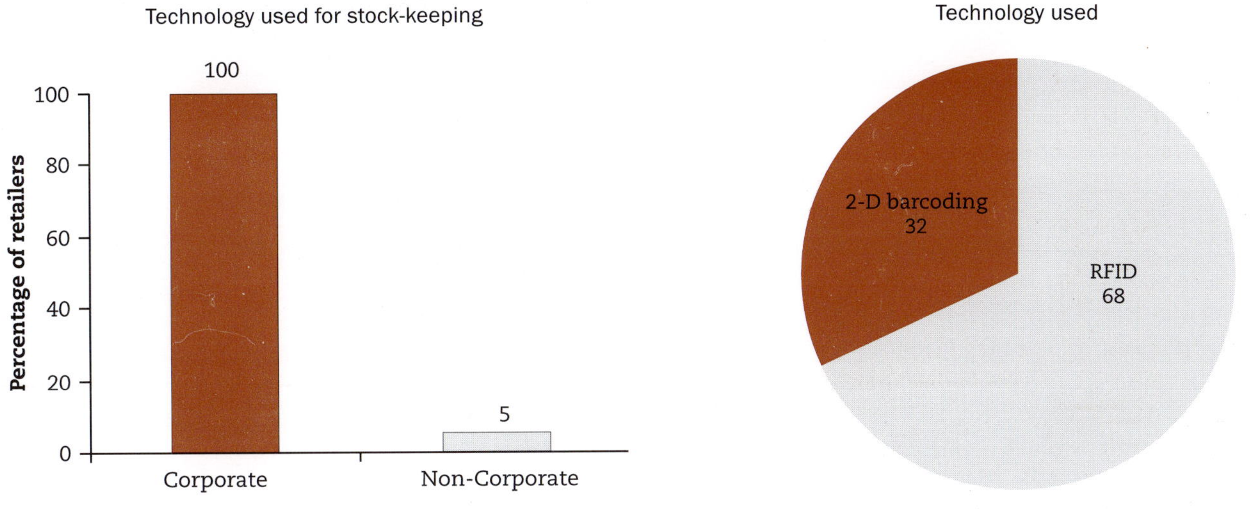

Figure 5.4

Backward Supply Chain in Non-corporate Retail by Segment

(in percentage)

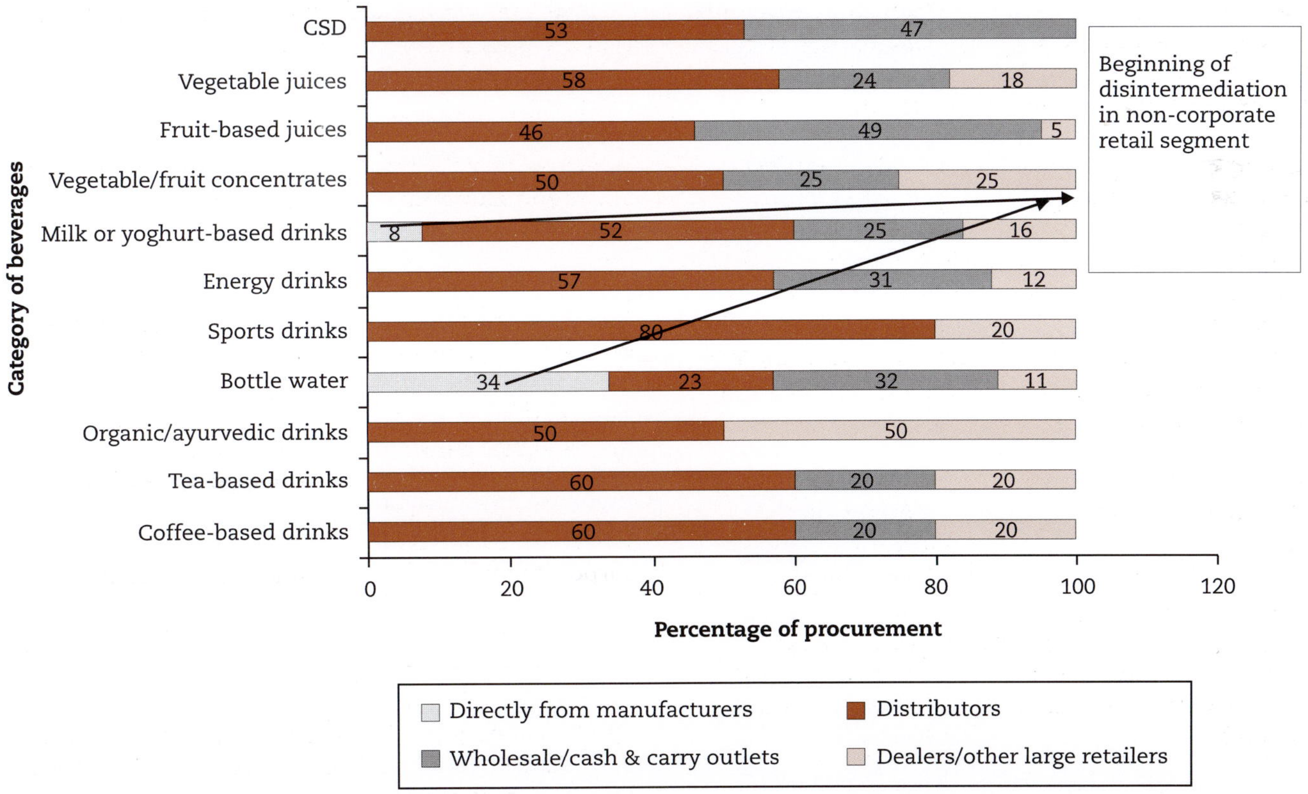

who have very limited market reach. Hence, it offers opportunities for small manufacturers to save on margins by removing intermediaries.

The buying process of corporate food retailers can be classified into the four categories shown in Figure 5.5.

All the corporate retailers surveyed use a combination of these buying processes. Items with a higher shelf life are routed through warehouses, whereas items with limited shelf life and which are sourced locally are supplied directly to retail outlets.

On average, around 57 per cent of corporate retailers source non-alcoholic beverages directly from manufacturers across different product categories, while 43 per cent source it from distributors (Figure 5.6). Thus, most of the sourcing is directly from manufacturers and the rest is from distributors; hence, they have fewer intermediaries in their backward procurement than non-corporate retailers.

Large retailers have also begun introducing private labels in beverage segments such as CSDs and fruit-based juices. This means that a manufacturer (which can be the retailer itself) makes products exclusively for a retailer, which is then sold under the retailer's brand name. Some private labels of leading retailers in the food and beverage segment are: Fresh & Pure (Big Bazaar), Feasters (More), Dairy Pure (Reliance Retail) and Smart Choice (Spencer's).

Corporate retailers often source raw materials directly from farmers and products from contract manufacturers for their private labels.

Box 5.1

Retailer-Manufacturer Tie-up for Private Labels

Big Bazaar, the hypermarket of Future Group, has a range of non-alcoholic beverages under its private label 'Tasty Treat.' Asian Lakto Industries Ltd., based in Ludhiana, supplies juices to Future Group for its private label 'Tasty Treat.' Asian Lakto earns about 20 per cent of its revenue of INR 70 crore from private labels. Earlier, the company relied on its plant in Ludhiana to supply juices and CSDs to retailers across India. To save on logistics costs and to supply retailers in the western and southern parts of India, it has invested INR 18 crore to start another plant near Bangalore with a daily handling capacity of 10,000 cases (one case contains 12 bottles). Thus, partnering with an organised retailer has helped the company grow.

Source: Compiled from primary survey.

Besides their own brands and established domestic brands, corporate retailers also sell imported international brands to cater to the needs of high- and high middle-income population of the country.

Storage

Since non-alcoholic beverages have a limited shelf life, proper storage is critical for maintaining consistent quality. Retailers need freezers, refrigerators, cold storage facilities, metal racks, etc., depending on the products they sell and their scale of operations. Manufacturers work closely with retailers for proper storage of non-alcoholic beverages. Large corporate manufacturers often provide non-corporate retailers with storage equipment, such as freezers and refrigerators. In the survey, about 84.5 per cent of non-corporate retailers said that corporate manufacturers supplied them with freezers. Corporate retailers generally have their own storage facilities.

In the survey, the majority of the retailers (56% of the non-corporate and 86% of the corporate) store small-sized packs of non-alcoholic beverages in refrigerators for consumers who prefer chilled beverages if they are to be drunk on the spot. For home consumption, large packs are generally used, which are not kept in the refrigerators.

5.3.2 Forward Linkages: Reaching Their Customers

The growing middle-class population in India provides ample scope for the growth of corporate as well as non-corporate retail. Both corporate and non-corporate retailers said that they are aware of their consumers' demand patterns. They said that rising incomes and purchasing power coupled with exposure to western culture have changed the consumption patterns of urban Indians, especially the young generation. The new generation of Indians in the post-reform period is more willing to try new cuisines, food and beverages and they are willing to experiment with products and brands. However, brand loyalty is low. The majority of the retailers said that Indian consumers are price-sensitive and they prefer discounts; promotional offers, advertisements and discounts rather than brand loyalty play a key role in determining consumer choice. In fact, there is no distinct brand preference for products that are close substitutes.

Both corporate and non-corporate retailers also stated that the demand pattern for certain categories of non-alcoholic beverages such as CSDs and energy

Figure 5.5

Buying Process of a Corporate Retailer

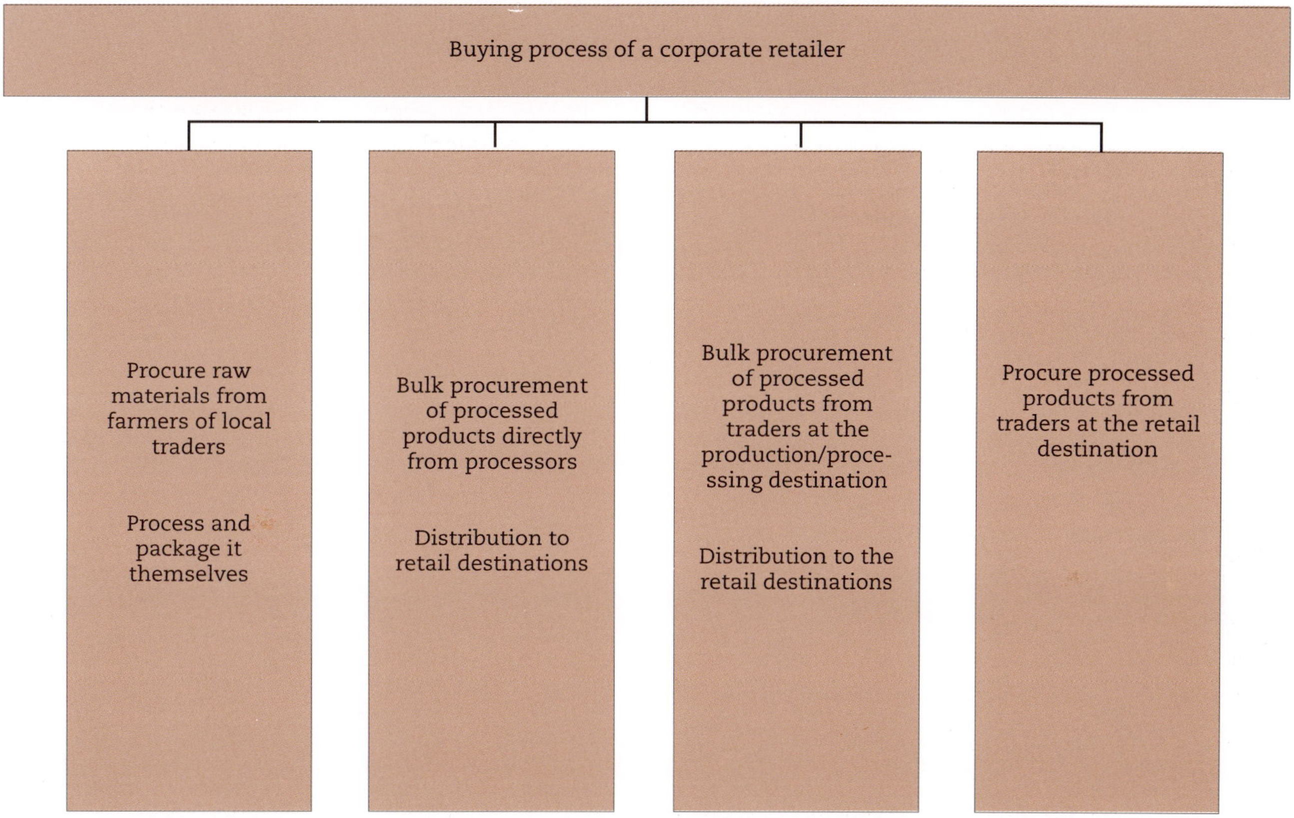

Figure 5.6

Backward Supply Chain in Corporate Retail by Segment

(in percentage)

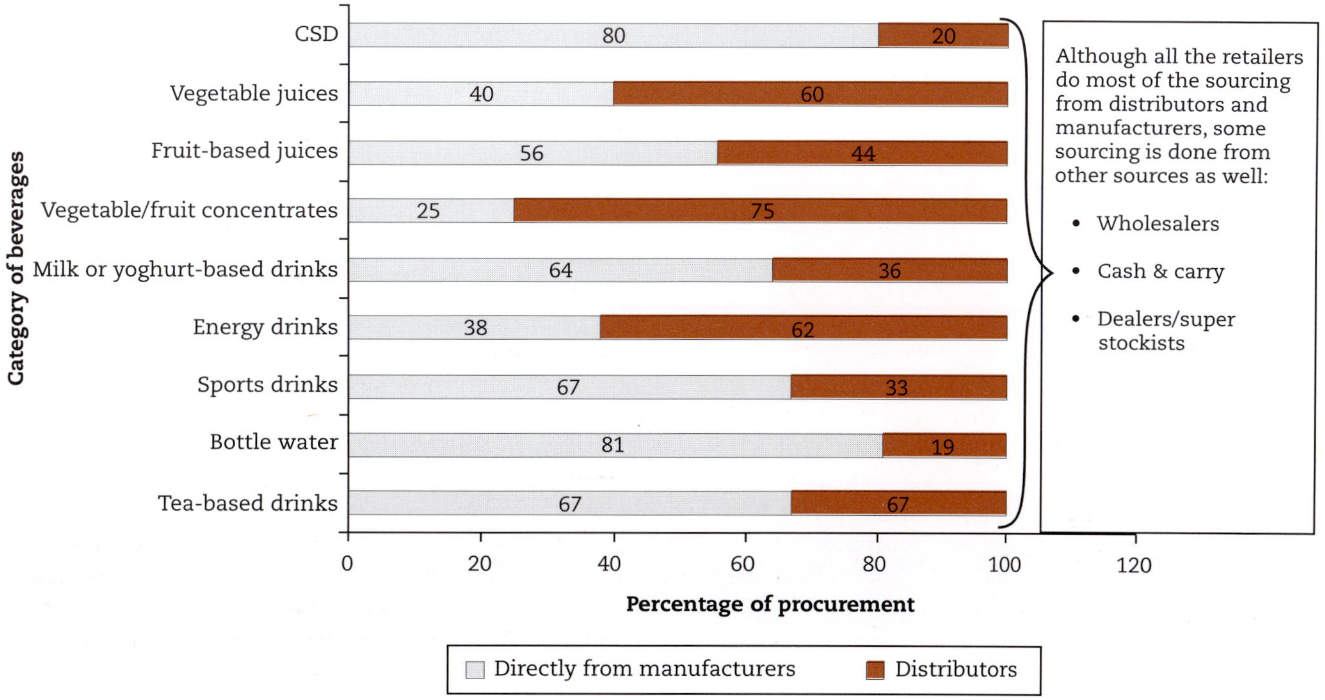

drinks is seasonal, while that for categories such as juices and bottled water remains constant through the year. For example, the demand for energy drinks rises during the time of examinations.

In both the corporate and non-corporate retail sectors, direct demand is higher than indirect demand. The non-corporate retailers said that more than 96 per cent of their non-alcoholic beverages are sold to end-consumers and the remaining 4 per cent is divided between business entities, such as restaurants and hotels, and educational institutions, such as schools and colleges. Corporate retailers said that 82 per cent of the non-alcoholic beverages are sold to end-consumers, around 8 per cent to business entities such as restaurants and hotels, and 10 per cent to educational institutions. Only a few retailers work with business entities and educational institutions, because this segment is generally handled by manufacturers, who work as direct suppliers.

In terms of product packaging, the majority of the retailers said that consumers prefer Tetra Paks, followed by PET bottles (31% of the corporate retailers and 26% of the non-corporate retailers). None of the corporate retailers mentioned glass as the preferred packaging of consumers, but 4 per cent of the non-corporate retailers did mention glass as the preferred packaging. This indicates a shift from glass to Tetra Pak, perhaps because of factors such as carrying convenience, hygiene and the perceived freshness of beverages in Tetra Paks.

The retailers were asked how they ensured the quality of the product and met consumer satisfaction. The majority of the corporate retailers have an in-house quality assurance team, while 63 per cent of non-corporate retailers said that they relied on government agencies such as food inspectors for their quality assurance.

Advertising and Marketing

Advertising and marketing are particularly important for non-alcoholic beverages as it increases product visibility and consumer's knowledge of the product. Corporate retailers are more proactive in this than non-corporate retailers; almost 44 per cent of the corporate retailers invested in advertising and marketing in the past three years compared with only 9 per cent of the non-corporate retailers. The survey found that corporate retailers spend almost 30 per cent more on advertising and marketing than non-corporate retailers. The survey participants also said that product advertising for beverages is mainly done by manufacturers or the brand owners (Figure 5.7).

Figure 5.7

Agency Responsible for Advertising

(in percentage)

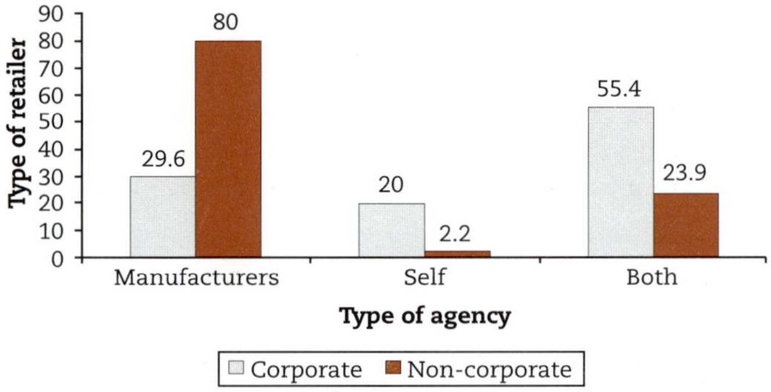

Note: This is a multiple-choice question.

To increase sales, sometimes retailers work with manufacturers to market the product to consumers.

5.4 Perceptions of Recent Regulations

Two recent government policy changes are likely to have a strong impact on the retail sector: the decision to allow FDI in multi-brand retail and the Food Safety and Standards Act (FSSA), 2006.

5.4.1 Impact of Permitting FDI in Multi-brand Retail

The existing studies show that corporate and non-corporate retail will co-exist in India, because of multiple needs and utility functions among various socioeconomic classes (Joseph and Soundararajan, 2009; Mukherjee and Patel, 2005).

The survey found mixed reactions among retailers to the new policy. More than 75 per cent of the corporate retailers believe that all the stakeholders—consumers, retailers and employees—will benefit from FDI inflows. They foresee an increase in investments to attract more customers as well as more products to sell. The majority of the non-corporate retailers (52%) feel that there will be a decrease in business with the advent of FDI, because food and grocery retail will become more corporatised (Figure 5.8). Further, a considerable percentage of non-corporate retailers (41%) perceive that they will have more products and brands to sell because with the entry of global retail chains, the number of manufacturers will grow. There has already been product and brand proliferation in India with companies such as Danone Food & Beverages (India) Private Limited recently launching new products.

Less than 50 per cent of the non-corporate retailers felt that there would be a decrease in prices or an improvement in product quality. More than 70 per cent of corporate and non-corporate retailers said that more pack sizes would become available (Figure 5.9).

Around 50 per cent of the non-corporate retailers mentioned that they would make investments to compete with corporate retailers and attract more customers.

Figure 5.8

Perceived Impact of FDI on Retail

(in percentage)

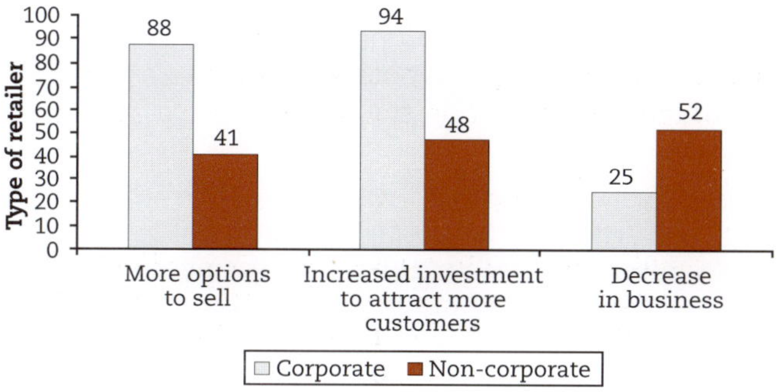

Figure 5.9

Perceived Impact of FDI on Products

(in percentage)

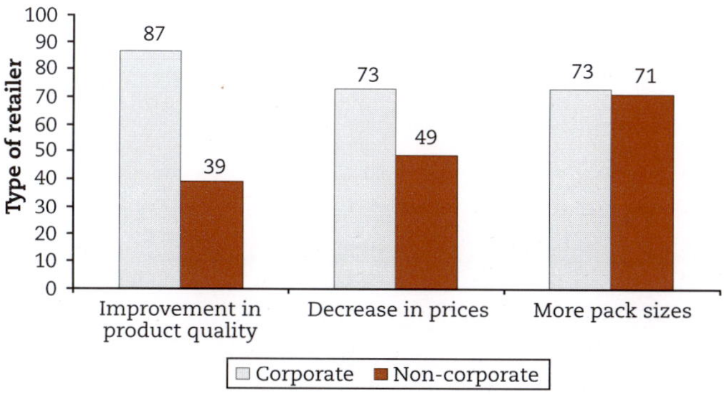

At the same time, retailers have a strong perception that FDI in multi-brand retail will benefit other stakeholders—employees, consumers, farmers and manufacturers. More than 50 per cent of them believe that instead of job losses, there would be skill upgrading and employees would get better salaries and employment options (Figure 5.10).

Figure 5.10

Perceived Impact of FDI on Employees

(in percentage)

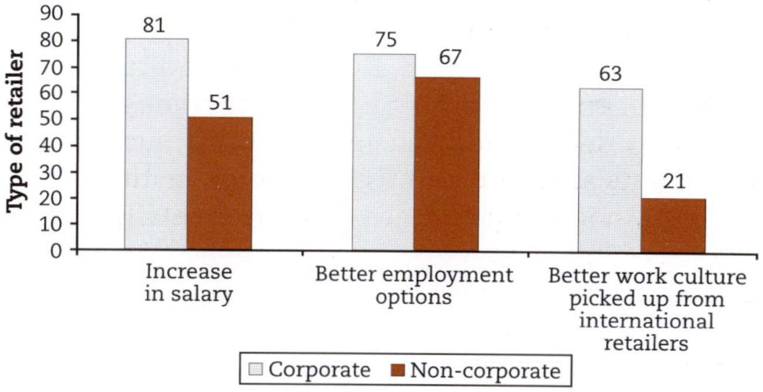

Both corporate and non-corporate retailers perceived that FDI in retail would have a positive impact on consumers (Figure 5.11). All the corporate retailers and more than 40 per cent of the non-corporate retailers thought that it would provide consumers with better product options. With the spread of corporate retail in various formats, consumers would have a greater choice of products at competitive prices. Both corporate and non-corporate retailers thought that the buying pattern of consumers would change. Most of the non-corporate retailers felt that there would be increased buying from corporate retailers. Some retailers felt that FDI in retail would lead to better promotion of brands.

Figure 5.11

Perceived Impact on Consumers

(in percentage)

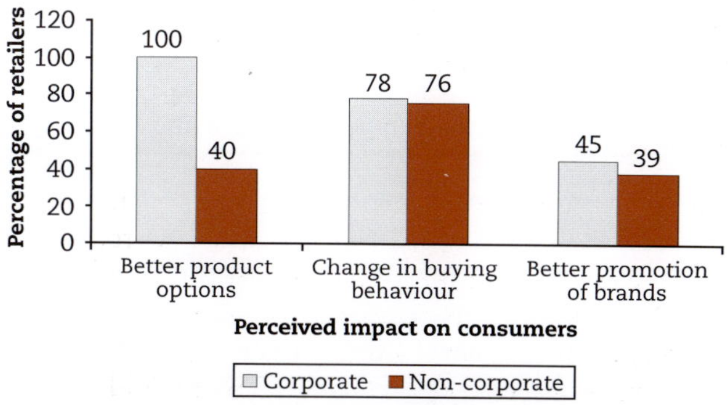

Both corporate and non-corporate retailers said that the entry of global players in the Indian food retail sector and the expansion of domestic retailers would have a direct, positive impact on farmers and manufacturers, if they are able to respond to the needs of the corporate retail sector. Specifically, farmers will have to make active efforts to improve and increase their agricultural output (quality and productivity) and establish an efficient infrastructure for grading, sorting, cleaning and storage. Smaller manufacturers, too, would have to scale up their operations and upgrade their technology. Corporate food retailers are likely to adopt direct sourcing models, in which they purchase farm produce in bulk, thereby reducing wastage and ensuring fair pay to the producers. Working with large corporate retailers would help technology percolation in the Indian manufacturing sector.

5.4.2 *Impact of the Food Safety and Standards Act (FSSA), 2006*

Indian food regulations comprise various food policies and food safety standards that have been enacted at different times and come under the ambit of different ministries in the Government of India (GoI) (see Chapters 3 and 7). The main law regulating food safety is the FSSA, 2006. However, the survey found that there is low awareness of this act among retailers; only 25 per cent of the non-corporate retailers and 44 per cent of the corporate retailers are aware of the food safety standards given in the FSSA, 2006 (Figure 5.12). At the same time, retailers are subject to checks by food inspectors; 75 per cent of the corporate retailers mentioned that food inspectors come for quality checks, while only 33 per cent of non-corporate retailers said that their stores had been visited by food inspectors. Corporate retailers reported no major problems caused by food inspectors' visits to their stores, but both corporate and non-corporate retailers reported the incidence of corruption and bribes.

Figure 5.12

FSSA, 2006: Awareness and Quality Checks

(in percentage)

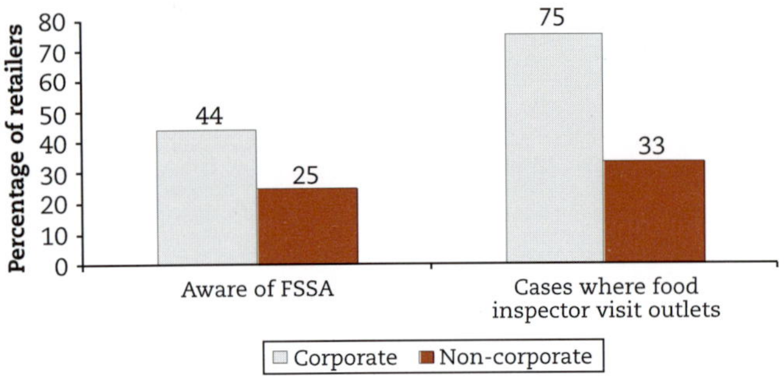

5.5 The New Retail Dynamics

The Indian retail sector is one of the fastest-growing sectors owing to a rising economy and large middle class. Due to its high growth potential, the sector has attracted a large number of Indian and foreign corporate players, thereby making India's retail structure more complex. Though this increased corporatisation is perceived as a threat by a large section of traditional or non-corporate retailers, the survey shows that with growing consumer demand in India, both corporate and non-corporate retail will co-exist.

The modernisation of retail is expected to increase competition for established manufacturers and brands, with retailers bringing in their own private labels. However, it has benefits for all the stakeholders including farmers, manufacturers and consumers.

- Corporate retail can help streamline the supply chain and enable direct sourcing from the farmers.
- It reduces delays, leakages and wastage of products in the supply chain. In a competitive scenario, these benefits can be passed on to consumers in terms of lower product prices.
- The presence of global retailers and their sourcing from India for the domestic and global market can create new opportunities for small and medium-scale manufacturers who can gain economies of scale and technology by their association with global retailers. Small and medium-scale manufacturers can also integrate into the global chains of the retailers by manufacturing their private labels.
- It provides better employment opportunities, with a better salary structure and skill upgrading for employees.
- It can lead to product and brand proliferation, which gives consumers more product options.

6

Consumers and their Demand Patterns

Although consumers are at the end of the supply chain for non-alcoholic beverages, they play a pivotal role in determining the sales of non-alcoholic beverages and thereby the revenue of the manufacturers and retailers. Their tastes and demand patterns determine the growth and development of the manufacture and retail of non-alcoholic beverages.

Before economic liberalisation in 1991, consumers in India had little choice in terms of products and brands. There were only a few commercial non-alcoholic beverages, and these were mainly fruit concentrates (such as the brand Kissan manufactured by Kissan Products Limited) and CSD brands manufactured by domestic companies (such as Campa Cola manufactured by Campa Beverages Private Limited and the brands Thums Up and Limca from Parle Products Limited). Post-liberalisation, a number of global manufacturers and Indian corporates ventured into the non-alcoholic beverage market. Several Indian corporates such as the Tata Group (with brands such as Himalayan in bottled water) and Dabur India Limited (with brands such as Real in juices) and corporate retailers and wholesalers such as Future Group (with the brand Tasty Treat) also ventured into the non-alcoholic beverage market. There have also been collaboration and joint ventures between manufacturers and retailers. For example, Bharti Enterprise has a joint venture with Del Monte Corporation for the juice brand Del Monte. The entry of both global and domestic corporate manufacturers and retailers improved the retail and distribution channels and increased consumer choice in terms of products and brands. All these factors affected the market dynamics and consumer behaviour in India (Paliwoda *et al.*, 2012).

Today, Indian consumers have a wide choice of products and brands; they are aware of products available in other countries through television, internet and other media, and are keen to experiment (Mukherjee *et al.*, 2012). With market conditions evolving and consumer behaviour changing, there has been an increase in brand competition across all product categories, leading to the entry and exit of brands. This has also led to changes in product pricing and promotion patterns. For instance, for products in the same category, companies have started similar product pricing, thus giving consumers a wide range of choice across different brands.

Post-liberalisation, the Indian economy has also become a more consumption-driven economy from the savings-oriented economy of the past. In 2007, India was the 12th largest consumer market, and consumer spending is expected to increase in the near future (Ernst & Young, 2012; McKinsey Global Institute, 2007). With growing consumerism, rising incomes, the proliferation of products and brands and the evolution of modern retail, the purchase and consumption of non-alcoholic beverages in India is likely to increase. This is expected to contribute to the growth of the Indian non-alcoholic beverage sector.

Given this background, this chapter analyses the purchase and consumption patterns of Indian consumers. It begins with an overview of Indian consumers and their consumption patterns for non-alcoholic beverages based on secondary data followed by a survey-based analysis of a select group of urban consumers. Since the focus of the report is on manufacturers of non-alcoholic beverages, this chapter is not intended to be a comprehensive consumer survey. The interviews with consumers are intended to understand their buying patterns.

6.1 Profile of Indian Consumers

Indian consumers are heterogeneous—their tastes and preferences for non-alcoholic beverages vary across different geographical regions, states, rural and urban areas and depend on factors such as their income, educational level and knowledge about brands. Their consumption patterns also differ from those of consumers in developed and developing countries, and they tend to spend a larger share of their earnings on food and grocery.[1]

A survey by the National Council of Applied Economic Research (NCAER) (2004-05) classifies Indian consumers into four categories: Deprived, Aspirers, Middle Class and Rich. Shukla (2010) used this classification to re-estimate the size of the Indian consumer class in the year 2009-10. From Table 6.1 it can be seen that between 2004-05 and 2009-10, the number of consumers in the Deprived category came down, whereas the size of the other three categories—Aspirers, Middle Class and Rich—has gone up. This result is corroborated by other studies (Meyer and Birdsall, 2012; Saxena, 2010), and the findings show that, in general, the number of people in the low-income group is decreasing, whereas it is rising in the middle and high-income groups.

1. The Boston Consulting Group (2012).

Table 6.1

Classification of Indian Consumers by Income, 2009-10

Consumer Class (annual household income at 2001-02 prices)	*Distribution of Households (in million)*		*Distribution of Households (in percentage)*		*Annual Growth (in percentage)*
	2001-02	2009-10	2001-02	2009-10	
Deprived (below INR 90,000)(below $2,000)	135.4	114.4	71.9	51.5	–2.1
Aspirers (INR 90,000-2,00,000) ($2,000-$4,000)	41.3	75.3	21.9	33.9	7.8
Middle Class (INR 2,00,000-10,00,000) ($4,000-$21,000)	10.7	28.4	5.7	12.8	12.9
Rich (over INR 10,00,000) (over $21,000)	0.8	3.8	0.4	1.7	21.4
Total	188.2	221.9	100.0	100.0	2.1

Note: These data are based on a pan-India survey of 63,016 households conducted by the NCAER (2004-05).

Source: Shukla (2010): 100, Table 5.2.

The pattern of consumption is also important. The breakdown of monthly consumer expenditure in the National Sample Survey shows that in 2009-10, within food consumption, beverages, refreshments and processed food accounted for about 13 per cent of the consumption in rural areas and about 18 per cent in urban areas (Table 6.2).

Table 6.2

Monthly per capita Expenditure by Item Group: All-India, 2009-10

(in INR)

Category	*Rural*	*Urban*
Beverages, refreshments and processed food*	78	159
Food total	600	881
Non-food		
Pan, tobacco and intoxicants	31	30
Fuel and light	85	138
Clothing and footwear	65	115
Education	38	161
Medical	57	99
Conveyance	36	112
Other consumer services	44	124
Miscellaneous goods, entertainment	53	113
Rent	5	115
Taxes and cesses	2	16
Durable goods	36	81
Non-food total	453	1104
All items	1,054	1,984

Note: * Includes purchased cooked meals.

Source: Compiled from the *National Sample Survey* 66th Round (July 2009 to June 2010), Report Number 541: 19.

In terms of quantity of consumption, the per capita consumption of packaged non-alcoholic beverages in India is much lower than in other countries, both developed and developing. For example, in packaged juices, India's per capita consumption is only 0.02 litres per annum compared to 42.2 litres in the USA and 1.5 litres in China.[2] In bottled water, India's per capita consumption is estimated to be 5 litres per annum, which is lower than the global average of 24 litres.[3] This is because there is a strong preference for homemade beverages and a large demand for a range of traditional beverages, such as coconut water and *nimbu pani* (lime drink). India also has a large unbranded beverage market, but the consumption of these beverages is not recorded. Hence, the data for packaged beverage consumption under-report the per capita beverage consumption.

In terms of pattern of consumption, there is a difference between rural and urban areas. Table 6.3 shows that overall consumption of non-alcoholic beverages was higher in urban areas than in rural areas in 2009-10.

The rural/urban distinction is one way to categorise consumers, but there is also tremendous variation in consumers' food habits and purchase behaviour across regions and even states [Mukherjee *et al.*, 2012; PricewaterhouseCoopers (PwC), 2011]. Consumption differs due to differences in income, level of education, health awareness, etc. In non-alcoholic beverages, this variation is compounded by

2. *http://www.himalayanbeverages.com/fruit-drink-industry.php* and *http://www.nationmaster.com/graph/foo_fru_jui_con-food-fruit-juice-consumption* (last accessed in July 2013).
3. *http://www.gits4u.com/water/water16.htm* (last accessed in July 2013).

Table 6.3

Monthly per capita Consumption of Non-alcoholic Beverages, Urban *versus* Rural, 2009-10

Category	*Urban*			*Rural*		
	Quantity (in 30 days)	*Value for 30 days (INR)*	*Number of households reporting consumption (per 1,000 households)*	*Quantity (in 30 days)*	*Value for 30 days (INR)*	*Number of households reporting consumption per 1,000 households)*
Tea cups (number)	6.389	20.93	492	3.767	9.89	386
Coffee cups (number)	0.184	0.84	22	0.044	0.14	7
Mineral water (litres)	0.348	1.09	21	0.019	0.06	4
Cold beverages: bottled/canned (litres)	0.092	3.27	77	0.02	0.66	25
Fruit juices and shakes (litres)	0.075	3.63	74	0.008	0.33	13
Other beverages: cocoa, chocolate, etc.	-	3.16	123	-	1.09	93

Source: Compiled from the *National Sample Survey* 66th Round (July 2009 to June 2010), Report Number 541: 47, 51.

the climatic diversity in the country, which explains the seasonality in demand for certain beverages in different regions of India. For instance, in Delhi, the demand for CSDs increases during the summer months, while in Tamil Nadu, the demand for CSDs remains the same through the year. Manufacturers and retailers in India have to take account of these variations in consumer tastes and preferences while reaching out to their consumers.

6.2 Survey: Methodology, Sampling and Objectives

A small survey of 220 consumers was conducted to understand their spending patterns, purchase behaviour, packaging preferences and perceptions of different regulations, such as FDI in multi-brand retail and Food Safety and Standards Act (FSSA), 2006. We also wanted to map their feedback with the survey findings for manufacturers and retailers. The consumers were spread across four cities—Delhi, Mumbai, Bangalore and Kolkata—with 55 respondents in each city. The interviews were based on a semi-structured questionnaire and lasted for more than an hour. Since the survey only covered four cities in India, it is not a representative sample of Indian consumers. Nevertheless, it indicates some key characteristics of consumers of non-alcoholic beverages.

The sample comprised 52 per cent males and the rest were female respondents. The majority of the respondents were between the ages of 35 and 50 and had a college degree, with an annual household income between INR 5,00,000 and 15,00,000. Thus, they were mainly in the socioeconomic classification (SEC) category A and B (see Annexure A-3.2).

Stratified random sampling was used to select the sample. Consumers were first classified by SEC categories and then a random sample of consumers from the four cities was selected under SEC categories A and B. The sample was selected to ensure that the surveyed consumers are informed about both global and domestic products and brands, acquainted with various forms of modern and traditional retail and aware of government policies on food and beverages such as food safety regulations and consumer protection acts. Further, a large percentage of homemakers were selected, since they drive the maximum in-home consumption of non-alcoholic beverages.

6.3 Findings of the Survey

The survey findings are discussed below. First, we cover expenditure on non-alcoholic beverages to identify current patterns in spending. The section on preferences analyses how often and from where consumers buy non-alcoholic beverages and the type of packaging they prefer; this helps retailers and manufacturers understand trends in consumer behaviour that affect the non-alcoholic beverage sector. The final section locates this sector in a wider socioeconomic context; it records consumer's views on government policies, such as allowing 51 per cent FDI in multi-brand retail and consumer awareness campaigns, in order to find out whether these play a role in their buying behaviour.[4]

6.3.1 Expenditure

Figure 6.1 shows how each income group allocates its expenditure in a month. The average of our sample shows that food constitutes the maximum share (around 30%) of the total monthly expenditure. Other studies show similar results (The Boston Consulting Group, 2012). One reason is that our sample largely concentrates on the middle-class group.

Figure 6.1

Allocation of Expenditure by Level of Household Income

(in percentage)

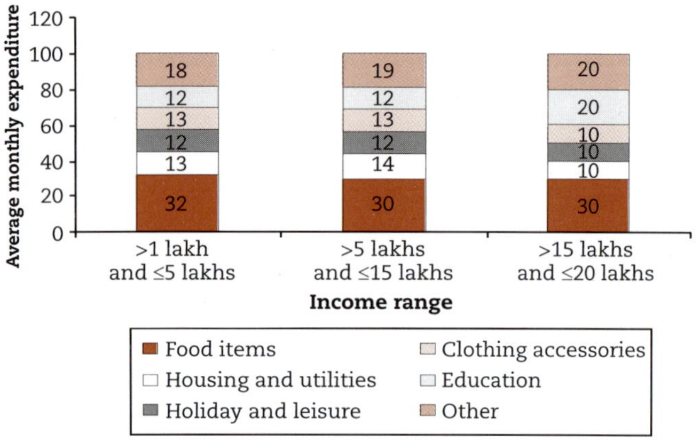

Within food, the expenditure on non-alcoholic beverages is in the range of 10-12 per cent for the consumers surveyed. In terms of average expenditure on product categories per household, the dominant categories are CSDs, fruit-based juices and milk/yoghurt-based beverages, with CSDs having the highest share (Figure 6.2). Consumers are gradually experimenting with new non-alcoholic beverages, such as energy drinks and organic drinks. They explained that most of them have in-house water-purifier facilities, and so they buy bottled water for on-the-go consumption. CSDs and fruit-based drinks are preferred, both for in-house and on-the-go consumption.

4. Although the survey included questions on brand preferences and brand knowledge, these data are not presented in this report.

6.3.2 Purchase and Consumption Behaviour

Information about consumers' purchase and consumption behaviour can help manufacturers and retailers customise their product offerings.

Frequency of Purchase. The majority of households buys non-alcoholic beverages once a week, but some households buy them every day. This shows that these non-alcoholic beverages have become part of consumer's regular purchase items (Figure 6.3).

Most respondents said that they have not yet bought product categories such as sports drinks, energy drinks, ready-to-drink (RTD) coffee and tea-based drinks. This indicates that these categories have not yet picked up, even in metro cities. This presents an opportunity for these categories to grow, since there is a sufficiently large untapped market for them.

Location of Purchase. Consumers were asked where they bought their non-alcoholic beverages. The maximum purchases for all categories are done at traditional or *kirana* stores (Table 6.4), but some purchases are done at other locations, such as hypermarkets and supermarkets. The table also shows whether consumers buy branded or unbranded beverages at these locations. Consumers generally buy branded products from both traditional stores and modern retail stores (supermarkets or hypermarkets). However non-branded products are generally purchased at traditional stores, restaurants and beverage chains, since modern retail formats do not store these products. This is particularly true of fruit and vegetable juices, tea/coffee-based drinks, and milk/yoghurt-based drinks.

An analysis of purchase locations by income category found that consumers in the higher income brackets are more likely to buy non-alcoholic beverages from hypermarkets and supermarkets. This is unlike other countries where low-cost multi-brand retail caters to middle and low-income consumers. There are several possible reasons why consumers continue to buy from traditional retail outlets. First, modern retail has not penetrated all consumer groups in India, so consumers still buy food and beverages largely through traditional outlets. Second, traditional retail outlets are closer to the home and require less travel. Third, in India, given the lack of large refrigeration and storage spaces in the home, it is easier to buy and store smaller packs. Nevertheless, in recent years, several value retailers have emerged in the corporate retail segment, who offers lucrative deals on non-alcoholic beverages. Our survey showed

Figure 6.2

Average Monthly Expenditure on Non-alcoholic Beverages

(in INR)

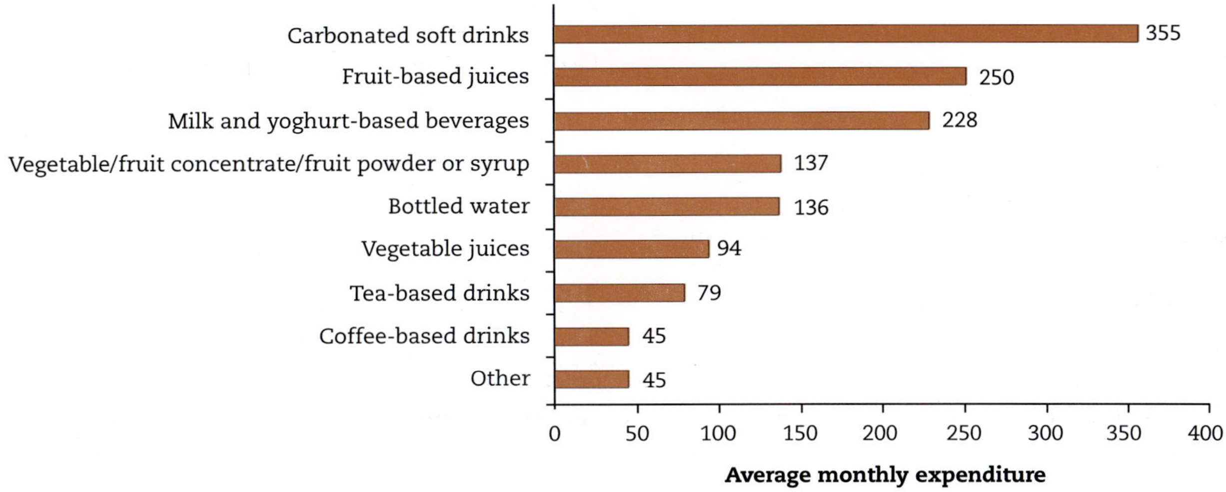

Note: 'Other' includes energy drinks, ayurvedic/organic drinks and sports drinks.

Figure 6.3

Frequency of Household Purchase by Product Category

(in percentage)

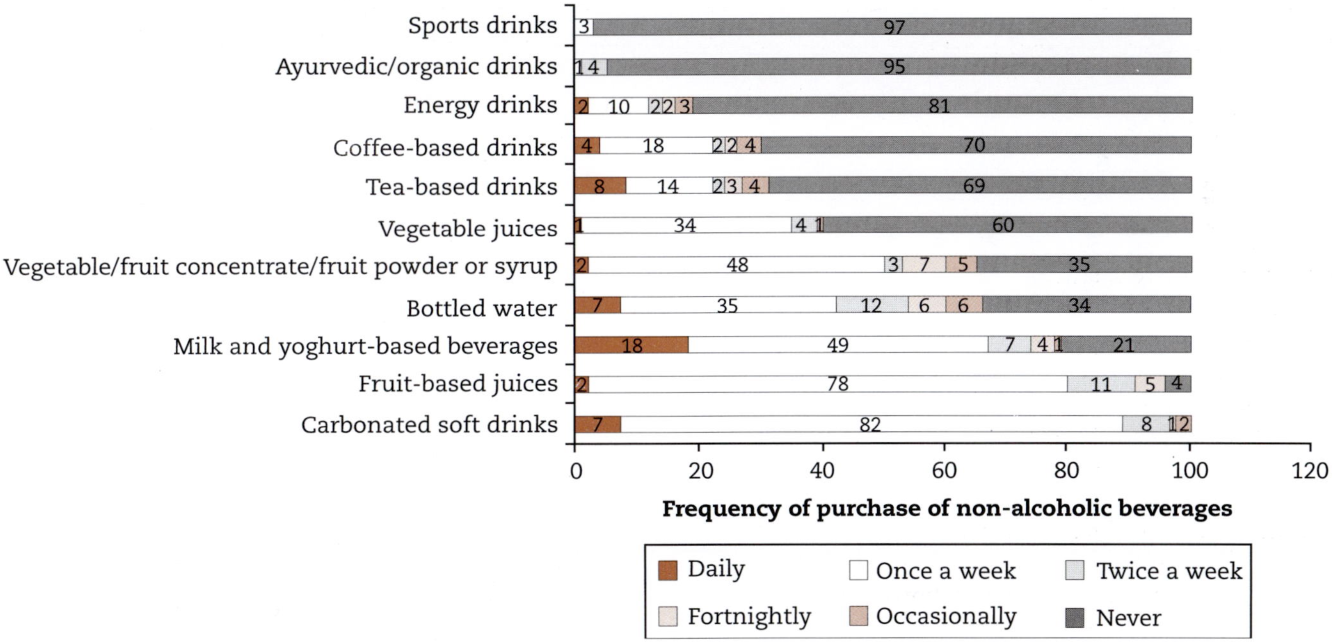

significant interest among Indian consumers in shopping at these retail outlets, primarily to avail of the discounts.

Location of consumption. This identifies whether consumers drink the beverages at home or outside the home. Consumption location varies for different categories of beverages. In the CSD category, location is split between the home and outside (restaurants, colleges, offices, 'on-the-go,' etc.). Consumption outside the home is greater in categories such as packaged drinking water, sports drinks and coffee-based drinks, since they tend to be drunk 'on-the-go';

Table 6.4

Types of Stores where Beverages are Bought

(in percentage)

Product Category	*Traditional Stores/ Kirana Stores*		*Hypermarket/ Supermarket*		*Specialty/Department Stores*		*Other**	
	Branded	*Non-branded*	*Branded*	*Non-branded*	*Branded*	*Non-branded*	*Branded*	*Non-branded*
Carbonated soft drinks	44	0	32	0	9	0	14	0
Vegetable juices	35	0	56	0	9	0	2	1
Fruit-based juices	40	2	37	0	9	0	13	5
Milk/yoghurt-based beverages	59	5	25	0	7	0	3	1
Energy drinks	63	0	18	0	9	0	10	0
Bottled water	57	0	12	0	7	0	23	0
Tea-based drinks	32	7	16	0	9	0	28	8
Coffee-based drinks	33	3	9	0	10	0	38	7

Note: This is a multiple-choice question.
* Restaurants and beverage chains.

home consumption is higher in categories such as fruit juices, fruit concentrates and vegetable juices (Figure 6.4).

Figure 6.4

Where Beverages are Consumed?

(in percentage)

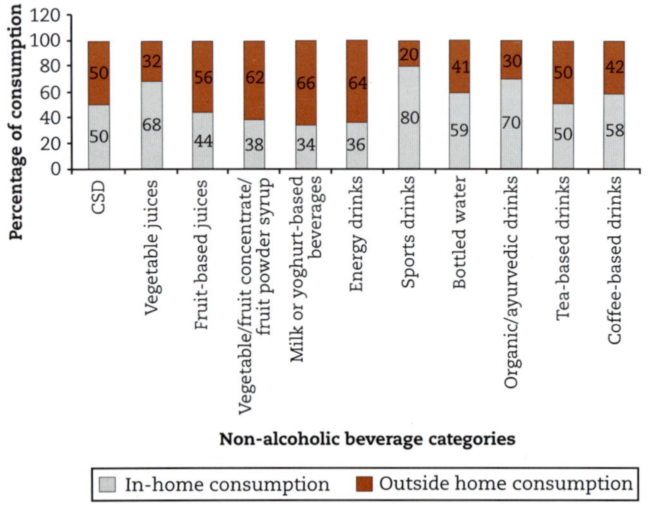

Attitude to Homemade Beverages. When consumers were asked about homemade beverages, it was seen that they prefer homemade beverages to packaged non-alcoholic beverages (Figure 6.5a), mainly because they perceive homemade beverages as more hygienic (Figure 6.5b).

Figure 6.5a

Prefer Homemade Beverages

(in percentage)

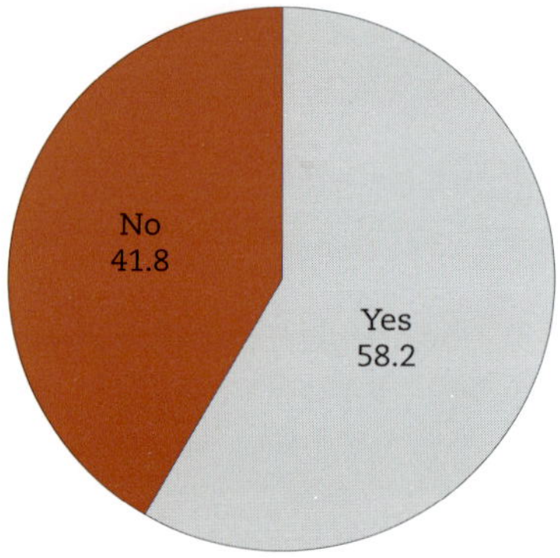

Figure 6.5b

Reasons for Preference

(in percentage)

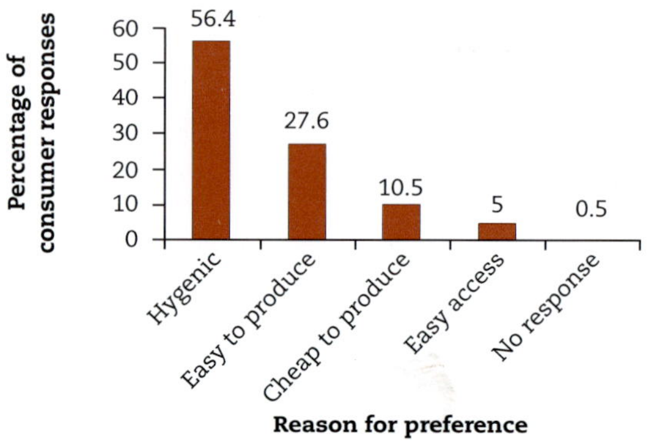

Packaging Preferences. Consumers were asked to rank seven types of packaging, with 1 being the most preferred (Figure 6.6). Around 73 per cent of the respondents ranked Tetra Paks as their preferred packaging option, followed by PET bottles (53%).

Figure 6.6

Packaging Preferences of Customers

(in percentage)

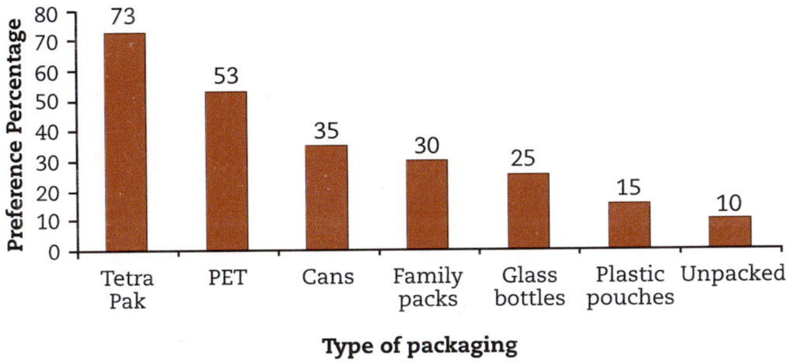

Note: This is a multiple-choice question

This pattern resembles the packing preferences of the retailers in the survey. Both the consumers and the retailers in the survey clearly preferred Tetra Pak, because it is convenient, prevents damage and retains the freshness of the beverages. In contrast, manufacturers in the survey preferred PET bottles. The difference could be due to the fact that retailers and consumers were surveyed in the metro cities, whereas the manufacturing surveys were held in metros as well as smaller cities and towns.

6.3.3 Perceptions

Modern Retail *vis-à-vis* Traditional Retail

To understand the perceptions of corporate retail among urban consumers in India, consumers were asked to rate modern retail outlets *vis-à-vis* traditional outlets in their cities on parameters such as retail infrastructure, time taken to clear bills and location, on a scale of 1-5 (1 is the highest rank). Based on the mean scores for each parameter, the ranks are given in Figure 6.7. There is little difference between the results across the four cities. However, the sample size is too small to draw any conclusion.

On the whole, modern retail outlets across all four cities score lower on the ability to bargain and ease in getting things exchanged/returned. Interestingly, they also scored low on the time taken to clear bills. This highlights the key strengths of traditional retail stores: they allow bargaining and offer exchange/return facilities, because they build interpersonal

Figure 6.7

Ranking of Modern Retail Outlets *versus* Traditional Outlets

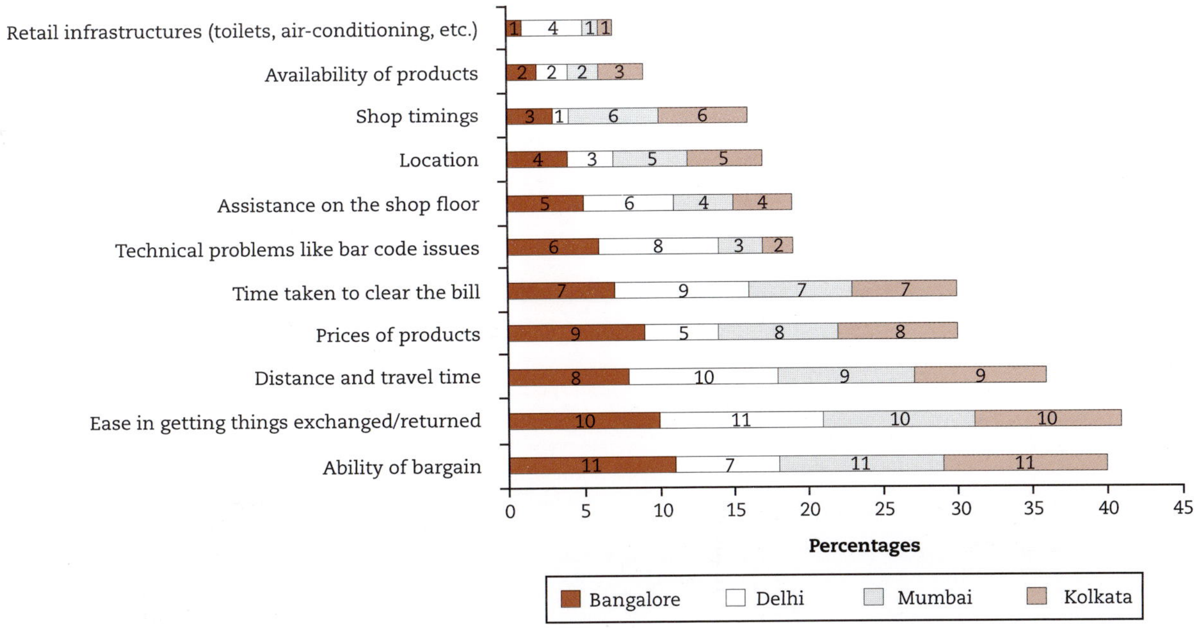

Note: 1=highest, 11=lowest.

relationships over time with customers in their neighbourhood. They also take less time for billing. These advantages of traditional retail help them compete with modern retail in India. However, in terms of infrastructure and availability of products, modern retail outlets across all the cities are rated higher. These findings confirm that since both corporate and non-corporate retailers offer different benefits to consumers, they can co-exist in India.

FDI in Multi-brand Retail

Consumers were asked about their views on the policy of allowing 51 per cent FDI in multi-brand retail. Most of the consumers perceived that the policy would benefit them. Almost 95 per cent of the consumers said that it would not only provide a wider choice of products and brands, but also get better deals and discounts on the products and brands (Figure 6.8). However, they also found the policy cumbersome and pointed out that it might not result in inflow of FDI or help streamline the agro supply chain.

Figure 6.8

Consumer Perceptions of FDI in Multi-brand Retail

(in percentage)

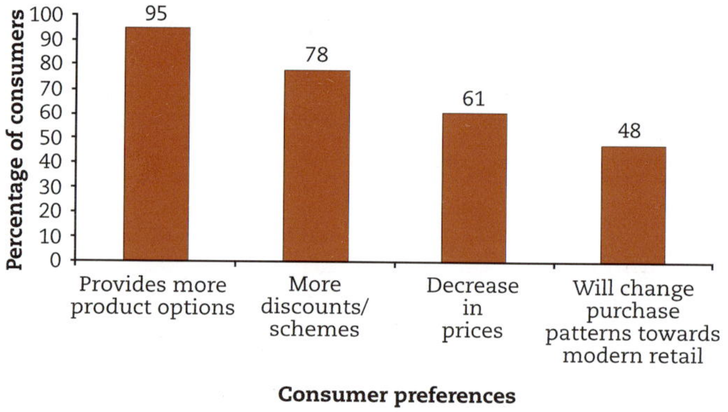

One important point that emerged is that 48 per cent of the total respondents mentioned that with the advent of modern retail, their purchase behaviour has changed in the direction of modern retail. They also pointed out that with the development of shopping malls, purchases of brands, frequency of purchase, amount of money spent on non-alcoholic beverages, etc., have increased (Figure 6.9).

Figure 6.9

Changes in Purchase Patterns due to Increased Number of Malls

(in percentage)

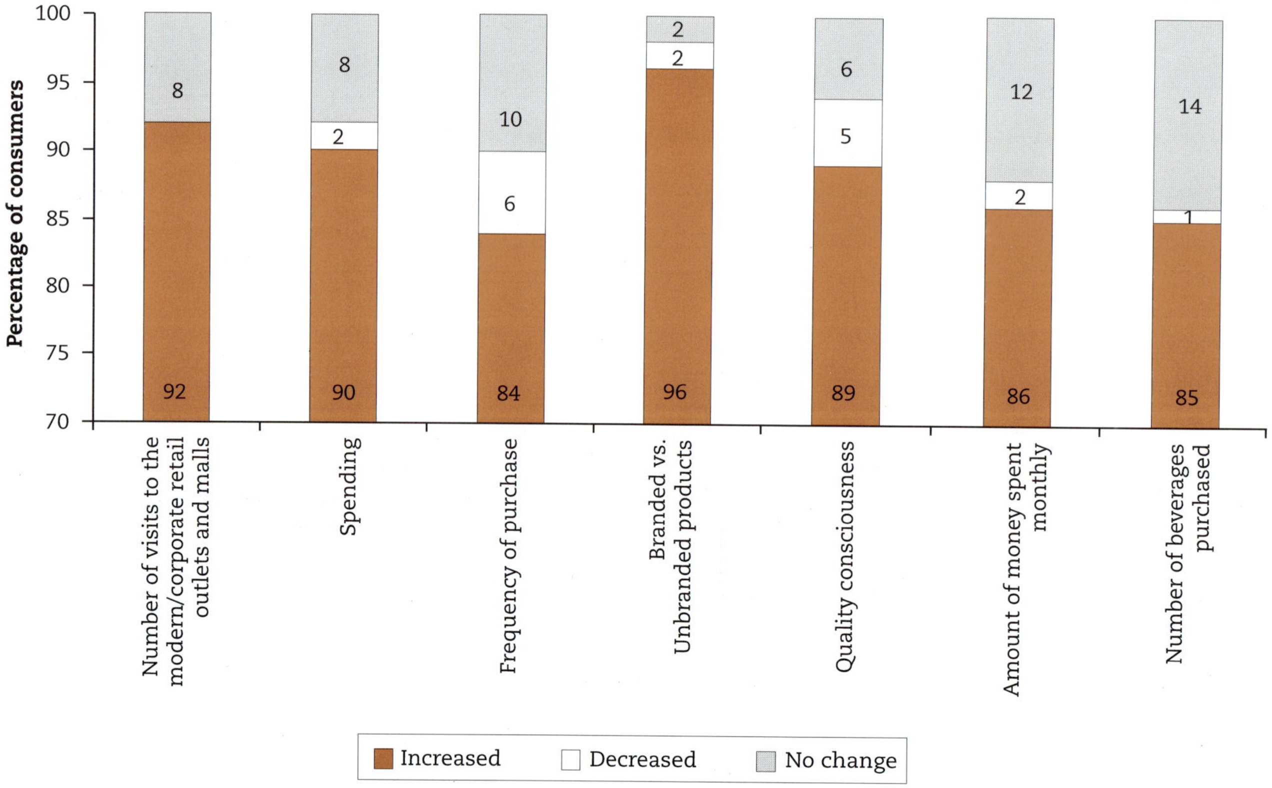

All these factors are likely to have a positive impact on the non-alcoholic beverage industry, since the growth in the number of malls and modern retail stores has enhanced their penetration as well as reach. Quality consciousness has also increased, perhaps because consumers can now see a variety of products on the shelves and make purchase decisions.

Consumer Awareness

Consumers were asked questions to gauge their knowledge of consumer protection acts. This is important for the non-alcoholic beverage sector, because there are several spurious products in this sector that can lead to health hazards. The survey indicated that even after 26 years of the Consumer Protection Act in India and several recent campaigns in the media such as 'Jago Grahak Jago,' only around 61 per cent of consumers in the sample were aware of these regulations and campaigns (Figure 6.10a). Unless consumers are aware and take a conscious decision not to buy spurious products, such products will continue to co-exist. Despite the limited number of campaigns on spurious products, about 60 per cent of the consumers felt that the recent consumer awareness campaigns have strongly increased their consumer awareness (Figure 6.10b). In general, consumer forums in India are weak and Indian consumers are less aware of their rights than global consumers.

Items Checked Before Buying a Beverage

Due to lack of awareness, consumers often do not check the expiry date, etc., when they buy non-alcoholic beverages. To check the level of consumer awareness, consumers were probed on the factors they consider before buying a beverage. It was found that most consumers are cautious about price and therefore they checked the maximum retail price (MRP) of the product in most cases (Figure 6.11). With increasing health awareness, consumers also check the ingredients and the date of manufacture.

Figure 6.11

Items Checked Before Buying a Non-alcoholic Beverage

(in percentage)

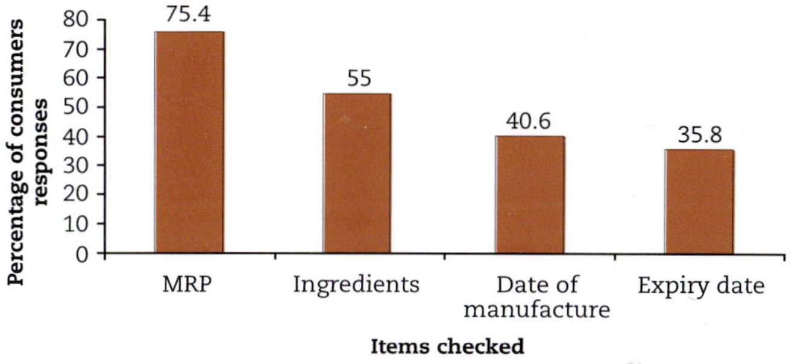

Note: This is a multiple-choice question.

Figure 6.10a

Aware of Consumer Awareness Campaigns

(in percentage)

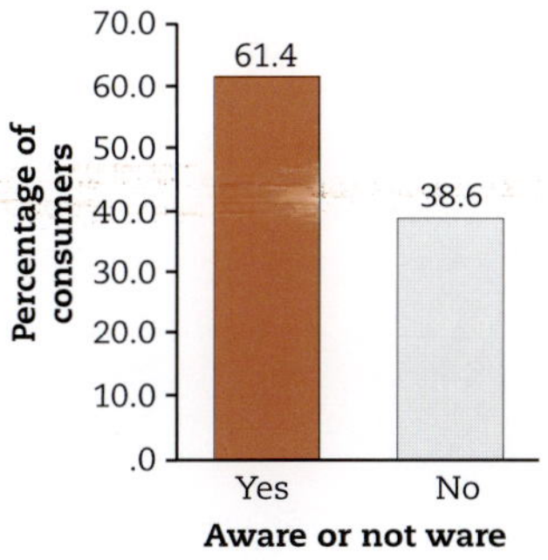

Figure 6.10b

Effectiveness of the Campaigns

(in percentage)

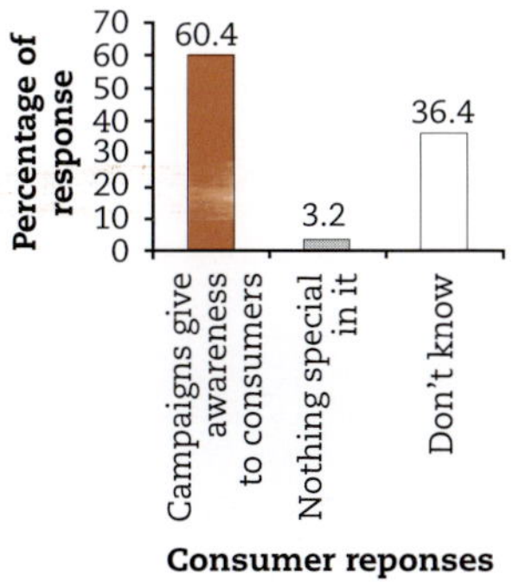

6.4 Conclusion

Overall, the analysis of the consumer data and the survey show that India is a large and unsaturated consumer market. With the growing economy, increasing incomes, evolving retail structure, wider choice and greater awareness about global and domestic brands, the size of the Indian consumer class is growing. The consumption and spending patterns of Indian consumers vary widely, both in comparison with their global counterparts as well as within India. Although they spend a significant amount of their earnings on food and grocery, owing to their preference for homemade beverages, their per capita consumption of non-alcoholic beverages remains lower than in other countries.

The chapter also highlights that as more multinationals and domestic companies enter the Indian manufacturing and retail market and as the income of consumers and level of consciousness increase, the consumption of non-alcoholic beverages is likely to increase. However, both traditional and packaged beverages will co-exist in the Indian market. There is likely to be a proliferation of products and brands. Indian consumers are still weighing the costs and benefits of different types of beverages, including branded and non-branded, and different retail formats, namely, modern retail *vis-à-vis* traditional retail. Although consumers support the expansion of modern retail, they still buy beverages largely from traditional retailers, due to their ability to bargain. Therefore, the price of a product still plays an important role in determining their purchase decisions.

The survey also shows that Indian consumers are still not fully aware about food safety, their consumer rights and consumer protection regulations.

Although they spend a significant amount of their earnings on food and grocery, owing to their preference for homemade beverages, their per capita consumption of non-alcoholic beverages remains lower than in other countries. Indian consumers are still weighing the costs and benefits of different types of beverages, including branded and non-branded, and different retail formats, namely, modern retail *vis-à-vis* traditional retail.

7

Barriers and the Way Forward

7.1 Introduction

This chapter examines the barriers faced by the non-alcoholic beverage sector in India and suggests the way forward. The sector faces some specific issues such as high and discriminatory taxes across different product categories, lack of availability of surface water, stringent environment regulations related to water that vary across states, spurious products and lack of implementation of regulations against spurious products. At the same time, since it is a part of the food processing industry, which is subsumed under the manufacturing sector, it faces the barriers affecting food processing in particular and manufacturing sector in general (see Figure 7.1). Given this structure, addressing the sector-specific and general barriers would not only help develop the non-alcoholic beverage sector, but also help the food processing sector in particular and the Indian manufacturing sector in general to grow and become globally competitive.

Figure 7.1

Selected Barriers Faced by the Non-alcoholic Beverage Sector

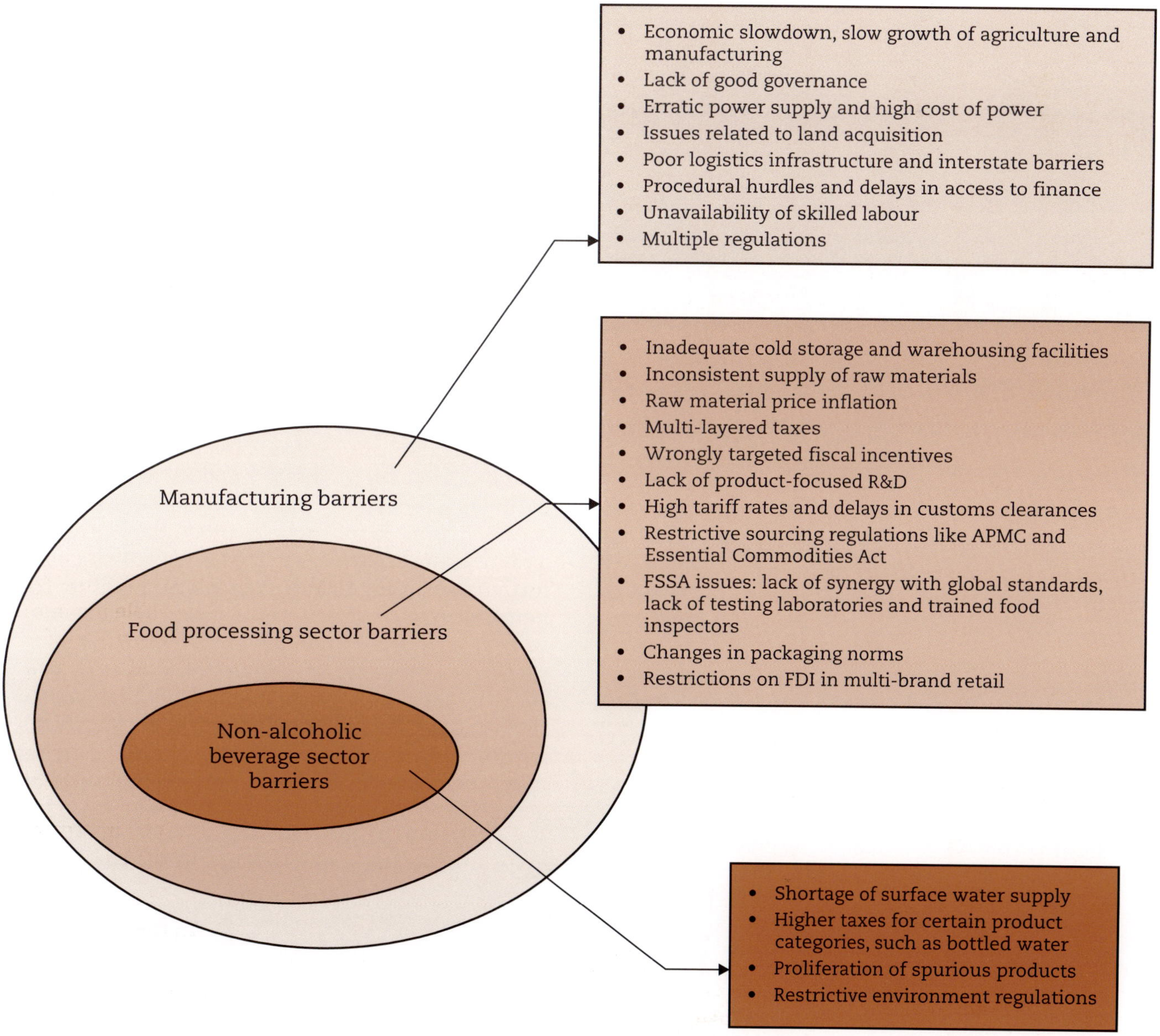

7.2 Barriers

The barriers discussed below were identified through the primary survey. Stakeholders were asked detailed questions about the barriers that they faced in the non-alcoholic beverage sector in India, and asked to rank the barriers and elaborate the impact of these barriers on their operations. An analysis revealed that some barriers are common across all stakeholders; these are mainly macroeconomic issues such as India's recent economic slowdown. Other barriers were specific to certain stakeholders, but interestingly, barriers for one stakeholder could be opportunities for another. For instance, restrictions on imports of fruits and vegetables may hamper the growth of the processed food industry due to scarcity in quality raw material, but they can benefit Indian farmers.

The next three sub-sections first discuss the general macroeconomic issues tabulate the rankings given to the barriers and finally examine each of the nine main barriers identified by the stakeholders.

7.2.1 General Macroeconomic Issues

Stakeholders identified several barriers due to poor macroeconomic performance, such as the recent economic slowdown, low investment, persistent inflation and a negative trade balance. These perceptions are supported by macroeconomic data and existing research.

India's growth rate has slowed in the past few years, and international organisations such as the International Monetary Fund (IMF) have projected a further slowdown. In 2010, India's GDP grew at 10.1 per cent, but the growth rate fell to 4.5 per cent in 2012 and is likely to be lower than that of developing Asia in 2014 (Table 7.1).

Table 7.1

GDP Growth Rates and Projections for India and Other Regions

Country/Region	2010	2011	2012	2013*	2014*
Emerging and developing markets	7.4	6.3	5.1	5.5	5.9
Developing Asia	9.5	8.0	6.6	7.1	7.5
China	10.4	9.3	7.8	8.2	8.5
India	10.1	7.9	4.5	5.9	6.4

Note: * Projected figures.

Source: Compiled from IMF (2013), *http://www.imf.org/external/pubs/ft/weo/2013/update/01/pdf/0113.pdf* (last accessed in May 2013).

Even when India's GDP was growing at a higher rate, the growth was not inclusive (Ganguly, 2011). The share of agriculture in India's GDP fell substantially from 33.2 per cent in 1993-94 to 16.9 per cent in 2009-10. However, the share of agriculture in GDP has not been commensurate with its share in employment. Agriculture still employs more than half of India's total population, although its share in India's employment declined from 62.8 per cent in 1993-94 to 53.2 per cent in 2009-10. At the same time, the services sector and manufacturing have not been able to create significant employment opportunities. Between 1993-94 and 2009-10, the share of the services sector in employment increased from 22 per cent to only 25.3 per cent, although its share in GDP increased from 44.8 per cent to 57.3 per cent (Mukherjee, 2013). This phenomenon has led to a situation of jobless growth (Kochhar *et al.*, 2006; Mehrotra *et al.*, 2013), with agriculture suffering from huge disguised unemployment and leading to low labour productivity.

The agricultural value chain in India is highly fragmented and is characterised by small land holdings, lack of irrigation facilities and lack of transport and storage infrastructure (Ganguly, 2011), leading to wastage. In 2009, only 35.1 per cent of India's total agricultural land was irrigated.[1] In addition, there are delays in irrigation projects. Approximately 77 major and 86 minor irrigation projects have been delayed, increasing the total cost of the projects by 231 per cent.[2]

Another cause for concern is the mismatch in demand and supply. The demand for agricultural products (processed or otherwise) has increased in India owing to the growing urban population and rising income levels, and it is likely to increase further. According to McKinsey Global Institute (2007), India's average real household disposable income will experience a compound annual growth rate (CAGR) of 5.6 per cent between 2005 and 2025. The government's rural employment generation schemes, such as the National Rural Employment Guarantee Act (NREGA), will also contribute towards an increase in rural income. All this will create significantly high demand for food among Indian consumers. On the supply side, India does not perform well in terms of agricultural yield or productivity. In 2010-11, both

1. *http://data.worldbank.org/indicator/AG.LND.IRIG.AG.ZS* (last accessed in May 2013).
2. *http://articles.timesofindia.indiatimes.com/2012-10-24/india/34707606_1_irrigation-projects-minor-irrigation-major-irrigation* (last accessed in May 2013).

fruit and vegetable productivity in India (11.7 and 17.3 tonnes per ha, respectively) was half that of the USA (22.2 and 31.4 tonnes per ha, respectively).[3] The non-performance of the manufacturing sector also affects supply. There has been a decline in the growth rate of India's manufacturing, from 10.1 per cent in 2005-06 to 1.9 per cent in 2012-13. This is despite the government coming up with various policies such as the National Manufacturing Policy, 2011, and the Special Economic Zone (SEZ) Act, 2005.

There is a low level of public investment in agro-supply chain infrastructure. In recent years, India has been suffering from a high fiscal deficit, which makes it difficult for the government to invest in infrastructure. Despite several government schemes and initiatives to increase private investments, there has not been any significant increase in the share of private investment in GDP, especially in rural infrastructure and the agro-processing sector, which are crucial for a stable agricultural supply chain (Table 7.2).

Table 7.2

Investment in Infrastructure as a Percentage of GDP

Type	2007-08	2008-09	2009-10	2010-11	2011-12
Public investment	4.2	4.7	4.9	5.0	5.1
Private investment	2.2	2.4	2.6	2.9	3.3
Total investment	6.4	7.1	7.5	7.9	8.3

Source: Compiled from *http://rbi.org.in/scripts/BS_SpeechesView.aspx?Id=655* (last accessed in May 2013).

According to the A.T. Kearney FDI Confidence Index, in 2012, India ranked as the second most attractive destination for FDI (after China) among 25 economies. However, the Inward FDI Performance Index of the United Nations Conference on Trade and Development (UNCTAD)[4] in 2010 ranked India at 97 among 141 countries, while Brazil was ranked at 69, China at 86 and Mexico at 84.[5] Thus, although India has the potential, it has not been successful in attracting FDI because of factors such as the difficult regulatory framework and the absence of long-term policies, non-implementation of policies, bureaucratic delays, centre-state divergence on investment-related policies, high levels of corruption and bribery and inflexible labour laws.[6] The World Bank's 'Ease of Doing Business Index'[7] has ranked India below other emerging markets such as China (Table 7.3). Due to these factors, even Indian companies are investing in other emerging countries such as China and Sri Lanka rather than in India in the food and beverage sector.

Table 7.3

Ease of Doing Business Index for Select Countries

Country	*Rank (2011)*	*Rank (2012)*
India	132	132
China	91	91
Brazil	128	130
Mexico	53	48
Thailand	17	18

Source: Compiled from World Bank, 'Ease of Doing Business Index,' *http://data.worldbank.org/indicator/IC.BUS.EASE.XQ* (last accessed in May 2013).

In terms of inflation, India's average inflation rate between 2000 and 2007 was 5.2 per cent, but between 2008 and 2012, it rose to 7.4 per cent. Average food inflation, which was only 3.8 per cent between 2007 and 2008, increased to an average yearly inflation of 10.1 per cent between 2011 and 2012 (Gulati and Saini, 2013). Therefore, consumers are facing high food prices and have to reduce their discretionary consumption, while for manufacturers, the cost of raw materials is rising, thereby squeezing their margins.

On the trade front, India's trade deficit in the non-alcoholic beverage sector increased from $3.3 million in 2001 to $60.0 million in 2011. Therefore, there is a pressure on the government to reduce the trade deficit by controlling imports and increasing exports. This can adversely impact access to raw materials for manufacturers.

7.2.2 The Survey

Manufacturers and retailers (both corporate and non-corporate) ranked several barriers on a 5-point scale, where the most critical barrier was given a rank of 5 and the least critical was 1. Table 7.4 shows the rank given to each barrier by type of stakeholder.

3. *http://mospi.nic.in/Mospi_New/upload/SYB2013/CH-9-HORTICULTURE/horticulture.pdf* (last accessed in May 2013).
4. UNCTAD's Inward FDI Performance Index is used to compare the relative performance of countries in attracting FDI inflows.
5. *http://unctad.org/Sections/dite_dir/docs/WIR11_web%20tab%2028.pdf* (last accessed in May 2013).
6. Ministry of Finance (2006).
7. 'Ease of Doing Business' ranks economies from 1 to 185, with the first place being the best.

Table 7.4

Barriers Ranked by Stakeholders in the Non-alcoholic Beverage Sector

Type of barrier	*Barrier*	*Corporate manufacturer*	*Non-corporate manufacturer*	*Corporate retailer*	*Non-corporate retailer*
Infrastructure	Inadequate surface water	5	4	1	1
	Power	5	5	5	5
	Land availability/real estate	5	4	5	3
	Transportation	4	4	4	3
	Cold chain infrastructure	4	5	4	2
	Warehousing	4	5	4	2
	Finance[8]	3	4	3	4
Raw materials	Inconsistency in supply/shortage of critical raw materials	5	5	3	1
	Inconsistent quality of raw materials	5	4	3	1
	Raw material price inflation	4	5	4	2
	Cost fluctuation	5	5	4	2
Labour	Availability of skilled workforce	4	3	4	1
	Labour regulations	4	2	4	1
Fiscal (taxes and incentives)	National taxes	5	4	4	2
	State taxes	5	4	5	3
	Delay in implementation of GST	5	5	5	4
	Lack of lucrative tax holidays and other schemes	3	4	1	1
Spurious and contaminated products	Proliferation of spurious and contaminated products	5	3	4	2
R&D, patents and copyright	Lack of R&D	4	3	3	NA
	Patent application filing	5	3	3	NA
Trade	High tariffs	5	3	5	2
	Hassles in custom clearances (bureaucratic issues, delays, etc.)	4	3	4	NA
Consumers	Low per capita consumption of non-alcoholic beverages	4	3	4	4
	Fluctuating demand	4	4	3	4
	Price sensitivity of the consumer	4	3	5	4
	Lack of information about consumer preferences	3	2	2	2
Regulations	Multiple regulations	5	4	5	5
	Sourcing regulations	4	4	4	2
	FSSA, 2006	3	4	4	5
	Restrictions on FDI in multi-brand retail	3	4	5	2
	Packaging regulations	4	3	3	2
	Environmental regulations	5	3	3	1

Note: 1. NA (not applicable) denotes that this particular sector is not directly engaged in this process and therefore is not impacted by the related issues.
2. Ranking is on a scale of 1-5; 5 is the most critical barrier and 1 the least critical.

Source: Compiled from the survey.

8. Includes access to bank loans/high interest rates/alternative financial options, etc. High interest rates on loans are a problem for both the corporate and non-corporate sectors. Access to finance is a problem faced by the non-corporate sector.

Below, we take up each of the nine main barriers, focusing on the impact on non-alcoholic beverage manufacturers.

7.2.3 Infrastructure Barriers

The infrastructure barriers are discussed below in terms of their importance for the non-alcoholic beverage sector.

- *Inadequate Water*. This is a key issue for non-alcoholic beverage manufacturers, since water plays a major role in their manufacturing processes. Due to the deficient supply of surface water, the industry is compelled to depend on ground water. According to the corporate manufacturers, this sector is generally held responsible for high ground water usage. However, respondents argued that of the total ground water consumed in the country, almost 80-85 per cent is used by the agricultural sector and only 6 per cent is used by the industry, of which the beverage industry's consumption is only 0.04 per cent. There is also lack of clear water usage policies in most Indian states, which enables local players to resort to unscrupulous practices by drawing agricultural water and selling it commercially. Finally, the respondents noted that in the absence of a stringent water harvest policy in India, continuous withdrawal of water for both commercial and personal use would soon affect ground water levels and the availability of surface water, impacting both agriculture and industrial growth.

- *Power*. Erratic power supply and voltage fluctuations (quality of the supply) affect all stakeholders. Respondents pointed out that even if rural areas get free power, the power cuts could be for as long as six hours. This restricts the use of certain machines and technologies and makes it difficult to have uniform temperature control in cold storages. Farmers have to visit the storage facilities often to personally inspect whether their produce is still of good quality. Approximately 36 per cent of the food and beverage firms suffer a loss of 11-20 per cent in their production due to intermittent power supply.[9]

  The inadequate power supply results in increasing dependence on power back-ups, such as diesel generators. Since India is a net importer of diesel and there is a steady rise in the price of diesel, the use of power back-ups increases operating costs for processed food companies. Almost 36 per cent of food and beverage companies experience a cost escalation of 21-30 per cent[10] due to the use of power back-ups and the large corporate manufacturers said that their cost of production has increased by 40 to 50 per cent. In the case of cold storage facilities, the increase in operational costs is passed on to users of the facility, such as farmers. The continuous use of diesel generators also affects the carbon footprint of the country. In the survey, several international companies that import final products from other countries for the Indian market voiced their unwillingness to set up manufacturing bases here due to these power problems.

- *Land*. In the 11th Five Year Plan the Indian government took initiatives to encourage the food processing sector such as setting up mega food parks, integrated cold chains, etc. However, these have not been successful primarily due to difficulties in getting land and the high level of land prices (see Planning Commission, 2012).

  Since land is a limited resource, there is always competition between the various purposes of use. In India, the amount of land required for urbanisation and industrialisation is huge; survey respondents estimated that by 2020, India would need 6.3 million ha of land for these purposes.[11] However, since most of the land available, especially in the south and east of India, is agricultural land, there is always a conflict between land use for industrial purposes and agricultural purposes. Moreover, landholdings in India are fragmented and there are no proper records of their availability, since titles to land are not clear and transparent. Due to these factors, purchasing land involves lengthy and difficult negotiations.

9. FICCI and BRIEF (2012).

10. FICCI and BRIEF (2012).
11. Inputs from the survey.

Several respondents pointed out that large projects have been stalled, because companies do not know what compensation package needs to be paid to the existing landowners. Often, the compensation packages are high by global standards. Globally, compensations for land constitute only 5 per cent of the total project cost, but in India it can be as high as 40 per cent, which makes the business less viable. Although the Indian government has recently passed the Land Acquisition Bill in order to facilitate the process of land acquisition, respondents felt that this would increase the compensation amount, since it covers all stakeholders dependent on the land and not the owners alone. Since land is a state subject, companies try to locate in states such as Gujarat where land acquisition is easier, but these companies may not be able to source all their raw materials from the state. They would have to transport it from other states, which increases their operating costs. Hence, the high cost of acquiring land in India discourages large-scale investments, especially in manufacturing.

- *Transportation*. The beverage industry primarily uses two modes of transportation—railways and roads—to move domestic goods. However, Indian Railways suffers from capacity constraints. Between 2003-04 and 2011-12, Indian Railways added around 6,000 km to the length of the railway tracks and the total route length increased from 63,221 km to only 64,600 km,[12] but this is not enough. Freight tariffs in the railways are also high compared with other countries (Mukherjee *et al.*, 2012). Moreover, due to its monopolistic nature and lack of regulatory oversight, Indian Railways lacks reliability and is deficient in terms of quality of operations, speed and customer orientation. The slow process of development of freight facilities, such as dedicated freight corridors (DFCs), has adversely impacted freight movement. The freight rates are high as they cross-subsidise the low passenger fares. Therefore, the industry prefers to use road transport, which is more expensive and less environment friendly.

Although the government has created the Golden Quadrilateral, its linkages with state and rural roads are yet to be developed. Transporting agricultural raw materials from rural areas requires well-developed stretches of rural roads and linkages with expressways, but in India, these are not well-connected, with stretches through habitations, crowded markets, etc. Heavy traffic and poor road conditions cause delays in transit that adversely impact the on-time supply of raw materials in the production process, leading to operational losses and requiring large stocks to be held in the inventory. Delays also lead to wastage in transit, as the majority of the raw materials are perishable. Raw materials like fruits and vegetables are often stacked tightly in gunny bags (instead of trays) and due to the poor road conditions, they get spoilt during the journey.

Some manufacturing companies pointed out that it takes almost seven days to transport material from Mumbai to Kolkata. Compared with international norms of 600-800 kilometres per day, Indian trucks and trailers can normally cover only 250-300 km per day. Most roads in India are designed to carry a maximum weight of 16.2 tonnes, whereas in the USA, the standard is 36 tonnes.[13] This affects the overall productivity of the sector. Lack of computerisation at check-posts and informal payments at interstate clearances increases transit time; this affects the life of the raw materials and increases logistics costs, which are then passed onto manufacturers and consumers.

In India, 8-tonne trucks are widely used, unlike the larger 40-foot trailers that are used by the beverage sector worldwide. This necessitates additional trips or additional trucks for transportation. Since international packaging does not apply in India due to the truck sizes and conditions, importers need to repackage their beverages for transportation within India. Moreover, most operators are small non-corporate businesses; almost 75 per cent of the trucking 'companies' are single-truck operators and almost 90 per cent of trucking companies have a turnover of less than INR 10 million (in the Indian road freight

12. *http://www.livemint.com/Politics/nF1j9j7b2QSKnYqtPyBzUL/Infrastructure-A-drag-on-the-economy.html* (last accessed in May 2013).

13. FICCI (2010).

industry worth about INR 1.42 trillion).[14] Due to their small size, these companies often depend on a large number of brokers and intermediaries to get contracts. These intermediaries dominate the market and often fix the freight rates. The truck operators do not have the capacity to invest in automation of processes, including handling of the beverages, which may lead to breakage/spoilage during loading and unloading.

- *Cold chain infrastructure*. Cold chain infrastructure is required for storing agricultural raw materials such as fruits, vegetables and milk. India has roughly 5,300 cold storages with a capacity of 23 million metric tonnes, but over 90 per cent of these are only suitable for storing potatoes.[15] In the survey, farmer organisations such as Bharat Krisak Samaj, manufacturers and retailers said that the cold storage facilities are fragmented, with small capacities and no temperature control.

  In terms of capacity and ownership, the private sector is the largest player in cold storage, followed by cooperatives and the public sector.[16] Industry associations pointed out that enormous investment is required to set up large international standard cold storage facilities with temperature controls; however, returns on this investment are very slow, since most of the farmers who use these facilities do not have the scale of production or the capability to pay for the facilities.

  Government incentives are also not viable. The government provides an income tax holiday on the income accrued in the first five years of setting up a cold storage. However, if a new entrant plans to open a fruit processing unit along with cold storage facilities, it takes almost five years to develop these facilities, during which they hardly earn any income.

- *Warehousing*. Non-corporate players dominate the warehousing sector. Currently, only 20 per cent of warehousing is in the formal sector and the government controls 70 per cent of the formal sector. Most warehouses in India have small capacities and lack barcoding and scanning facilities. Therefore, the benefits from quality warehousing, such as stock management (to prevent demand-supply imbalances), cannot be accrued optimally.

  The corporate sector's interest in investing in the warehousing industry has been low due to bureaucratic delays, the cumbersome process and low rates of return. The Planning Commission (2009) highlighted that to set up warehousing facilities in India, companies need to comply with as many as 20 different procedures, thus making the process very time-consuming (270 days) compared with countries like Korea where there are 11 procedures that can be completed in 56-60 days and the USA where there are 19 procedures that can be completed in 65-70 days. There are also other barriers such as acquiring land, lack of prescribed standards of services and trading conditions for operators in warehouses (other than those governed by the Customs Act) and no uniformity in warehousing standards across states.

- *Finance*. Access to finance is very important, especially for the non-corporate sector. Several non-corporate players said that although the government has proclaimed the sector a 'priority sector,' several procedural hurdles delay the disbursement of loans from financial institutions. Due to the high transactions costs involved in loan disbursements (almost 6-7% of the total loan amount) and high volatility in farm loans,[17] small entrepreneurs fail to get sufficient credit to start their business. They also pointed out that financial institutions often refuse to finance projects, citing seasonality, perishability and high-term loan requirements. These difficulties often compel small processors to borrow from private lenders, who may charge exorbitant interest rates, thereby affecting the profitability of the project.

To summarise, the infrastructure hurdles in India seriously affect the growth of various food processing sub-sectors, including the non-alcoholic beverage sector. Due to these problems, several international companies continue to import their brands rather than setting up manufacturing bases in India.

14. CII and KPMG (2007).
15. PHD Chamber and Yes Bank (2012).
16. Ibid.
17. Small-value loans made to farmers for agriculture or allied activities or small-scale industries. For details, refer to FICCI (2010).

7.2.4 Raw Materials

Inconsistency in the quantity and quality of raw materials, especially agricultural raw materials, is a problem for both corporate and non-corporate manufacturers. To some extent, it also affects corporate retailers, who may have their own private label for non-alcoholic beverages and want control over the entire supply chain. The non-corporate retailers said that they are not affected by the quantity and quality of raw material. This may be because they usually procure processed products and/or have less information. Nevertheless, although they have given a lower rank based on their perceptions, they are likely to be affected by raw material supply and price inflation.

- *Inconsistent Supply of Critical Raw Material.* The major concern remains inconsistency or shortage in the supply of critical raw materials, especially agricultural produce. The non-alcoholic beverage industry uses a range of agricultural raw materials from fruits and vegetables to sugar. Inconsistent supply can arise from low agricultural productivity, crop failure, restrictions on imports, restrictions on interstate mobility, commodity hoarding, etc. Table 7.5 shows that although overall production of fruits and vegetables in India has grown by 4.2 per cent and 4.5 per cent, respectively, in the past two decades, the productivity of fruits has declined by 0.2 per cent and in the case of vegetables, it has increased by only 1.7 per cent. In contrast, demand has increased, which has led to a rise in food prices.

Table 7.5

Growth Rate by Area, Production and Yield (Fruits and Vegetables) in the Past Two Decades

(in percentage)

	1990s	2000s	All Periods
Fruits			
Area	3.1	6.7	4.4
Production	4.4	7.4	4.2
Productivity	1.2	0.6	–0.2
Vegetables			
Area	2.1	1.3	2.8
Production	5.2	6.4	4.5
Productivity	3	2.1	1.7

Source: Compiled from Sharma and Jain (2011): 32, 40, tables 14 and 17.

Nin-Pratt *et al.* (2009) found that the total factor productivity (TFP)[18] of India's agriculture changed from –0.42 in the pre-reform period[19] to 0.54 in the post-reform period. Compared to this, in China, the TFP changed from –2.7 in the pre-reform period to 3.4 in the post-reform period. The main reason for the higher TFP in China is that the number of workers per hectare in India increased at a much faster rate compared with China, whereas the total land available for agriculture did not increase at that rate. Therefore, Indian agriculture became highly fragmented, with a large number of small holders.

- *Lack of Processable Quality Raw Materials.* Almost all stakeholders raised concerns about the quality of produce. Manufacturers and farmer associations pointed out that fruits and vegetables must be of a certain quality to make them processable, which India lacks. For example, West Bengal produces a huge quantity of pineapples, but the processing plants do not get the raw materials to process them into a consistent value-added product.[20] The technology used to process agricultural raw materials in India is quite low compared with other countries. The survey found that in India, only 7 per cent of the annual production is processed, compared with 23 per cent in China, 65 per cent in the USA and 83 per cent in Malaysia. The farmer associations also said that due to the small sizes of their holdings, most Indian farmers do not have the capacity to invest in superior quality high-value seeds, modern farm machinery and processes such as grading, sorting, harvesting or storage.

- *Raw Material Price Inflation and Cost Fluctuations.* Wastage and low productivity have led to rising prices for raw material. Raw material for the entire food processing industry is quite expensive and accounts for more than 50 per cent of the total input cost.

18. TFP is the variable that accounts for the effect on output not caused by traditionally measured inputs like land or labour. The inputs used to measure TFP can be technology, efficiency, etc.
19. Both India and China launched agricultural reforms between 1979 and 1985.
20. West Bengal State Food Processing and Horticulture Development Corporation Limited (2012).

Other factors, such as variations in climatic conditions, agricultural hoarding, control on distribution of products due to regulations such as the Essential Commodities Act, 1955, and restrictions on imports, have contributed to fluctuations in the availability of key agricultural raw materials, and led to fluctuations in their prices.

7.2.5 Labour Factors

The lack of skilled labour is a problem for both corporate manufacturers and retailers. To adequately train manpower, companies make large investments in designing and running training programmes. The industry pointed out that the central and state governments have hardly any specialised training facilities for labourers in the food processing industry.

The multiplicity of labour market regulations at the state and central levels affects operations for both manufacturers and retailers in the corporate sector. A global manufacturer pointed out that the Punjab government restricts employees from working more than 40 hours a week or eight hours a day, which affects the productivity of company employees. In Haryana, there are restrictions on employing women despite the central government's efforts to promote women empowerment. In addition, trade unions and interference by political parties impact the manufacturing sector, especially the corporate sector. Labour regulations are less of a barrier for the non-corporate sector, especially retailers, since most businesses are family-run, with family members working as employees.

7.2.6 Fiscal Barriers

- *Taxes*. India has a quasi-federal governance structure. The implications of this, especially in the case of taxes, are quite significant due to the multiplicity of taxes and differences in tax incidence across states. The survey found that the sector faces multiple and multi-layered taxes, most of which are imposed at the state level. There is considerable variation in the taxes imposed by different states and the taxes are discriminatory across product categories.

  Certain non-alcoholic beverages such as bottled water and CSDs face higher taxes than juices and other processed foods. This can be seen in Table 7.6, which presents the central value added tax (CENVAT) rates and value added tax (VAT) rates in some states for different categories of non-alcoholic beverages.

Table 7.6

CENVAT and VAT Rates for Different Categories of Non-alcoholic Beverages (2013)*

	CSD	*Juices*	*Bottled water*
CENVAT	7.4	4.02	6.8
VAT			
Maharashtra	20	5	12.5
Gujarat	15	5	15
Punjab	22.6	6.1	14.3
Haryana	13.1	5.3	13.1
Himachal Pradesh	13.8	5	13.8
Tamil Nadu	14.5	5	14.5
Karnataka	14.5	5.5	14.5

Note: *These rates are net of abatement.
Source: Based on data provided by Indian Beverage Association (IBA) members.

The corporate sector argued that in India the availability of clean drinking water is a problem and, therefore, bottled water should be treated as a necessity product and not a luxury commodity. Good quality drinking water ensures the health of consumers. Other stakeholders agreed and said that ideally bottled water should not be taxed at all or at the most taxed at par with juices.

Apart from these taxes, there are several state and local/municipal level taxes and levies such as *mandi/samiti* taxes, Octroi (in Mumbai) and Way Bill (West Bengal) that increase the tax burden for producers and consumers. All these taxes increase the cost of products by around 30-40 per cent, which is then passed on to consumers. Table 7.7 shows a hypothetical cost structure for a non-alcoholic beverage.

According to corporate manufacturers, such multi-level taxation makes it difficult to establish uniform pan-India prices and complicates the production process. For instance, a global multinational company pointed out that their own plants in India supply the cans used for packaging beverages. For the company-owned bottling subsidiary, the supply of cans implies a stock transfer within the company; hence, they are not required to pay sales taxes. However, for the company's authorised bottling partners, the supply of cans implies sales of products, which requires them to pay sales tax. This creates severe complications in pricing the same product produced by the company-owned bottling entity and the authorised bottling partners.

Table 7.7

Cost Structure of Packaged Beverages

Particulars	*Packaged beverages*
MRP	(X+Y+Z)+A+B+C+D+E+F
VAT	4-20 per cent of (X+Y+Z) = D
Excise Cess	3 per cent = F
CENVAT (4-7 per cent)	4-7 per cent = E
Retailer's margin (15 per cent of total cost)	15 per cent of (X+Y+Z) = C
Distributor's margin (7 per cent of total cost)	7 per cent of (X+Y+Z) = B
Transporter's margin (10 per cent of total cost)	10 per cent of (X+Y+Z) = A
Total manufacturing cost (includes taxes on transportation of raw materials and finished beverages between states)	(X+Y+Z)
Manufacturing and distribution cost	Z
Packaging cost	Y
Raw materials cost	X

Note: The manufacturing cost, packaging cost and raw materials cost are hypothetical. It is used to show the effect of tax on the maximum retail price (MRP) of a packaged beverage.

Source: Compiled from the survey and *http://www.eximguru.com/excise-duty/22-chapter-22-beverages-spirits-and.aspx* (last accessed in May 2013).

Indirect taxes also affect the cost of production. For instance, packaging material is taxed heavily. A 16 per cent excise duty is levied on packaging materials used for non-alcoholic beverages.

- *Incentives*. The tax holidays provided by the government are often ineffective in helping food processing units. For instance, companies involved in processing, preserving and packaging fruits and beverages get 100 per cent tax exemption on profits they make in the first five years of starting of business.[21] However, due to the long gestation period, companies may not be able to accrue profit in the first five years. Similarly, the Indian government offers a 10-year income tax holiday to food parks with processing facilities,[22] but often corporates do not earn income in the initial years of their operations to get this benefit.

  Corporate manufacturers in the survey argued that the incentives are also wrongly designed. For instance, the plot size of food parks is 50 acres and beverage manufacturers are allotted plots of 5-10 acres. However, the average size of a corporate beverage manufacturing plant is 35-50 acres, so the allocated plots do not meet their requirements. It appears that most food parks are meant for small and medium enterprises (SMEs) and, accordingly to survey participants, India does not have schemes/incentives to support large-scale food processing. Due to other complications such as sourcing products and machinery from domestic tariff areas (DTAs) and selling to the DTAs, several corporate manufacturers do not wish to relocate to facilities such as special economic zones (SEZs) that offer tax incentives, which reduces the effectiveness of this incentive.

- *Implementation of GST*. Due to the fragmented tax regime and piece-meal tax benefits, the Indian food processing sector is experiencing a low level of corporatisation. Even the corporate sector has to work with the non-corporate sector in the contract manufacturing model and their supply chains have to be fragmented due to the complicated tax structure. Several corporate players and even some non-corporate players pointed out that to ease out the fragmented tax system, the Indian government should implement the Goods and Services Tax (GST) and should treat the non-alcoholic beverage sector at par with the other processed food industries. This would also help resolve the supply chain issue. However, due to disagreements between the central and state governments, the implementation of GST is getting delayed,

21. *http://mofpi.nic.in/images/File/TaxRelief_FPISector_140213.pdf* (last accessed in June 2013).
22. *http://mofpi.nic.in/images/File/FICCI%20Data/FDI/FDI.pdf* (last accessed in June 2013).

which is a major concern for both the corporate and non-corporate sectors.

7.2.7 Spurious Products

A key problem for the non-alcoholic beverage sector, especially the corporate sector, is spurious products, especially in segments such as bottled water. There is a lack of enforcement of consumer protection regulations and often spurious and contaminated products enter the market, causing health hazards and creating problems for the original brands. Industry estimates show that counterfeit/spurious products account for 23.4 per cent of the total size of the fast-moving consumer goods (FMCG) industry (packaged goods), which results in a loss of approximately INR 5,660 crore to the exchequer, besides impacting the brand image of the companies and the health of consumers.

7.2.8 R&D, Patents and Copyright

All corporate manufacturers, some non-corporate manufacturers and some corporate retailers feel that applying for and getting patents for innovative food and beverage products is a difficult and time-consuming process in India.

- *Research and Development*. The Ministry of Food Processing Industries (MoFPI) has introduced several schemes to promote R&D in the Indian food processing industry. However, this has not increased the processing of quality fruits and vegetables or its productivity, and manufacturers have to largely depend on imports.

  Farmer organisations and manufacturers pointed out that despite having good public research institutes in India, most of the research is de-linked from farmers and industry and there is no attempt to make the products commercially viable. The research institutes do not focus on a particular product category and there has been no major breakthrough in agriculture research in India. In contrast, other countries have based their research and innovation on products and animals of Indian origin and have succeeded. For instance, Latin American countries have imported cows of Indian origin, because they are the hardiest variety, and have conducted extensive research on how to increase their milk productivity. They have succeeded, whereas in India the productivity of the same variety of cows is declining. Respondents also pointed out that even introducing new and productive varieties of fruits and vegetables seeds imported from abroad has not worked due to the lack of supportive research and innovations.

  Farmer organisations such as Bharat Krisak Samaj and some Indian companies pointed that research in fruits and vegetables requires almost 5-10 years; thus, the benefits of research can be realised only after a time gap. They also observed that fruit cultivation is expensive and requires a long gestation period. The lack of proper research and financial support makes it difficult for farmers to increase the quantity and quality of their production.

  Several multinationals pointed out that they have in-house R&D facilities and are willing to collaborate with government research institutes to raise the quality and quantity of agricultural raw materials in India. However, the public institutes follow a long and complicated procedure for a new project. At times, the quality of research is not at par with global standards. Multinationals said that they are willing to work directly with farmers in India to ensure a consistent supply of processing-quality raw materials for their own food and beverage products. However, they face several barriers, such as restrictions imposed by certain state governments on allowing contract farming. The majority of the incentives offered by the Indian government to encourage R&D are directed towards small-scale industries, and large companies, especially international companies, do not gain much from them.

- *Patents and Copyright*. The survey found that obtaining patents for a new product in India is an enormous problem for both SMEs and corporate manufacturers. The application procedure has a long gestation period. There is a lack of awareness and under-utilisation of patent information by business people and SMEs, because it is perceived as only applicable to scientists and researchers. In addition, SMEs face problems accessing patent information, and online patent services are quite expensive. Most large companies file patents in the USA and now in countries like China.

7.2.9 Trade Barriers

High import tariffs along with hassles and delays in getting clearances from customs and other authorities are a major problem for those engaged in international trade (corporate manufacturers, importers, corporate retailers, etc.). These are not as much of a problem for the non-corporate sector, because they are less likely to directly import their products.

- *Tariff Rates*. The structure of India's tariffs is quite complex. The import tariff structure is composed of four components, namely, basic duty, countervailing duty or additional duty (applied on all imports except for alcoholic beverages and intended to match the excise duty applicable on domestic products), special additional duty (applicable on top of the basic customs duty and the countervailing duty) and education cess. All these duties escalate the cost of imported products. Table 7.8 illustrates the total duty that an importer needs to pay to import orange juice worth INR 100 into India.

Table 7.8

Duty Structure for an Importer of Orange Juice

Particulars	*Orange Juice (in INR)*
Total import value (assessable value)	101
Basic customs duty (30%) (A)	30.3
Countervailing duty (6%) (B)	7.8
Education cess (3%) (C)	1.1
Special additional duty (4 per cent, ad valorem) (D)	5.6
Total customs duty (A+B+C+D)	44.9

Source: Calculated from information in the survey and *http://www.eximguru.com/calculator/calculatecustomduty.aspx?1=30&2=&3=6&4=4&5=&6=3&hscode=2009* (last accessed in May 2013).

There is also wide disparity in India between the bound tariff rates on agricultural products in the World Trade Organization (WTO), which are quite high (average 118.3%), and the applied tariff rates (average 30%). The Indian government frequently uses this disparity to adjust the level of protection in the market, which creates considerable confusion among importers. India also uses quantitative restrictions or quotas for agricultural raw materials such as sugar, dairy products, fruits and vegetables. This implies that only certain quantities of imports are allowed at certain tariff rates. In addition, to keep domestic prices stable, the Indian government often changes the tariff rates on essential products such as sugar, which creates problems in supply (Gulati *et al*., 2013).

Several corporate manufacturers pointed out that India imposes restrictions on the import or use of sweeteners such as Stevia, which is used globally. Since India imposes quantitative restrictions on the domestic sale of sugar by levying a sugar quota, the market price for sugar remains quite high. Moreover, the trade policy for sugar in India frequently changes depending on availability and erratic political lobbying. In such a scenario, restrictions on the use of these sweeteners by food processors hurt their operations.

Since the non-alcoholic beverage sector, especially in fruit and vegetables juices, is highly dependent on imports, high tariff rates and the complicated execution of tariff policies create several problems for their operations. India has signed a range of free trade agreements (FTAs) and comprehensive trade agreements with neighbouring countries such as Sri Lanka, the Association of Southeast Asian Nations (ASEAN) countries and countries in East Asia, such as Korea and Japan. These trade agreements have provisions for duty-free imports of processed food and beverages. Hence, corporate manufacturers, including domestic companies, resort to methods such as tariff jumping[23] to take advantage of these FTAs. This leads to a loss in domestic investment as well as FDI. Unlike India (where there is no single reference for different tariff lines and FTA tariffs), in New Zealand and Singapore, there a single reference point that a trading company can visit to check on the tariff lines and FTA tariffs. With India entering into several FTAs and with different tariff lines under different FTAs, imports have become very complicated for manufacturers.

23. Tariff-jumping: The establishment of a production facility in a foreign country, through FDI or licensing, and then importing the product on zero or lower tariff for the home country market using the FTA.

Further, the Indian government imposes high import duties on raw materials for allied sectors such as the packaging industry, which affects manufacturers and bottlers. For instance, it was pointed out that the import duty for polyethylene terephthalate/high-density fiberboard (PET/HDF) raw materials is in the order of 27 per cent, which affects the cost structure of bottlers.

- *Customs Clearances.* Several international manufacturers and importers pointed to problems with ports and port clearances. Port clearance in India takes almost 14 days compared with countries such as Singapore where it takes only 24 hours. This can be attributed to the lack of mechanisation and the presence of multiple clearance authorities, lack of coordination between these authorities and the lack of clarity on beverage standards and classifications. For instance, one global multinational pointed out that in the case of energy drinks, even if they manage to get clearances from the central Food Safety and Standards Authority of India (FSSAI), they face challenges in getting clearances from state-level authorities due to the lack of coordination between the two departments. Due to these delays, beverage consignments need to be stored at the port. However, beverages have a short shelf life and due to the lack of adequate storage conditions inside the ports, beverages get spoilt, leading to huge losses for the companies.

  International logistics companies pointed out that in India customs regulations restrict the transportation of perishable products through express delivery (courier mode) and companies have to choose cargo delivery, which is a longer process. The smooth transportation of imported products depends on customs officers. If they feel there is any problem with the product, they may draw a sample and send it for testing to the accredited lab, which is usually not within the port premises. As a result, clearances take time and affect the shelf life of the products.

  The survey also found out that despite the modernisation of Indian airports, they are lacking in terms of cargo space and cargo facilities. For instance, the airports at Chennai, Mumbai and Delhi have only three cargo terminals compared with nine in Singapore and six in Korea.[24] Warehousing facilities are also small and congested, and there is no cold storage facility. Domestic terminals do not even have covered storage spaces, in which case during rainy season or hot summer months, non-alcoholic beverages spoil. There are also no facilities for internal transfer of cargo between domestic and international terminals and, unlike other international airports, Indian airports do not have logistics parks or free-trade zones.

7.2.10 Consumers

Indian consumers have low per capita consumption of non-alcoholic beverage and their demand fluctuates. They are highly price sensitive and there is a lack of information on their preferences. This is a significant problem for both corporate and non-corporate manufacturers and retailers.

- *Low per capita Consumption.* Several corporate manufacturers pointed out that per capita consumption of non-alcoholic beverages is low in India (9.51 litres in 2010)[25] compared with other emerging countries such as China and Mexico. Per capita consumption of fruit juices in India is only 0.02 litres compared with China that has attained a level of 1.5 litres,[26] and per capita consumption of packaged drinking water in India is only 16.2 litres compared with 250 litres in Mexico and 95 litres in China—Hong Kong.[27] They observed that only one per cent of beverage consumers in India drink packaged beverages. This limits the growth potential of the market for non-alcoholic beverages.

  This is despite the fact that income levels in India are rising and 31 per cent of consumer spending is on food and beverages. Corporate manufacturers attributed the low level of consumption of packaged juice and packaged drinking water to factors

24. For details, see Mukherjee *et al.* (2012a).
25. AM Mindpower Solutions (2011).
26. *http://mofpi.nic.in/ContentPage.aspx?CategoryId=547* (last accessed in May 2013).
27. *http://articles.economictimes.indiatimes.com/2012-07-03/news/32524033_1_bottled-water-water-market-capita-consumption* (last accessed in May 2013).

such as price sensitivity, preference for home-made beverages and the low level of health-consciousness among Indian consumers. Indian consumers are not aware that packaged juices and drinking water are safe for consumption and provide health benefits. Therefore, companies feel the need for an increase in consumer education and awareness.

- *Fluctuations in Demand*. Demand for non-alcoholic beverages such as CSDs is sporadic, unlike for necessities such as milk and milk products. In India, consumption of these non-alcoholic beverages is seasonal, with high demand in the summer months and low demand during winter. The survey found that CSDs, energy drinks, sports drinks, etc., are usually consumed 'on the go.' In the peak summer season (April to July), sales of CSDs increase by almost 30-40 per cent.[28] According to the survey, consumption of energy drinks and sports drinks increases particularly when there are examinations and sports events. This fluctuation is a cause of worry for non-alcoholic beverage manufacturers as well as retailers because a drop in demand during the off-season results in idle capacities across the entire supply chain. To counter this, companies need to plan their production cycle to cater to the high demands of the peak season and manage inventories during the off-season.

- *Low Brand Loyalty and Price Sensitivity*. The survey found that Indian consumers generally demonstrate low brand loyalty. In the sample of 200 consumers surveyed across four cities (Delhi, Mumbai, Bangalore and Kolkata), only 1.4 per cent checks the name of the brand while buying a beverage. Price sensitivity is another problem for corporate manufacturers and retailers. Companies need to price their products carefully, because a rise in price can cause demand to drop. Corporate manufacturers also pointed out that due to this high degree of price sensitivity, Indian consumers are often attracted to unpackaged beverages that may not be safe for consumption.

- *Lack of Information about Consumer Preferences*. Indian consumers have very heterogeneous tastes, and preferences for food and beverages vary across regions. Keeping this in mind, companies need to invest regularly in market research and innovation to come up with products that cater to Indian tastes.

7.2.11 Regulatory Barriers

The survey found that India's food and beverage sector is governed by multiple regulations that cover sourcing, the supply chain and food safety. These regulations are implemented by states, even though the central government may design them. As a result, the regulatory environment may vary across states. The variations in the regulatory structures in different states increase compliance costs and make it difficult for companies to set up a smooth supply chain. Almost all the stakeholders pointed out that fragmentation in India's agro-supply chain is in areas where the central government has limited regulatory control. In addition, there is a lack of co-ordination between the central and state government bodies responsible for modelling and implementing the regulations, which increases the confusion of stakeholders in the processed food and beverage sector. There is a lack of awareness about the various regulations such as FSSA, 2006, among stakeholders, especially in the non-corporate sector.

The extent to which each stakeholder is affected by the different regulations depends on their involvement in the value chain of the food processing industry. For instance, a non-corporate retailer is affected less by the different sourcing regulations compared with other stakeholders. They are most affected by food safety regulations, because it is difficult for them to keep up with the procedural and compliance changes. In this section, we discuss the major regulations that impact the industry that were highlighted by stakeholders during the survey.

- *Sourcing Regulations*. Both corporate and non-corporate manufacturers and corporate retailers pointed out that sourcing regulations, including the APMC (reformed in 2008) and the Essential Commodities Act, 1955, seriously impact the sourcing of raw materials as well as finished products.

---

28. *http://www.just-drinks.com/news/late-monsoon-rains-in-india-edges-up-soft-drink-consumption_id67766.aspx* (last accessed in May 2013).

Table 7.9

Current Status of the APMC Act in Indian States

State of Reforms	*States/Union Territories*
States/UTs where APMC Act reforms have been done for direct marketing; contract farming and markets in private/co-op sectors	Andhra Pradesh, Arunachal Pradesh, Assam, Goa, Gujarat, Himachal Pradesh, Jharkhand, Karnataka, Maharashtra, Mizoram, Nagaland, Orissa, Rajasthan, Sikkim, Uttarakhand and Tripura
States/UTs where APMC Act reforms have been done partially	Direct marketing: Delhi, Madhya Pradesh and Chhattisgarh
	Contract farming: Chhattisgarh, Punjab, Haryana, Madhya Pradesh and Chandigarh
States/UTs where there is no APMC Act and hence do not require reform	Bihar,* Kerala, Manipur, Andaman & Nicobar Islands, Dadra & Nagar Haveli
States/UTs where the APMC Act already provides for the reforms	Tamil Nadu
States/UTs where administrative action has been initiated for the reforms	Meghalaya, Haryana, J&K, West Bengal, Delhi, Uttar Pradesh and Puducherry

Note: *APMC Act repealed with effect from September 1, 2006.
Source: Compiled from Press Information Bureau (2012): 130-31, table 5.2.

Agricultural Produce Marketing Committee Act (APMC), 1963 (reformed in 2003).[29] Under the APMC Act, 1963, state-controlled *mandis* have witnessed a steady increase in the number of wholesalers and traders or middlemen. On average, survey participants pointed out that fruits and vegetables pass through six to seven middlemen before reaching manufacturers. Most *mandis* suffer from poor storage, handling and processing facilities and lack marketing channels. In addition, there is a lack of modern weighing equipment. Around 15-25 per cent of the total produce sold *via* the APMC route gets wasted due to multiple intermediaries and poor *mandi* infrastructure. Moreover, an agricultural commodity moving from one state to another attracts a tax or '*mandi* fee' every time it enters a new regulated market. Therefore, the cost at which the produce is available to the manufacturer rises by almost 60-70 per cent. These factors lead to poor farm-market linkages and impact the supply chain of any food processing company (for details, refer to Pachouri, 2013).

In response to these problems, the central government amended the APMC Act in 2003, which allows direct marketing of agricultural produce, contract farming, direct sourcing and the development of market infrastructure by private players. However, since implementation of these reforms continues to be a state subject, some states have still not adopted the amended act. Table 7.9 shows the present status of the reforms in the APMC Act in different states.

In some states, processors need to pay a '*mandi* cess' to procure fruits and vegetables even if they do not use the services of the *mandis*. This discourages direct sourcing by manufacturers. Industry associations argued that fruits and vegetables could be exempted from *mandi* cess since they contribute to only around 7 per cent of the *mandi* earnings. Moreover, farmer associations pointed out that the APMCs have a strong political presence. The governments at the centre and state levels acknowledge this, and states such as Madhya Pradesh, Maharashtra and Uttarakhand are in the process of exempting fruits and vegetables from the list of agricultural products that require *mandi* cess to be paid.

29. The APMC act was modelled in 1963 by the Indian government to address inefficiencies in agricultural markets and implemented at the state level. Under the act, each state had an agricultural produce marketing committee that was responsible for a particular market area (*mandi*) and the act mandated the sales of agricultural products through these market areas with a market fee charged for each transaction, which would be used for development and maintenance of *mandis* by the authorities. The act also prohibited direct selling of agricultural produce to consumers including exporters, processors or retail chain operators by the farmers. The act was amended in 2003.

Essential Commodities Act 1955. This act regulates and controls the production, distribution and pricing of essential commodities. Although the central government designed the act, the powers to implement it lie with the state governments. The state governments issue various control orders to regulate different aspects of trading in essential commodities including interstate movement of goods. Both corporate and non-corporate manufacturers and corporate retailers pointed out that since the implementation powers lie with the states, they can control the production and distribution of the listed commodities in both domestic as well as international markets. This act restricts easy availability and interstate movement of certain commodities such as sugar, which is a key raw material for the non-alcoholic beverage industry. For instance, in the case of 'levy sugar,' all sugar mills have to supply part of their produce to the Food Corporation of India (FCI) at a price set by individual state governments. This is a concern for manufacturers and corporate retailers. Like the APMC Act, the implementation of this act varies widely between states. In most cases, the latest information is not available at the state level, which creates complications for food and beverage processors. Also, most states require prices to be displayed in the local language, which can be difficult for companies.

The Minimum Support Price. The minimum support price (MSP) is the minimum price that has to be paid to farmers for certain produce such as sugar. A very high MSP for sugar may increase costs and hurt the profitability of non-alcoholic beverage manufacturers.

Figure 7.2

Awareness about FSSA, 2006

(in percentage)

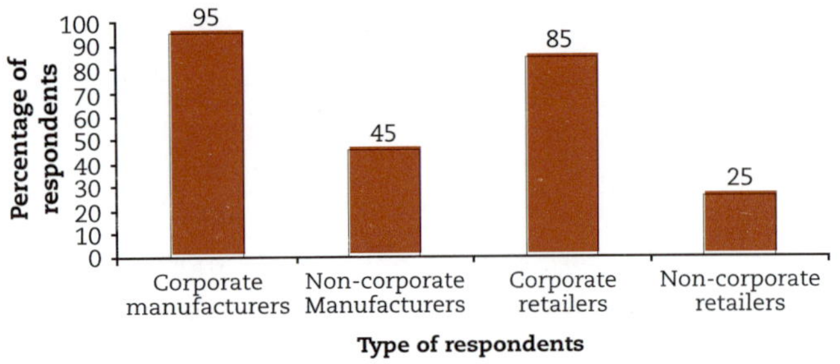

- *FSSA, 2006*.[30] The survey found high levels of awareness of this act among corporate manufacturers and retailers, but low awareness in the non-corporate sectors (Figure 7.2).

Corporate retailers, manufacturers and industry bodies agreed that the act, if implemented, would benefit the processed food and beverage sector, but they listed certain problems. First, the act lacks supply chain traceability. It does not cover farmers and, therefore, does not cover inspection/regulation of products that are supplied by farmers. Hence, adulteration due to the presence of insecticides or pesticides at the farm level is not governed, and other stakeholders in the supply chain can be held responsible for this. In a training manual prepared for food safety regulators, the FSSAI agrees on the importance of supply chain traceability as a preventive strategy in food quality and safety management. It observes that supply chain traceability is necessary to search for the cause of non-conformity and the ability to recall a product, if required. It also mentions the limitations of implementing traceability methods in India where small/marginal farmers produce agricultural raw materials in very low volumes and marketable volumes are built up at various collection centres before being taken to processing areas (FSSAI, 2010).

Second, the classification and categorisation of food and beverages in India differ from global categorisation. This creates problems of parity and definitional synergy for global companies, especially those involved in imports of food and beverages. The additive approval process is not aligned at the global level. For instance, several globally approved additives used in processed food and beverages are not approved under the additive approval process in the act. The problem arises at the time of customs clearance.

International companies pointed out that as per Schedule 4 of FSSA, 2006, separate licences are required for the manufacture and distribution of different categories of

30. Refer to Box 3.1, Chapter 3.

foods and beverages including proprietary foods, genetically modified foods, health supplements, functional foods and special dietary foods. Moreover, separate licences are required for the states and the centre, which complicate the licence application and approval.

Companies with global operations also pointed out that as per the act, testing of all foods and beverages should be done in accredited laboratory. However, most states do not have adequate funds to set up a lab and the central government has not permitted any additional budget to the states for this purpose. There is also a lack of qualified food inspectors. Initially the act mandated food inspectors to have a background in nutrition and food, but the lack of qualified people and pressure from trade unions led to a change in the requirement, making recruitment more flexible and allowing the recruitment of food inspectors from other science streams (such as physics). Lack of knowledge and experience among the inspectors might create inefficiencies.

- *FDI in Multi-brand Retail*. Both corporate and non-corporate manufacturers consider the fragmented retail structure in India as a barrier. However, corporate manufacturers do not consider FDI in multi-brand retail a major reform measure, because they generally distribute their products through non-corporate retailers—'*kirana* stores.' Non-corporate manufacturers, especially small-scale enterprises, were optimistic about opening up multi-brand retail since they felt that large supermarkets would also stock their brands along with global brands and this would increase their visibility to consumers.

  Corporate retailers expressed concerns about the conditions associated with the policy. Multinational corporate retailers pointed out that investment in back-end operations is difficult for retailers who only deal with front-end retail (they source the product from other sources and sell it in the market). Some of them already have wholesale operations and have invested in back-end operations; they now prefer to invest in front-end retail. This condition will turn away many foreign retailers who have plans to open only retail stores and not to set up manufacturing facilities or invest in infrastructure and the supply chain. They expect to source from contract manufacturers and other large manufacturers and use the existing logistics network and other supporting infrastructure in the country instead of investing in it. The retailers also had concerns regarding the sourcing conditions from the SMEs. The Indian government tried to address these concerns by reviewing and relaxing the SME sourcing conditions in August 2013 (for details refer to Annexure A-3.1, section: multi-brand retail, part-d). Though these changes may prove to be beneficial for multinational food and grocery retailers, the SME sourcing conditions still remain a concern for specialised and high-end food and beverage retailers. These products require substantial investments and large scales of operation for production, which are not available in SME sourcing. In addition, multinational food and beverage retailers, especially those operating in the high-end and specialised segments, have strict quality control measures for sourcing of products, which SMEs may find difficult to comply with. Moreover, since policy implementation has been left to state governments, retailers feel it would create confusion and uncertainty, as some states may not implement the policy, thereby leading to regional heterogeneity. Overall, there is lukewarm response to this policy. All stakeholders argued that this policy, in its present format, would not bring in the desired FDI, help to streamline the supply chain or help to reduce inflation.

- *Packaging and Labelling Regulations*. Packaging and labelling requirements for processed foods and beverages are governed by several sectors including the FSSA, 2006, Bureau of Indian Standards (BIS) and Department of Consumer Affairs, who may change the regulations as per their requirements. Since companies usually maintain labelling stocks for 6-8 months, they face problems if they are required to change the labels according to different acts. Retailers importing products into India face a challenge, because they need to repackage to meet Indian standards. Previously, companies were allowed to do the packaging and labelling in bonded warehouses in India; however, now they are required to package and label the goods abroad. Since this is expensive, several companies have stopped importing products.

The standard weights and units in which a packaged food or beverage product can be sold in India are governed by the Legal Metrology Act, 2009 (which replaces the Standards Weights and Measures rules, 1977). Companies involved in the production and sale of powdered beverages pointed out that under the current Packaged Commodity rule and the Legal Metrology Act, 2009, food and beverages can only be sold in certain standard sizes that have to be printed on the package in specific units. For instance, while previously companies involved in producing powder for beverages could print 'number of glasses' to denote the quantity of beverage, under the new act, they need to specify the quantity in grams. Companies observed that converting 'number of glasses' to grams might result in odd package sizes that may affect their promotional activities. The Legal Metrology Act also does not account for shrinkages in the weight of food and beverage products due to weather conditions. If the weight is found to be below the printed weight, the company is held responsible.

- *Environment Regulations*. Environment regulations create problems for both corporate and non-corporate manufacturers and retailers. Companies face barriers in setting up business in places close to their sourcing areas due to several environmental restrictions. In India, the major environment acts that impact the food and beverage processing industry include the Environmental Protection Act, 1986, the Plastics (manufacture, usage and waste management) Rules, 2009, the Water (Prevention and control of pollution) Act, 1974, amended in 1988, the Water (prevention and control of pollution) Cess Act, 1977, amended in 2003, and the Air (prevention and control of pollution) Act, 1981, amended in 1987.

  According to the survey, manufacturing units are classified under three categories—'Green,' 'Orange' and 'Red'—by the Ministry of Environment and Forests, Government of India (GoI), under the Central Action Plan. The categorisation depends on the intensity of pollution created by the industries, with 'Green' being the least and 'Red' being the highest polluting industry. State Pollution Control Boards also classify industries under similar categories to grant consent for operations. While the Ministry of Environment and Forests places the non-alcoholic beverage manufacturing units in the Orange category as with most other food and food processing industries, several State pollution control boards place these units in the Red category with highly polluting chemical industries (Table 7.10).

Table 7.10

Classification of Non-alcoholic Beverage Manufacturing Units by the Central Government and Some State Pollution Control Boards

Ministry/Department	*Categorisation of Non-alcoholic Beverage Manufacturing Units*
Ministry of Environment and Forests, Government of India	Orange
Gujarat State Pollution Control Board	Red
Karnataka State Pollution Control Board	Red
Haryana State Pollution Control Board	Red
Himachal Pradesh State Pollution Control Board	Orange
Maharashtra Pollution Control Board	Red
Orissa State Pollution Control Board	Orange
Punjab Pollution Control Board	Red
Tamil Nadu Pollution Control Board	Red
Tripura State Pollution Control Board	Red
West Bengal Pollution Control Board	Red

Source: Authors' compilation from *http://envfor.nic.in/legis/ucp/ucpsch8.html* (last accessed in July 2013) and State Pollution Control Board websites.

  Large manufacturers also said that they face barriers in obtaining environmental clearance to set up a manufacturing unit. Under the present policy, the Ministry of Environment and Forests identifies any non-alcoholic beverage manufacturing facility with built-up area equal to or above 20,000 square metres as a construction or building project, and includes it in the list of eight industries, which includes the chemical fertiliser industry, man-made fibre industry

Figure 7.3

Impact of Government Policy Initiatives on the Growth of the Non-alcoholic Beverage Industry

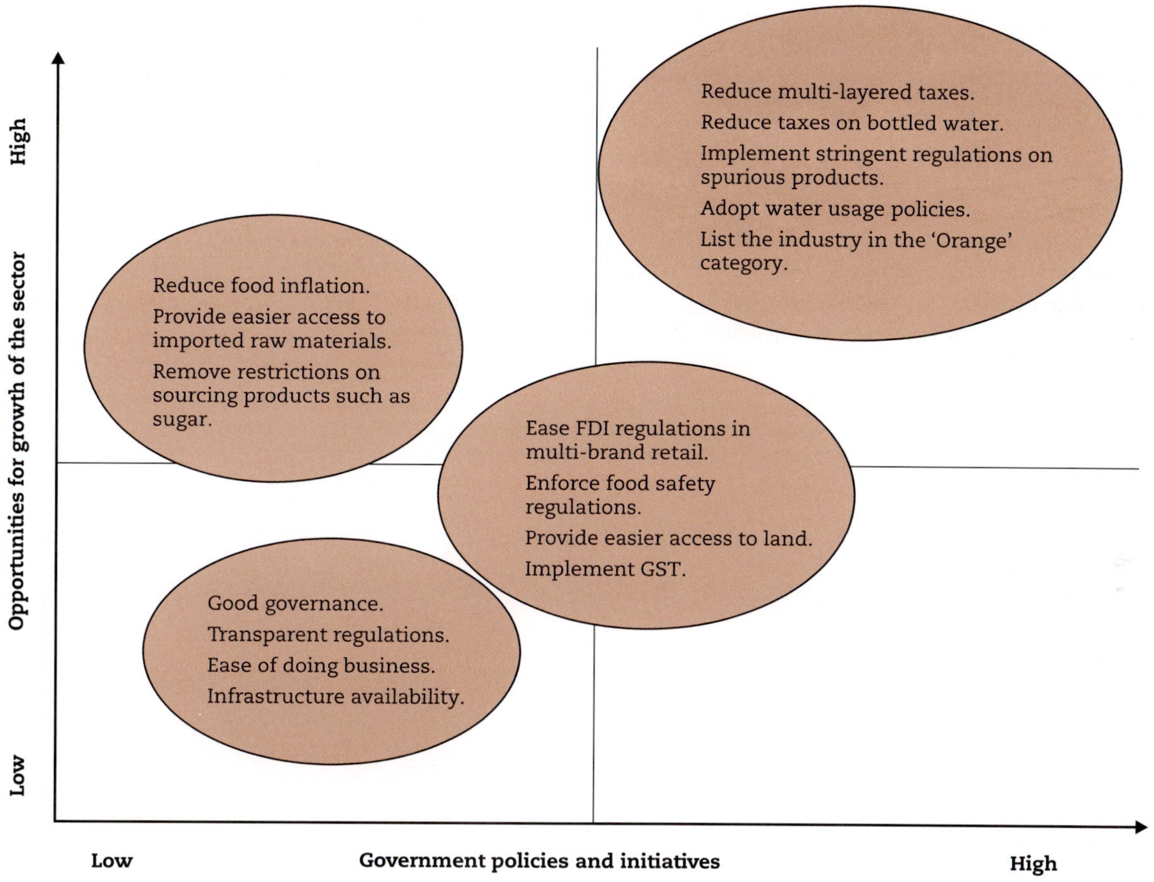

and sugar industry, that require prior environmental clearance. This delays project implementation.[31]

Almost 86 per cent of the non-corporate manufacturers surveyed lack awareness about recent changes in environment regulations in India. When asked about the ban on plastics, 80 per cent of them do not feel that the ban on plastic bags has affected their business. However, those who feel the impact of the ban pointed out that plastic bags are easy to procure and less expensive than paper bags. In the case of retailers, almost 60 per cent of corporate retailers feel that the ban on plastic bags has not affected the sector or their business particularly and they feel that this will be good for a healthy environment.

This discussion highlights key issues faced by the non-alcoholic beverage sector. In light of the discussion, we present a broad set of reforms to increase the confidence of investors, increase competitiveness in manufacturing and develop India as a global sourcing hub for non-alcoholic beverages.

7.3 The Way Forward

Survey respondents suggested some reforms that could help the non-alcoholic beverage sector grow, enhance productivity, make the sector globally competitive and develop India as an agro-processing and production hub. The respondents clearly identified the measures that would help the industry grow at a rapid pace in the short run and those that would benefit the Indian manufacturing sector in general. These are presented in Figure 7.3. The figure

31. Source: Survey inputs and *http://www.indiawaterportal.org/sites/indiawaterportal.org/files/Environmental%20Impact%20Assessment_%20Notification_Ministry%20of%20Environment%20and%20Forests_2006.pdf* (last accessed in August 2013).

shows that good governance structure, transparent regulations and the removal of bureaucratic procedures and red tape are required for the growth and development of an efficient manufacturing sector in India. The non-alcoholic beverage sector will be helped by targeted measures such as streamlining the tax system to have a low and uniform tax across food and beverage categories, implementing GST, implementing stringent regulations to curb spurious products and listing the industry in the 'Orange' category for environment clearances.

- *Good Governance and Simple, Transparent Regulations*. The Indian government has initiated several institutional and regulatory reforms to attract greater private and foreign investment and help in the overall development of manufacturing and the food processing sector. However, stakeholders pointed out that these should be implemented in a supportive business environment that is investor friendly and well-governed. Several studies have found that good governance is key to the growth of any industry [for details, see Confederation of Indian Food Trade and Industry (CIFTI), 2010], and this is demonstrated by the success of agro-processing companies such as Amul and McCain Foods (India) in states such as Gujarat. According to industry stakeholders, especially manufacturers, these ventures have been successful due to the business friendly environment in the state with a clear policy, quick clearance procedures, supportive tax regime and absence of corruption and red tape. Greater coordination is needed between state and central government departments responsible for granting clearances and the process needs to be streamlined by developing single-window clearance facilities across the supply chain.[32] In this, India can replicate or emulate global best practices. For instance, New Zealand and Singapore have implemented single-point clearance for all products at the ports. In these countries, any company importing a particular product accesses the country's relevant website and chooses the product from an harmonised system (HS) code list at the six-digit level. Accordingly, no-objection certificates, clearances, sample testing, etc., can be done online. The procedures are completed before the product physically reaches the port, which reduces delays and wastage.

  Regulations should be transparent and predictable. In food and beverage retail, the gestation period is long and hence regulatory certainty is important for investment. A Planning Commission study in 2011 also highlighted the need for stable and predictable regulations that would promote competition within a sector and attract investment.[33] For instance, retailers pointed out that conditions such as the requirement of sourcing products from SMEs or the need for a huge investment in back-end infrastructure might have dampened the interest of foreign retailers who were otherwise willing to come to India. Even though the government has made several clarifications to the industry on the multi-brand retail FDI regulations, the industry remains sceptical.

- *Taxes and Subsidies*. Reforms in taxes and subsidies are crucial for the growth of the non-alcoholic beverage sector. These reforms can be classified as below:

(i) *Remove multiple taxes and implement GST*: The major tax issues in India are the multiplicity of taxes and variation in taxes across states. There is an urgent need to streamline the system by introducing a single tax or the GST. In fact, most stakeholders said that speedy implementation of the GST is the single biggest reform in India that can help develop the pan-India supply chain, reduce wastage and ensure price consistency. With proper implementation of GST, manufacturers would be able to locate their processing units in states with easier availability of raw materials and companies would be able to operate on a hub-and-spoke model. They added that when deciding on the GST rates for the non-alcoholic beverage sector, India should take examples from other countries such as the UK, Canada, Australia and France where food (including any processed or un-processed food and beverages) is subject to zero or lower tax rates.

32. FICCI (2010).

33. *http://12thplan.gov.in/forum_description.php?f=9* (last accessed in May 2013).

(ii) *Uniform tax rates for all non-alcoholic beverage categories*: The non-alcoholic beverage sector should have uniform and low tax across different product categories. At present, bottled water faces very high VAT rates in different states (12-15%) compared to juices (5-6%), and even the CENVAT rates vary for the two categories, with 4.02 per cent for juices and 6.8 per cent for bottled water. All respondents argued that the bottled water taxes should be reduced to the level of juices since it is a 'necessity' consumption and a source of safe and hygienic drinking water. Reducing the tax will enable the industry to reduce prices, which will increase affordability. The consumers, in fact, argued that since it is difficult to get good quality drinking water in India, bottled water should be subsidised rather than taxed.

(iii) *Balancing taxes and subsidies*: The Indian corporate sector is subject to very high corporate tax, which is increased by the imposition of several cesses. While the tax burden is increasing on the one hand, on the other hand, the government offers various incentives to corporates, including income tax holidays to invest. The centre and state governments compete in giving subsidies, but many of these subsidies are piecemeal. Instead of multiple taxes and multiple subsidies, the industry argued that the Indian government could have a single lower corporate tax as Singapore does, and it would then not need subsidies. In fact, several respondents said that the Indian government should remove the various cesses charged on non-alcoholic beverages, especially on juices and bottled water. This may eliminate the need for extra subsidies given to this sector. It would also reduce the propensity to avoid tax, allow industry to grow and increase the tax base. A single and transparent tax system reduces compliance costs and the incidence of corruption and bribery.

(iv) *Assessing the impact of subsidies and taxes*: The survey found that several tax concessions and subsidies given to the non-alcoholic beverage sector are not aligned to industry requirements. While the government wants large-scale investment in the food processing sector, subsidies are targeted at small-scale industries and to a certain extent prohibit scale expansion. Hence, the Indian government should first consult with industry and understand their requirements and then design the subsidies. The subsidies should enable SMEs to grow and benefit from economies of scale. Also, as a member of the WTO, India should be careful about giving subsidies, since they are actionable under the WTO. For this purpose, the tax advisers in the Ministry of Commerce and the Ministry of Finance should have adequate knowledge of WTO rules and the two ministries should co-ordinate. This would enable the government to design a set of smart input subsidies that are WTO non-actionable. These can then become part of the 2014 Foreign Trade Policy of the Department of Commerce. Further, the erratic imposition of taxes and rules, such as Minimum Alternate Tax (MAT) and General Anti-Avoidance Rule (GAAR), leads to operational uncertainties and has adversely impacted the confidence of foreign and domestic investors. Although the SEZ Act clearly states that companies will benefit from MAT exemptions, MAT has been imposed in SEZs. The government has deferred GAAR, which has brought in some industry confidence, but the industry is worried that it could be imposed in future. Issues related to transfer pricing have also dampened investor confidence. Foreign companies are worried about investing in such an uncertain fiscal environment. The government should thoroughly study the impact of levying taxes or withdrawing benefits on investment before imposing them.

- *Regulatory Reforms*. The regulatory reforms needed by the sector can be classified under the following categories:

(i) *Reforms needed to establish a smooth supply chain*: An effective supply chain can be ensured if the GST is implemented and the APMC Act is implemented evenly across all states. The latter can be done by amending the model APMC Act to make contract farming and direct marketing mandatory in states that have not implemented it. Gulati and Saini (2013) have highlighted the need for models such as farmer-producer organisations (FPOs) in this regard. A report by the Ministry of Agriculture in 2013 stressed the need for state governments to amend the APMC Act and allow the direct sale of farm produce by organisations such as FPOs and facilitate contract farming arrangements between FPOs and bulk buyers such as food processors.[34] These models can remove middlemen from the supply chain and make agricultural procurement much smoother. In addition, fruits and vegetables should be exempted from APMC cess. Since it constitutes a small proportion of APMC earnings, it would not make a difference to the APMC revenue, but would encourage private players to procure directly from farmers. It would benefit the industry, farmers and consumers by reducing the number of intermediaries and associated costs in the process. All industry bodies have proposed that fruits and vegetables should be de-listed from the list of products that require the APMC cess. They also argued that there is a need to dismantle the controls and regulations on the production and distribution of commodities such as sugar under the Essential Commodities Act, 1955. This would enable free movement and easy procurement of sugar, which is an essential ingredient for manufacturers of non-alcoholic beverages.

(ii) *Ensuring quality, traceability and food safety through regulation*: The FSSA, 2006, aims to provide comprehensive regulation with respect to food safety and standards, but it does not cover farmers. Survey participants said that complete traceability of the supply chain is necessary. To address this issue, the FSSAI has suggested alternatives such as group farming with an internal control system and record keeping. For this, documentation of the inputs and practices in producing agricultural as well as processed products need to be maintained so that possible sources of contamination could be identified. There is also a need for proper tagging and labelling of agricultural products that provide information on the source of the product (see FSSAI, 2010). States such as Tamil Nadu and Maharashtra have already implemented steps such as cattle tagging to ensure the safety of the milk produced;[35] these should be implemented on a pan-India basis. There is also an urgent need to build up testing laboratories in all the states and have qualified food inspectors for proper implementation of these regulations. While most corporates support these regulations, they are worried about their implementation.

(iii) *Environment regulations*: Many state pollution control boards classify non-alcoholic beverage manufacturing units with other heavily polluting industries in the 'Red' category, whereas other food processing sectors are classified in the moderately polluting 'Orange' category. The non-alcoholic beverage sector should be classified in the 'Orange' category. There are also significant state-wise variations in environment regulations. In some states, the use of plastic is allowed, while in others it is banned. This leads to problems in establishing pan-India operations. There have to be synergies across state-level policies in environment regulations across the country.

(iv) *Proper water usage policies*: In order to protect ground water levels and surface water availability in India, states should adopt proper water usage policies. This would arrest unscrupulous practices such as withdrawal of agricultural water for commercial purposes.

(v) *Packaging regulations*: Some regulations such as the Legal Metrology Act, 2009, require beverage companies to package products in pre-specified sizes. Most beverage companies plan their inventories six months in advance. The imposition of such laws leads to losses due to wastage. These acts should be imposed in a phased manner with some 'grace' period (at least one year) for the companies to change their packaging.

(vi) *Strong measures to curb counterfeit and spurious products*: To prevent the spread of counterfeit products, the government needs to bring in stringent laws and implement stronger enforcement of the existing regulations. There should be stricter penalties for spurious products and fast-track courts for legal issues related to spurious products. The law enforcement authorities require consistent training and awareness campaigns, and there is also a need to increase consumer awareness so that they are better able to identify spurious

34. Ministry of Agriculture (2013).

35. *http://www.ictinagriculture.org/sourcebook/module-12-improving-food-safety-and-traceability* (last accessed in May 2013).

products. At present, the government feels that it is the responsibility of the industry to check spurious products. However, since there is a large non-corporate sector and a small corporate sector, it is not possible for the corporate sector to check spurious products. This should be the government's responsibility.

(vii) *Other regulations*: Several reforms, such as labour reforms, are pending in India and their implementation varies across states. A consistent labour policy with the flexibility to hire and fire, ease in employing women, etc. is important for the growth of manufacturing in India.

Overall, the discussion on reforms shows that most of them have to be conceived and implemented at the state level. In a quasi-federal governance structure, uniformity in state-level regulation requires significant centre-state coordination and willingness.

- *Need for Infrastructure*. The poor quality of infrastructure is a major barrier for the manufacturing sector in general. The reforms that would facilitate the growth of the non-alcoholic beverage sector are given below:

(i) *Power*: Shortages and the high price of power are the main infrastructure hurdles. The government should do away with the system where industry cross-subsidises agriculture by paying a higher price for power. There should be a clear policy of uninterrupted and consistent power supply at least in designated industrial clusters, SEZs, etc.

(ii) *Railways*: There is a need to speed up the process of building the DFCs and to increase the efficiency of the Indian Railways, which is the most environment friendly mode of transportation (Mukherjee *et al.*, 2012b). Respondents pointed out that Indian Railways has land and space, but there is a need to develop cargo facilities at railway stations with adequate storage facilities and dedicated spaces that provide logistics infrastructure, such as warehouses, cold chains and parking facilities for trucks. The cross-subsidisation of freight charges with passenger charges has led to high freight charges and loss of the country's global competitiveness.

(iii) *Roadways*: In terms of roadways, the problems are related to both connectivity and movement of traffic. Respondents pointed to the need to modernise road infrastructure, especially in smaller cities and rural areas that can develop as processing hubs and are the key suppliers of agricultural raw materials. There is an urgent need to connect the 'Golden Quadrilateral' with state highways, district and rural roads and establish linkages with key exports points, such as the Chennai port, for smoother movement of freight. Roads also need to be properly maintained by establishing road management units and taking steps for effective traffic control, as recommended by the Thangaraj Committee in the National Road Transport Policy.[36]

(iv) *Implementing a Green Channel system*: Even if the GST is implemented, the long wait time at check-posts will continue due to the lack of computerisation at check-posts and the various clearances required. For pan-India operations it is important to do away with various entry barriers such as the Way Bill and Octroi levied by different states, which increase the wait time at check-posts. The speed of traffic movement will increase and wastage will be reduced by replacing the manual check-posts with computerised ones that have a 24x7 manning facility. There is an urgent need to adopt a single-window clearance system at the check-posts. India can adopt the concept of 'Green Channels' as has been done by European Union (EU) member states; under this system, payments are made online and, by producing the receipt at the check-post, trucks can pass through without queuing to pay toll charges. The concepts of smart cards at check-posts and proper driver's licences are a pre-requisite. A national register should be developed for all vehicles and traders that frequently use the service. All these will help in faster movement of freight, especially those with a single destination. If adopted, it can considerably reduce wastage of fruits and vegetables and also save time and fuel costs.

36. *http://morth.nic.in/writereaddata/sublinkimages/ROAD_TRANSPORT_POLICY7406816237.htm* (last accessed in May 2013).

Currently, this has been adopted by states such as Gujarat.[37]

(v) *Airports*: There is an urgent need to develop more logistics parks and better cold chain facilities at Indian airports to store perishable commodities. There is also a need to develop linkages between domestic and international airports, and express delivery services should be allowed to operate in the fresh produce segment to ensure faster transportation for perishable commodities (Mukherjee *et al.*, 2012b).

(vi) *Warehousing and Cold Chains*: The development of warehouses and cold chains under private initiatives can be encouraged through allocation of concessional land by state industrial corporations, single-window clearances, implementation of pan-India quality standards, etc.

- *Land Reforms for Successful Agro-processing Projects*. Most infrastructure constructions in India have been delayed due to land acquisition issues. In addition, the manufacturing sector faces very high prices for land. The SEZs, National Manufacturing Zones and industrial clusters have not been successful in India primarily due to problems in land acquisition, allotment of land for specific purposes, the price of land and availability of allied connectivity such as roads and railways to manufacturing projects. The survey found that one way to tackle and reduce the problem of land availability would be to maintain a computerised system of recording allocation of land and land ownership at the state government level. Information on non-irrigated and wasteland that can be used for industrial purposes should be provided through the same or a similar portal. This finding is supported by studies [Asian NGO Coalition (ANGOC), 2013; Sethi, 2006]. In states such as West Bengal, land is available with state industrial corporations, but industry finds it difficult to access that land.

  The price of land and the compensation to be paid to the owner are high—the cost is around 40 per cent for industries located close to urban areas in India compared to the global average of 5 per cent. Land acquisition is highly political in India. To tackle the problem of adequate compensation for land acquisition, a well-maintained record of land ownership for calculating compensation, keeping in mind industry and farmers' requirements, can be effective. For instance, Ghatak and Ghosh (2011) pointed out that in the case of farmland being acquired by industry, the displaced farmers could be given an opportunity to decide whether they want compensation in cash or as land. However, the compensation package is still unclear in India and is compounded by the problems that land holdings are non-transparent and a lot of black money is involved in the transactions. The government wanted to come up with a clear policy, but the Land Acquisition Bill is pending in the Parliament. Industry argued that it would not be viable for them to pay the level of compensation stated in the Land Acquisition Bill and unless the government helps them acquire land at competitive prices and provides the allied infrastructure, manufacturing in India will not grow.

  In India due to high and escalating land prices, industry wants to own the land. Therefore, they have shown little interest in locating in agro-parks and SEZs where units cannot own land. While designing its incentive schemes, the government has to take this into consideration.

- *Reduce Inflation*. There is a need to reduce agricultural inflation. Apart from the implementation of the APMC reforms and reducing the number of intermediaries, another factor that can reduce agricultural inflation is reducing India's fiscal deficit. This can be done by rationalising different subsidies, such as fuel, food and fertiliser subsidies. A recent study observes that if fertiliser subsidies are given directly to farmers based on the total area of land they hold (prioritising small and marginal farmers), it could save almost INR 20,000 crore, thus reducing the fiscal deficit (Gulati and Saini, 2013). The government has allowed FDI in retail with the view to curb inflation. However, with the restrictive conditions in the policy, it is unlikely that it would lead to an inflow of FDI or lower food price inflation in India. The timely implementation of the

37. Ministry of Road Transport and Highways (2011).

GST is a more crucial reform for increasing sourcing from all over the country and for establishing a pan-India supply chain. Unless the GST covers agricultural commodities, private players cannot help reduce inflation. In India, a major cause of inflation is supply bottlenecks. The government should take measures to increase farm productivity, provide flexible import conditions and take steps to minimise wastage in the farm sector. All these will help overcome supply shortages and regulate inflation.

- *Rationalise Import Duties and Trade Policies.* Since India is globalising, there has been an increase in the number of FTAs and comprehensive trade agreements signed by the country. Since India's tariffs in agriculture are among the highest in emerging markets, tariff reduction is an important element in most of these trade agreements. However, so far there has not been any major study on the impact of tariff reduction in India's recent trade agreements. With trade agreements, multinationals and domestic companies are free to relocate to any country with which India has signed an agreement and which has a better manufacturing facility and ease of doing business. They can then import the product into India. Therefore, India should have a more rational domestic tariff policy and lower tariffs for key imports. The majority of the respondents highlighted the need for a long-term, predictable, agri-trade policy and a liberalised tariff regime. The trade policies should be equally focused on exports and imports, keeping in mind the requirements of both producers and consumers. Since many raw materials available in India are not of adequate quality, it is important for the government to impose moderate duties and special exemptions and grants on imports of such products used in manufacturing. Some experts suggest that domestic agriculture prices in India should be determined on the basis of global agricultural price trends, accounting for both long-term changes and short-term fluctuations. They also highlight the need to abolish quantitative restrictions or quotas on commodities such as sugar, since these are inefficient and make the trade policy biased.

- *Encourage Product-Focused R&D.* Research in the agriculture sector needs to be commercialised. Even though there are dedicated agriculture research institutes, there are very few path-breaking research outcomes. There is a need to develop high-yielding varieties (HYVs) and better quality agricultural products that serve as raw materials for the non-alcoholic beverage industry, particularly in the case of fruits and vegetables like oranges, mangoes, litchis and tomatoes. Both government and private participation is needed at various levels. The size of farms, irrigation facilities, quality of seeds and technology are important for enhancing yield. There is a need to encourage contract farming and cooperative farming (since individual farm sizes are small). These types of farming have to be made legal so that the corporate sector is interested in investing. There can be a partnership between state governments, corporates and farmer associations through public-private partnership models as in countries such as Vietnam.

  Increased investment in developing R&D facilities at different levels is essential and the research should be product-focused. The government should encourage investments in developing R&D facilities in existing universities and research institutes rather than creating new ones, and facilitate interaction between domestic and foreign companies and Indian research organisations. The government can offer incentives to manufacturers that have developed in-house R&D facilities for product innovation and development. At present, large manufacturers, especially global manufacturers, are not encouraged to do R&D in India through policy initiatives. The government needs to discuss this with the industry to understand their requirements and attract more foreign investment in R&D. R&D should also encourage more public-private partnerships, taking the example of successful ventures in other emerging economies. In addition, the government should educate farmers and, if required, offer them benefits for cultivating HYVs on their farms. Special benefits can be extended to farmers with small holdings who agree to consolidate their farms with neighbouring farms and grow HYVs. Respondents also highlighted the need for transparency in the process for obtaining patents within India. This will encourage innovation in the agricultural sector.

7.4 Conclusion

India's food processing sector is one of the key sectors for economic prosperity and the non-alcoholic beverage sector is a key component of the food processing industry. The sector is driven by the growing number of middle-class consumers who are willing to experiment with new products. India has an agricultural production base that can supply the raw materials for the non-alcoholic beverage sector. The sector has been identified as a sunshine sector by the Indian government. However, there are certain areas of concern for the non-alcoholic beverage sector in India that restrict the growth of the sector.

In an emerging economy like India where agriculture remains a large employer, the growth of the non-alcoholic beverage sector can generate significant employment and help in the country's economic growth. For this, the sector needs both domestic and foreign investment. Even though India is a preferred consumer market, it has failed to attract investment in non-alcoholic beverage manufacture and retail and in the food processing industry, in general. Given this, if the reforms highlighted in the chapter are implemented, they will help the sector in its growth and also increase India's global competitiveness in food processing. Specifically, for the growth of the non-alcoholic beverage sector, India should (a) streamline its multi-layered tax policy and have a single low tax across all product categories, (b) have facilitating environment regulations and regulations to counter spurious products and protect consumer interests and (c) have policies to facilitate water usage. In addition, other reforms impacting the food sector such as those related to quality and supply of raw materials, food safety and packaging regulations would help the non-alcoholic beverage sector grow. A stable macroeconomic condition, good and transparent governance and better infrastructure will make the Indian manufacturing sector globally competitive. Since India is in the process of implementing the FSSA, 2006, and other regulations that are likely to impact the food and beverage sector including the non-alcoholic beverage sector, the country can learn from global best practices. It is important to note that proper implementation of regulations and pan-India consistency in regulations are crucial for the success of this sector. It is also important to understand that although in developed countries regulations related to food safety standards, consumer and environment protection are more stringent than in developing countries such as India or China, they are also more transparent and better implemented, which has enabled the non-alcoholic sector to grow and reach its potential. India lags behind China and other emerging markets in receiving investment in this sector, creation of employment, exports and FDI inflows. India today is not a part of the global production network in the non-alcoholic beverage manufacturing sector, despite its rich base in raw materials. If the reforms discussed in this chapter are implemented, they would enable India to become part of the global processed food value chain, increase employment, enhance and diversify exports and lead to FDI inflows and higher domestic investment.

Bibliography

AM Mindpower Solutions (2011). *Indian Non-alcoholic Beverages Market Outlook to 2015: Rising Health Consciousness among Consumers*. India: The Market Publishers Ltd.

Accenture (2012). *Compete or Collaborate? Meeting the Challenge of Private Label Brands*. United States. *http://www.accenture.com/SiteCollectionDocuments/PDF/Accenture-Outlook-Compete-or-collaborate-Meeting-the-challenge-of-private-label-brands.pdf* (accessed in June 2013).

AC Nielsen (2012). *Nielsen Retail Audit*. USA.

ANGOC (2013). *Country Land Monitoring Report: India*. Philippines: ANGOC. *http://www.angoc.org/portal/wp-content/uploads/2013/01/31/cso-land-reform-monitoring-in-asia/India_Country_Report.pdf* (accessed in June 2013).

ASSOCHAM and Yes Bank (2012). *FDI in Retail: Advantage Farmers*. New Delhi: Food and Agribusiness Strategic Advisory and Research, Yes Bank. *http://www.assocham.org/arb/general/Background-FDI-Retail.pdf* (accessed in June 2013).

Biswas, A. and A. Sen (1999). "Coke vs. Pepsi: Local and Global Strategy", *Economic and Political Weekly* 34(26): 1701-08.

Britannia Industries Limited (2012). *Britannia in Every Heart: Annual Report 2011-12*. *http://www.britannia.co.in/Annual_Report_2012.pdf* (accessed in June 2013).

Business Monitor (2011). *India Food and Drink Report (Q32011)*. United Kingdom.

CIFTI (2010). *Industry Challenges in Food Regulations*. New Delhi: FICCI. *http://www.ficci.com/SEDocument/20057/FICCI_Survey_on_Industry_Challenges_in_Food_Regulations_F.pdf* (accessed in June 2013).

CII and KPMG (2007). *Skill Gaps in India's Logistics Sector: A White Paper*. India. *http://www.kpmg.de/docs/Skill_gaps_in_the_Indian_Logistics_Sector_A_white_paper.pdf* (accessed in June 2013).

CSO (2008). *National Industrial Classification (All Economic Activities)*. New Delhi: MoSPI. *http://mospi.nic.in/mospi_new/upload/nic_2008_17apr09.pdf* (accessed in June 2013).

————. (2013). *Press Release: Quick Estimates of Index of Industrial Production and Use Based Index for the Month of April 2013 (Base 2004-05=100)*. New Delhi: MoSPI. *http://mospi.nic.in/mospi_new/upload/t2_new.pdf* (accessed in June 2013).

Dabur India Limited (2012). *Earth Our Most Important Stakeholder: Dabur India Limited Business Responsibility Report 2011-12*. New Delhi. *http://www.dabur.com/en/Investors1/Annual_reports/2011-12/Dabur-BR-Report-2012.pdf* (accessed in June 2013).

Ernst & Young (2012). *Ready for the Transition: Ernst & Young's 2012 Attractiveness Survey India*. Greater China: Ernst & Young Emerging Markets Center. *http://emergingmarkets.ey.com/wp-content/uploads/downloads/2012/03/india-attractiveness-final-version1.pdf* (accessed in July 2013).

FICCI (2010). *Bottlenecks in Indian Food Processing Industry: Survey 2010*. New Delhi. *http://www.ficci.com/SEDocument/20073/Food-Processing-Bottlenecks-study.pdf* (accessed in June 2013).

FICCI BRIEF (2012). *Lack of Affordable and Quality Power: Shackling India's Growth Story*. New Delhi: FICCI. *http://www.ficci.com/Sedocument/20218/Power-Report2013.pdf* (accessed in June 2013).

FICCI and KPMG (2007). *Processed Food and Agribusiness: Opportunities for Investment in India*. India: KPMG. *http://www.in.kpmg.com/pdf/Processed%20Food%20%20Final.pdf* (accessed in June 2013).

FICCI and Technopak (2008). *Land of Opportunities: The Food Industry in India*. New Delhi: FICCI. *http://cifti.org/Reports/Ficci_Technopak%20'08.pdf* (Accessed in June 2013).

FSSAI (2010). "Food Safety Regulations and Food Safety Management", *Training Manual for Food Safety Regulators*. Vol. II. New Delhi: Food Safety and Standards Authority of India. *http://www.fssai.gov.in/Portals/0/Training_Manual/Volume%20II-%20Food%20Safety%20Regulators%20and%20Food%20Safety%20Management.pdf* (accessed in June 2013).

Gandhi, V.P. and N.V. Namboodiri (2002). "Fruit and Vegetable Marketing and its Efficiency in India: A Study of Wholesale Markets in the Ahmedabad Area", *Indian Institute of Management Ahmedabad Working Paper* No 2002-12-05. Ahmedabad. *http://www.iimahd.ernet.in/assets/snippets/workingpaperpdf/2002-12-05vasantgandhi.pdf* (accessed in June 2013).

Ganguly, R. (2011). "Analysis of Pro-poor Agriculture Value Chains in Maharashtra: Preliminary Findings", *IGIDR Project Series PP-069-9b. Workshop on Policy Options and Investment Priorities for Accelerating Agricultural Productivity and Development in India*. India International Centre, New Delhi. November. *http://www.igidr.ac.in/newspdf/srijit/PP-069-09b.pdf* (accessed in June 2013).

Ghatak, M. and P. Ghosh (2011). "The Land Acquisition Bill: A Critique and a Proposal", *Economic and Political Weekly* 46(41): 65-72.

Groupe Danone (2012). *Danone 11 Registration Document Annual Financial Report 2011*. Labrador, France. *http://danone11.danone.com/static/pdf/Registration_Document_2011.pdf* (accessed in June 2013).

Gulati, A. and S. Saini (2013). "Taming Food Inflation in India', *Discussion Paper* no. 4. New Delhi: Commission for Agricultural Costs and Prices, Ministry of Agriculture. April. *http://cacp.dacnet.nic.in/Food_Inflation.pdf* (accessed in June 2013).

Gulati, A., S. Jain and A. Hoda (2013). "Farm Trade: Tapping the Hidden Potential", *Discussion Paper* no. 3. New Delhi: Commission for Agricultural Costs and Prices, Ministry of Agriculture. *http://cacp.dacnet.nic.in/Agri-Trade_DP.pdf* (accessed in June 2013).

Hargitt, B. (2006). "Introduction", in David P. Steen and Philip R. Ashurst (eds.), *Carbonated Soft Drinks: Formulation and Manufacture*. Oxford: Blackwell Publishing Ltd.

IAMR (2012). *Employment in the Food Processing Industry*. New Delhi.

Images (2013). *India Retail Report 2013*. New Delhi.

IMF (2013). *World Economic Outlook Update: Global Upturn in Global Growth During 2013*. Washington, D.C. *http://www.imf.org/external/pubs/ft/weo/2013/update/01/pdf/0113.pdf* (accessed in December 2012)

IS Advisors (2012). *Non Alcoholic Beverage Industry in India (2011-2015)*. July. Ireland: Research and Markets.

Joseph, M., N. Soundararajan, M. Gupta and S. Sahu (2008). *Impact of Organized Retailing on the Unorganized Sector*. New Delhi: Indian Council for Research on International Economic Relations. *http://dipp.nic.in/english/publications/reports/icrier_report_27052008.pdf* (accessed in July 2013).

Joseph, M. and N. Soundararajan (2009). *Retailing in India: A Critical Assessment*. New Delhi: Academic Foundation.

Joshi, K. (2009). "Processed Food and Beverage Industry: An Overview", *S&T and Industry T3-106, National Institute of Science Technology and Development Studies* 2011. New Delhi.

Karan, A. K. and S. Selvaraj (2008). "Trends in Wages and Earnings in India: Increasing Wage Differentials in a Segmented Labour Market", *ILO Asia-Pacific Working Paper Series*. New Delhi. *http://www.ilo.org/wcmsp5/groups/public/---asia/---robangkok/documents/publication/wcms_098852.pdf* (accessed in June 2013).

Karlsen, K. M., P. Olsen and K.A-M. Donnelly (2009). "Implementing Traceability: Practical Challenges at a Mineral Water Bottling Plant", *British Food Journal* 112(2): 187-97.

Kashyap, P. and S. Raut (2005). *The Rural Marketing Book*. New Delhi: Dreamtech Press.

Kochhar, K., U. Kumar, R. Rajan, A. Subramanian and I. Tokatlidis (2006). "India's Pattern of Development: What Happened, What Follows?", *Journal of Monetary Economics* 53(5): 981-1019.

Kraft Foods Inc. (2011). *Creating A More Delicious World: Our 2010 Report*. USA. *http://www.kraftfoodscompany.com/SiteCollectionDocuments/pdf/kraftfoods_responsibility_report.pdf* (accessed in June 2013).

————. (2012). *2011 Fact Sheet*. USA. *http://www.kraftfoodscompany.com/SiteCollectionDocuments/pdf/kraft_foods_fact_sheet.pdf* (accessed in June 2013).

Krause Fund Research (2012). *Consumer Staples: PepsiCo Inc.* University of Iowa. *http://tippie.uiowa.edu/krause/spring2012/pep_sp12.pdf* (accessed in June 2013).

MarketLine (2010). "Soft Drinks: Global Industry Guide", *Datamonitor*, April. United Kingdom.

————. (2011). "Soft Drinks: Global Industry Almanac", *Datamonitor*, June. United Kingdom.

McKinsey Global Institute (2007). *The 'Bird of Gold': The Rise of India's Consumer Market*. India: McKinsey & Company. *http://www.mckinsey.com/locations/india/mckinseyonindia/pdf/India_Consumer_Market.pdf* (accessed in June 2013).

Mehrotra, S. and A. Gandhi (2013). "Turnaround in India's Employment Story", *Economic & Political Weekly* 48(35): 87.

Meyer, C. and N. Birdsall (2012). *New Estimates of Indian Middle Class: Technical Note*. Washington, D.C.: Center for Global Development. *http://www.cgdev.org/doc/2013_MiddleClassIndia_TechnicalNote_CGDNote.pdf* (accessed in July 2013).

Michael, T. and V.R. Nedunchezhian (2012). "Impact of Media on Consumers' Brand Preference: A Study on Carbonated Beverage Market with Reference to Coca-Cola", *European Journal of Social Sciences* 29(2): 233-43.

Ministry of Agriculture (2013). *Policy and Process Guidelines for Farmer Producer Organisations*. New Delhi: Department of Agriculture and Co-operation. *http://agritech.tnau.ac.in/pdf/fpo_policy.pdf* (accessed in June 2013).

Ministry of Finance (2006). *Investment Strategy for India: Investment Commission Report*. Investment Commission, Ministry of Finance. February. *http://finmin.nic.in/reports/InvestmentCommissionReport.pdf* (accessed in June 2013).

Ministry of Road Transport and Highways (2011). *Report of the Sub-Group on Policy Issues*. September. *http://morth.nic.in/writereaddata/linkimages/Policy%20Issues-9224727324.pdf* (accessed in June 2013).

MoFPI (2005). "Volume 1: Vision Strategy and Action Plan for Food Processing Industries in India", and "Volume 2: Strategy and Action Plan for Food Processing Industries in India", *Vision 2015*. Report prepared by Rabo India Finance Pvt. Ltd. April. New Delhi. *http://mofpi.nic.in/H_Dwld.aspx?KYEwmOL+HGpoo8DlNeKVV9Ovc/epY+sr3kZVvH4grl13fQ3Hl1cRUg==* (accessed in July 2013).

————. (2012). *Annual Report 2011-12*. New Delhi. *http://mofpi.nic.in/H_Dwld.aspx?KYEwmOL+HGpoo8DlNeKVV3fE4aW5+awTGdnZC9kP6BhMZcHG2sQhVA==* (accessed inJuly 2013).

————. (2013). *Annual Report 2012-13*. New Delhi. *http://mofpi.nic.in/H_Dwld.aspx?KYEwmOL+HGpoo8DlNeKVV3fE4aW5+awTGdnZC9kP6BjgyfUUMx3Nkw==* (accessed in June 2013).

Mukherjee, A. (2013). "Services Sector in India", *Asian Development Bank (ADB) Economics Working Paper Series* No. 352. Available at: *http://www.adb.org/sites/default/files/pub/2013/ewp-352.pdf*

Mukherjee, A. and N. Patel (2005). *FDI in Retail Sector: India*. New Delhi: Academic Foundation.

Mukherjee, A. and T.M. Goyal (2012). "Employment Conditions in Organised and Unorganised Retail: Implications for FDI Policy in India", *Journal of Business and Retail Management Research* 6(2).

Mukherjee, A., D. Satija, T.M. Goyal, M.K. Mantrala and S. Zou (2012a). "Are Indian Consumers Brand Conscious? Insights for Global Retailers", *Asia Pacific Journal of Marketing and Logistics* 24(3): 482-99.

Mukherjee, A., P. Pal, S. Mitra, R. Goswami and S. Dutta (2012b). *Facilitating Trade and Global Competitiveness: Express Delivery Services in India*. New Delhi: Oxford University Press.

National Accounts Statistics (2011). *http://mospi.nic.in/Mospi_New/upload/web_NAS_2011/pdf%20files/intro-eng.pdf* (accessed in June 2013).

National Commission on Population (2006). *Population Projections for India and States 2001-2026: Report of the Technical Group on Population Projections*. Constituted by the National Commission on Population', Census of India 2001. New Delhi. *http://nrhm-mis.nic.in/UI/Public%20Periodic/Population_Projection_Report_2006.pdf* (accessed in April 3, 2012).

National Skill Development Corporation (NSDC) (2009). *Human Resource and Skill Requirements in the Food Processing Sector (2022): A Report*. A study by ICRA Management Consulting Services Limited, NSDC, New Delhi. *http://www.nsdcindia.org/pdf/food-processings.pdf* (accessed in June 2013).

NCAER (2001). *An Analytical Framework of the Carbonated Soft Drink Industry in India*. New Delhi.

————. (2004-05). *National Survey of Household Income and Expenditure (NSHIE)* 2004-05. Data-Documentation, NCAER, New Delhi. *http://www.ncaer.org/NSHIE-Data-Documentation.pdf* (accessed in June 2013).

Nestlé S.A (2012). *Annual Report 2011*. *http://www.nestle.com/asset-library/Documents/Library/Documents/Annual_Reports/2011-Annual-Report-EN.pdf* (accessed in June 2013).

Neves, M.F., P. Milan, V.G. Trombin and F.C. Pereira (2011). "Market Drivers of Global Beverage Consumption in 2010: Opportunities for a New Positioning of the Juice Category", *IFAMA 2011 Forum and Symposium*. May. Frankfurt, Germany. *https://www.ifama.org/events/conferences/2011/cmsdocs/2011SymposiumDocs/429_Symposium%20Paper.pdf* (accessed in June 2013).

Nin-Pratt, A., B. Yu and S. Fan (2009). "The Total Factor Productivity in China and India: New Measures and Approaches", *China Agricultural Economic Review* 1(1): 9-22.

Pachouri, A. (2013). "Poor Farm-Market Linkages in India's Agriculture Value Chains", *Farmers Forum* 13(1): 55-6.

Paliwoda, S., T. Andrews and J. Chen (2012). *Marketing Management in Asia*. New York: Routledge.

PepsiCo Inc. (2012). *The Power of PepsiCo: 2011 Annual Report*. USA. *http://www.pepsico.com/annual11/downloads/pep_ar11_2011_annual_report.pdf* (last accessed in June 2013).

Pfitzer, M. and R. Krishnaswamy (2007). "The Role of the Food and Beverage Sector in Expanding Economic Opportunity", *Economic Opportunity Series*, Harvard Kennedy School. *http://www.fsg.org/Portals/0/Uploads/Documents/PDF/Role_of_Food_and_Beverage_Sector_in_Economic_Opportunity.pdf?cpgn=WP%20DL%20-%20Role%20of%20Food%20and%20Bev%20Sectors%20in%20Econ%20Opp* (accessed in July 2013).

PHD Chamber and Yes Bank (2012). *India's Cold Chain Sector: A Diagnostic and Prescriptive Study*. New Delhi: Food and Agribusiness Strategic Advisory and Research (FASAR) and Yes Bank.

Press Information Bureau (PIB) (2012). *State of India's Agriculture 2011-12*. March. New Delhi. *http://pib.nic.in/archieve/others/2012/mar/d2012031306.pdf* and *http://pib.nic.in/archieve/others/2012/mar/d2012031306.pdf* (accessed in June 2013).

Planning Commission (2009). *Report on Working Group on Logistics*. New Delhi: Government of India. *http://planningcommission.gov.in/reports/genrep/rep_logis.pdf* (accessed in June 2013).

———. (2012). *Draft Report of Working Group Food Processing Industries for 12th Five Year Plan*. New Delhi: MoFPI, Government of India. *http://planningcommission.nic.in/aboutus/committee/wrkgrp12/wgrep_fpi.pdf* (accessed in June 2013).

PwC (2011). *Winning in India's Retail Sector: Factors for Success*. PwC Brand and Communications, India. *http://list2.pwc.fr/assets/files/lettre_retail-and-consumer/pwc_winning_in_india_retail_sector_1.pdf* (accessed in June 2013).

Ramaswamy, V.S. and S. Namakumari (2009). *Marketing Management: Global perspective in Indian Context*. New Delhi: Macmillan.

Rao, S.L. (2000). "India's Rapidly Changing Consumer Markets", *Economic and Political Weekly* 35(40): 3570-72.

Ray, T. and Nagabhushana (2012). "Coca Cola in India: A Study on Product Portfolio and Distribution Adaptation", *International Journal on Research in Finance and Marketing* 2(2): 360-78. *http://www.euroasiapub.org/IJRFM/Feb2012/29.pdf* (accessed in June 2013).

Rabobank (2012). *Best of Times, Worst of Times: Global Beverage Outlook, 2012*. Netherlands.

Saxena, R. (2010). *The Middle Class in India*. Germany: Deutsche Bank Research. *http://www.dbresearch.de/PROD/DBR_INTERNET_DEPROD/PROD0000000000253735.pdf* (accessed in June 2013).

Sethi, M. (2006). "Land Reform in India: Issues and Challenges", in P. Rosset, R. Patel and M. Courville (eds.), *Promised Land: Competing Visions of Agrarian Reform*. Oakland, CA: Food First Books. pp-73-92.

Sharma, V.P. and D. Jain (2011). "High-Value Agriculture in India: Past Trends and Future Prospects", *Indian Institute of Management Ahmedabad Working Paper* No. 2011-07-02. *http://www.iimahd.ernet.in/assets/upload/faculty/678631189High%20Value%20Agri.%20Working%20Paper.pdf* (accessed in June 2013).

Shukla, R. (2010). *How India Saves, Earns and Spends: and Saves: Unmasking the Real India*. New Delhi: NCAER and Sage Publications.

Simchi-Levi, D., P. Kaminsky, E. Simchi-Levi and R. Shankar (2007). *Designing and Managing the Supply Chain*. New York: McGraw Hill.

Singh, B. and K. Agrawal (2012). "Impact of Advertisements on the Brand Preference of Aerated Drinks", *Asia Pacific Journal of Marketing and Management Review* 2(2): 147-60.

Sinha, P.K. and S.K. Kar (2007). "An Insight into the Growth of New Retail Formats in India", *Indian Institute of Management Ahmedabad Working Paper* No 2007-03-04. *http://iimahd.ernet.in/assets/snippets/workingpaperpdf/2007-03-04_PKSinha.pdf* (accessed in June 2013).

Tandon, S., M.R. Landes and A. Woolverton (2011). "The Expansion of Modern Grocery Retailing and Trade in Developing Countries", United States Department of Agriculture. *http://www.ers.usda.gov/media/118890/err122.pdf* (accessed in June 2013).

Technopak (2010). *Technopak Perspective: A Quarterly Report by Technopak Volume 3/2010*. India. *http://www.technopak.com/resources/Food/Technopak%20F%20and%20B%20Outlook_June%202012.pdf* (accessed in June 2013).

The Boston Consulting Group (2012). *The Tiger Roars: An In-depth Analysis of How a Billion Plus People Consume*. India. *http://www.indiaretailing.com/upload/ContentImage/Market_Research_pdf/The_Tiger_Roars.pdf* (accessed in July 2013).

The Coca-Cola Company (2011). *The Coca-Cola Company 2010/11 Sustainability Report: Reasons to Believe*. USA. *http://assets.coca-colacompany.com/c0/08/c6bcf57247b2b17f8ba87abafa87/TCCC_2010_2011_Sustainability_Report_Full.pdf* (accessed in June 2013).

———. (2012a), *Passionately Refreshing A Thirsty World 2011 Annual Review*. USA. *http://www.coca-colacompany.com/annual-review/2011/pdf/TCCC_2011_Annual_Review.pdf* (accessed in June 2013)

———. (2012b). *Coca-Cola 2011/2012 GRI Report A Companion to the 2011/2012 Sustainability Report*. USA. *http://www.coca-colacompany.com/sustainabilityreport/downloads/2012-sustainability- report.pdf* (accessed in June 2013)

West Bengal State Food Processing and Horticulture Development Corporation Limited (2012). "Introduction", in *Food Processing Industries Survey, West Bengal*. *http://www.ipshabengal.com/admin/upload_tender/1352713356Introduction.pdf* (Acessed in June 2013)

Yadav, P., O. Stapleton and L.N. van Wassenhove (2013). "Learning from Coca-Cola: Comparing Medicine and Consumer Product Supply Chains in the Developing World", *Stanford Social Innovation Review* (Winter): 51-55.

Useful Links

http://data.worldbank.org/indicator/NY.GDP.MKTP.CD (accessed in June 2013).

http://data.worldbank.org/indicator/IC.BUS.EASE.XQ (accessed in June 2013).

http://data.worldbank.org/indicator/AG.LND.IRIG.AG.ZS (accessed in June 2013).

http://unctad.org/Sections/dite_dir/docs/WIR11_web%20tab%2028.pdf (accessed in May 2013).

http://comtrade.un.org/db/ (accessed in June 2013).

Annexures

Annexure A-1.1

Classification of the Non-alcoholic Beverage Sector According to the United Nations Central Product Classification (CPC)

CPC (provisional)	*CPC (version 2)*	*HS Code*
Food products, beverages and tobacco, textiles, apparel and leather products (CPC 2)	Food products, beverages and tobacco, textiles, apparel and leather products (CPC 2)	Preparations of vegetables, fruit, nuts or other parts of plants (HS Code 20)
Meat, fish, fruit, vegetables, oil and fat (CPC 21)	Meat, fish, fruit, vegetables, oil and fat (CPC 21) Prepared and preserved vegetables, pulses and potato (CPC 213) Vegetable juice (CPC 2132) Tomato juice (21321) Other vegetable juices (21329)	
Fruit juices and vegetable juices (CPC 214)	Prepared and preserved fruits and nuts (CPC 214)	Fruit juices (including grape must) and vegetable juices unfermented and not containing added spirit (HS Code 2009)
Fruit juices and vegetable juices (CPC 2140)	Fruit juices (CPC 2143) Orange juice (CPC 21431) Grapefruit juice (CPC 21432) Pineapple juice (CPC 21433) Grape juice (CPC 21434) Apple juice (CPC 21435) Other fruit juices n.e.c (CPC 21439)	Orange juice (HS Code 20091100) Grapefruit juice (HS code 20091900) Pineapple juice (HS code 20093900) Tomato juice (HS code 20095000) Grape juice (HS code 20096000) Apple juice (HS code 20096900) Mango juice (HS code 20098010) Mixtures of juices (HS code 20099000)
Dairy products (CPC 22)	Dairy products and egg products (CPC 22)	Birds' egg; natural honey; edible products of animal origin, not elsewhere specified or includes
Processed liquid milk and cream (CPC 221)	Processed liquid milk and cream (CPC 221)	Milk and cream, not concentrated nor containing added sugar or other sweetening matter (HS code 401)
Processed liquid milk (CPC 2211)	Processed liquid milk (CPC 2211)	Of a fat content, by weight, not exceeding 1 per cent (HS code 4011000)
Cream, fresh (CPC 2212)	Cream, fresh (CPC 2212)	Of a fat content, by weight, exceeding 1 per cent but not exceeding 6 per cent (HS code 4012000)
Other dairy products (CPC 229)	Other dairy products (CPC 222)	Of a fat content, by weight, exceeding 6 per cent (HS code 4013000)
Milk and cream, concentrated or containing added sugar or other sweetening matter, other than in solid form (CPC 2292)	Milk and cream, concentrated or containing added sugar or other sweetening matter, other than in solid form (CPC 2222)	Milk and cream, concentrated or containing added sugar or other sweetening matter (HS code 402)
Milk and cream, concentrated or containing added sugar or other sweetening matter, other than in solid form (CPC 22920)	Evaporated milk (CPC 22221)	In powder, granules or other solid forms, of a fat content, by weight not exceeding 1.5 per cent (HS code 40210)
	Condensed milk (CPC 22222)	Skimmed milk (HS code 4021010)
	Milk and cream n.e.c (CPC 22229)	Milk food for babies (HS code 4021020) Other, in powder, granules or other solid forms, of a fat content, by weight exceeding 1.5 per cent (HS code 4021090)

contd...

...contd...

CPC (provisional)	*CPC (version 2)*	*HS Code*
		Not containing added sugar or other sweetening matter (HS code 4022100)
		Other (HS code 40229)
		Whole milk (HS code 4022910)
		Milk for babies (HS code 4022920)
		Other (HS code 4022990)
		Not containing added sugar or other sweetening matter (HS code 40291)
		Condensed milk (HS code 4029110)
		Other (HS code 4029190)
		Other (HS code 40299)
		Whole milk (HS code 4029910)
		Condensed milk (HS code 4029920)
		Other (HS code 4029990)
Yoghurt and other fermented or acidified milk or cream (CPC 2293)	Yoghurt and other fermented or acidified milk or cream (CPC2223)	Buttermilk, curdled milk and cream, yoghurt, kephir and other fermented or acidified milk and cream (HS code 403)
		Yoghurt (HS code 4031000)
		Other (HS code 40390)
		Buttermilk (HS code 4039010)
		Other (HS code 4039090)
Beverages (CPC 24)	Beverages (CPC 24)	Beverages, spirits and vinegar (HS code 22)
Soft drinks; bottled mineral water (CPC 244)	Soft drinks; bottled mineral water (CPC 244)	Waters, including natural or artificial mineral waters and aerated waters, not containing added sugar (HS code 2201)
Waters (including mineral water and aerated water), not sweetened nor flavoured except natural water; ice and snow (CPC 2441)	Bottled waters, not sweetened or flavoured (CPC 2441)	Mineral waters and aerated waters (HS code 220110) Mineral water (HS code 22011010) Aerated water (HS code 22011020) Other (HS code 220190) Ice and snow (HS code 22019010) Other (HS code 22019090)
Other non-alcoholic beverages (CPC 2449)	Other non-alcoholic beverages (CPC 2449)	Other fermented beverages (e.g., cider Perry mead); mixtures of fermented beverages and non-alcoholic beverages (HS code 2206)

Source: Authors' compilation from

UNCPC Provisional: *http://unstats.un.org/unsd/cr/registry/regcst.asp?Cl=9&Lg=1*

UNCPC (Version 2): *http://unstats.un.org/unsd/cr/registry/docs/CPCv2_structure.pdf*

HS code: *http://dgftcom.nic.in/licasp/itchs2012/itemdetail.asp*

Annexure A-3.1

Conditions for FDI in Retail

Retail mode	*Conditions*
Single-brand Retail	(1) Foreign investment in single-brand product retail trading is aimed at attracting investments in production and marketing, improving the availability of such goods for the consumer, encouraging increased sourcing of goods from India, and enhancing the competitiveness of Indian enterprises through access to global designs, technologies and management practices. (2) FDI in single-brand product retail trading would be subject to the following conditions: a. Products to be sold should be of a 'single brand' only. b. Products should be sold under the same brand internationally, i.e., products should be sold under the same brand in one or more countries other than India. c. 'Single brand' product retail trading would cover only products that are branded during manufacturing. d. A non-resident entity or entities, whether owner of the brand or otherwise, shall be permitted to undertake single brand product retail trading in the country, for the specific brand, directly or through a legally tenable agreement, with the brand owner for undertaking single brand product retail trading. The onus for ensuring compliance with this condition shall rest with the Indian entity carrying out single-brand product retail trading in India. The investing entity shall provide evidence to this effect at the time of seeking approval, including a copy of the licensing/ franchise/sub-licence agreement, specifically indicating compliance with the above condition. The requisite evidence should be filed with the Reserve Bank of India (RBI) for the automatic route and Secretariat for Industrial Assistance (SIA)/Foreign Investment Promotion Board (FIPB) for cases involving approval. e. In respect of proposals involving FDI beyond 51 per cent, sourcing of 30 per cent of the value of goods purchased will be done from India, preferably from micro, medium and small-scale enterprises or MSMEs (micro, small and medium enterprises), village and cottage industries, artisans and craftsmen in all sectors. The quantum of domestic sourcing will be self-certified by the company, to be subsequently checked, by statutory auditors, from the duly certified accounts which the company will be required to maintain. This procurement requirement would have to be met, in the first instance, as an average of five years' total value of the goods purchased, beginning 1st April of the year during which the first tranche of FDI is received. Thereafter, it would have to be met on an annual basis. For the purpose of ascertaining the sourcing requirement, the relevant entity would be the company, incorporated in India, which is the recipient of FDI for the purpose of carrying out single-brand product retail trading. f. Retail trading, in any form, by means of e-commerce, would not be permissible for companies with FDI engaged in the activity of single-brand retail trading. (3) Application seeking permission of the government for FDI exceeding 49 per cent in a company that proposes to undertake single-brand retail trading in India would be made to the SIA in the Department of Industrial Policy and Promotion (DIPP). The applications would specifically indicate the product/product categories that are proposed to be sold under a 'single brand.' Any addition to the product/product categories to be sold under 'single brand' would require fresh approval from the government. In the case of FDI up to 49 per cent, the product/product categories proposed to be sold except food products could be provided to the RBI. (4) Applications would be processed in the DIPP to determine whether the proposed investment satisfies the notified guidelines, before being considered by the FIPB for government approval.
Multi-brand Retail	(1) FDI in multi-brand retail trading, in all products, will be permitted subject to the following conditions: a. Fresh agricultural produce, including fruits, vegetables, flowers, grains, pulses, fresh poultry, fishery and meat products, may be unbranded. b. Minimum amount to be brought in as FDI by the foreign investor would be $100 million. c. At least 50 per cent of total FDI brought in the first tranche of $100 million, shall be invested in 'backend infrastructure' within three years, where backend infrastructure will include capital expenditure on all activities, excluding that on front-end units; for instance, backend infrastructure will include investment made towards processing, manufacturing and distribution, design improvement, quality control, packaging, logistics, storage, warehouse, agriculture market produce infrastructure, etc. Expenditure on land cost and rentals, if any, will not be counted for purpose of backend infrastructure. Subsequent investment in the backend infrastructure would be made by the MBRT retailer as needed, depending upon its business requirements.

contd...

...contd...

Retail mode	*Conditions*
	d. At least 30 per cent of the value of procurement of manufactured/processed products purchased shall be sourced from Indian MSMEs, which have a total investment in plant and machinery not exceeding $2 million. This valuation refers to the value at the time of installation, without providing for depreciation. The 'small industry' status would be reckoned only at the time of first engagement with the retailer and such industry shall continue to qualify as a 'small industry' for this purpose even if it outgrows the said investment of $2 million, during the course of its relationship with the said retailer. Sourcing from agricultural cooperatives and farmer's cooperatives would also be considered in this category. The procurement requirement would have to be met, in the first instance, as an average of five years' total value of the manufactured/processed products purchased, beginning 1st April of the year during which the first tranche of FDI is received. Thereafter, it would have to be met on an annual basis.
	e. Self-certification by the company, to ensure compliance with the conditions at serial nos. (b), (c) and (d) above, which could be cross-checked, as and when required. Accordingly, the investors shall maintain accounts, duly certified by statutory auditors.
	f. Retail sales outlets may be set up only in cities with a population of more than 10 lakh as per the 2011 Census or any other cities as per the decision of the respective state governments, and may also cover an area of 10 km around the municipal/urban agglomeration limits of such cities; retail locations will be restricted to conforming areas as per the master/zonal plans of the concerned cities and provision will be made for requisite facilities such as transport connectivity and parking.
	g. The government will have the first right to procurement of agricultural products.
	h. The above policy is an enabling policy only and the state governments/Union Territories would be free to take their own decisions in regard to implementation of the policy. The establishment of the retail sales outlets will be in compliance with applicable State/Union Territory laws/regulations, such as the Shops and Establishments Act, etc.
	i. Retail trading, in any form, by means of e-commerce, would not be permissible, for companies with FDI, engaged in the activity of multi-brand retail trading.
	j. Applications would be processed in the DIPP to determine whether the proposed investment satisfies the notified guidelines, before being considered by the FIPB for government approval.

Source: Extracted from 'Consolidated FDI Policy (Effective from April 5, 2013)', DIPP, Ministry of Commerce and Industry, Government of India and Press Note Nos. 5 and 6 (2013 Series), DIPP, Ministry of Commerce and Industry, Government of India.

Annexure A-3.2

Socioeconomic Classification (SEC) Grid

Education/Occupation	*Illiterate*	*School up to 4 years/Literate but No Formal Schooling*	*School (5-9 yrs)*	*SSC/ HSC*[a]	*College but not Graduate*	*Graduate/ Post-graduate General*	*Graduate/ Post-graduate Professional*
Unskilled worker	E2	E2	E1	D	D	D	D
Skilled worker	E2	E1	D	C	C	B2	B2
Petty worker	E2	D	D	C	C	B2	B2
Shop owner	D	D	C	B2	B1	A2	A2
Entrepreneur (employees none)	D	C	B2	B1	A2	A2	A1
Entrepreneur (employees < 10)	C	B2	B2	B1	A2	A1	A1
Entrepreneur (employees > 10)	B1	B1	A2	A2	A1	A1	A1
Self-employed professional	D	D	D	B2	B1	A2	A1
Clerical/Salesman	D	D	D	C	B2	B1	B1
Supervisory level	D	D	C	C	B2	B1	A2
Officers/Executives (Junior)	C	C	C	B2	B1	A2	A2
Officers/Executives (middle/senior)	B1	B1	B1	B1	A2	A1	A1

Note: [a]: SSC: senior secondary; HSC: higher secondary.

Source: Authors' compilation from Ramaswamy and Namakumari (2009), table 17.2, p. 275.